DISLIKE-MINDED

CRITICAL CULTURAL COMMUNICATION

General Editors: Jonathan Gray, Aswin Punathambekar, Adrienne Shaw
Founding Editors: Sarah Banet-Weiser and Kent A. Ono

Dangerous Curves: Latina Bodies in the Media
Isabel Molina-Guzmán

The Net Effect: Romanticism, Capitalism, and the Internet
Thomas Streeter

Our Biometric Future: Facial Recognition Technology and the Culture of Surveillance
Kelly A. Gates

Critical Rhetorics of Race
Edited by Michael G. Lacy and Kent A. Ono

Circuits of Visibility: Gender and Transnational Media Cultures
Edited by Radha S. Hegde

Commodity Activism: Cultural Resistance in Neoliberal Times
Edited by Roopali Mukherjee and Sarah Banet-Weiser

Arabs and Muslims in the Media: Race and Representation after 9/11
Evelyn Alsultany

Visualizing Atrocity: Arendt, Evil, and the Optics of Thoughtlessness
Valerie Hartouni

The Makeover: Reality Television and Reflexive Audiences
Katherine Sender

Authentic™: The Politics of Ambivalence in a Brand Culture
Sarah Banet-Weiser

Technomobility in China: Young Migrant Women and Mobile Phones
Cara Wallis

Love and Money: Queers, Class, and Cultural Production
Lisa Henderson

Cached: Decoding the Internet in Global Popular Culture
Stephanie Ricker Schulte

Black Television Travels: African American Media around the Globe
Timothy Havens

Citizenship Excess: Latino/as, Media, and the Nation
Hector Amaya

Feeling Mediated: A History of Media Technology and Emotion in America
Brenton J. Malin

The Post-Racial Mystique: Media and Race in the Twenty-First Century
Catherine R. Squires

Making Media Work: Cultures of Management in the Entertainment Industries
Edited by Derek Johnson, Derek Kompare, and Avi Santo

Sounds of Belonging: U.S. Spanish-language Radio and Public Advocacy
Dolores Inés Casillas

Orienting Hollywood: A Century of Film Culture between Los Angeles and Bombay
Nitin Govil

Asian American Media Activism: Fighting for Cultural Citizenship
Lori Kido Lopez

Struggling for Ordinary: Media and Transgender Belonging in Everyday Life
Andre Cavalcante

Wife, Inc.: The Business of Marriage in the Twenty-First Century
Suzanne Leonard

Homegrown: Identity and Difference in the American War on Terror
Piotr Szpunar

Dot-Com Design: The Rise of a Useable, Social, Commercial Web
Megan Sapnar Ankerson

Postracial Resistance: Black Women, Media, and the Uses of Strategic Ambiguity
Ralina L. Joseph

Netflix Nations: The Geography of Digital Distribution
Ramon Lobato

The Identity Trade: Selling Privacy and Reputation Online
Nora A. Draper

Celebrity: A History of Fame
Susan J. Douglas and Andrea McDonnell

Fake Geek Girls: Fandom, Gender, and the Convergence Culture Industry
Suzanne Scott

Locked Out: Regional Restrictions in Digital Entertainment Culture
Evan Elkins

The Digital City: Media and the Social Production of Place
Germaine R. Halegoua

Distributed Blackness: African American Cybercultures
André Brock

Beyond Hashtags: Racial Politics and Black Digital Networks
Sarah Florini

Race and Media: Critical Approaches
Edited by Lori Kido Lopez

Dislike-Minded: Media, Audiences, and the Dynamics of Taste
Jonathan Gray

Dislike-Minded

Media, Audiences, and the Dynamics of Taste

Jonathan Gray

NEW YORK UNIVERSITY PRESS
New York

NEW YORK UNIVERSITY PRESS
New York
www.nyupress.org

© 2021 by New York University
All rights reserved

References to Internet websites (URLs) were accurate at the time of writing. Neither the author nor New York University Press is responsible for URLs that may have expired or changed since the manuscript was prepared.

Library of Congress Cataloging-in-Publication Data
Names: Gray, Jonathan (Jonathan Alan), author.
Title: Dislike-minded : media, audiences, and the dynamics of taste / Jonathan Gray.
Description: New York : New York University Press, [2021] | Series: Critical cultural communication | Includes bibliographical references and index.
Identifiers: LCCN 2020051055 | ISBN 9781479809264 (hardback) | ISBN 9781479809981 (paperback) | ISBN 9781479810000 (ebook) | ISBN 9781479809998 (ebook)
Subjects: LCSH: Mass media—Audiences. | Social media. | Likes and dislikes. | Aesthetics.
Classification: LCC P96.A83 G675 2021 | DDC 302.2301—dc23
LC record available at https://lccn.loc.gov/2020051055

New York University Press books are printed on acid-free paper, and their binding materials are chosen for strength and durability. We strive to use environmentally responsible suppliers and materials to the greatest extent possible in publishing our books.

Manufactured in the United States of America

10 9 8 7 6 5 4 3 2 1

Also available as an ebook

To Matthew Gray,

who taught me how to dislike.

Thanks, big brother.

CONTENTS

Introduction: Media Studies: Click Dislike … 1

1. The Audience for Dislike … 27
2. What's Wrong and What's Missing … 67
3. Fallen from Grace, or, When Sequels Attack … 107
4. Performing Identity through Dislike … 136
5. The Multiplicities of Dislike … 176

Conclusion: The Rhythms of Dislike … 213

Acknowledgments … 223

Notes … 227

References … 239

Index … 253

About the Author … 259

Introduction

Media Studies: Click Dislike

One day, when I logged into Facebook, an interesting notification told me that my posts had now been "liked" fifty-nine thousand times. I am certainly flattered by the notion that my witticisms, pictures of my daughter, political rants, and comments about Star Wars have brought fifty-nine thousand brief instances of pleasure to people. Undoubtedly Facebook shared this news with me to provoke exactly this reaction and to encourage me to keep posting, to mildly delight or somewhat amuse the next fifty-nine thousand. But what Facebook didn't tell me is how often my posts have brought displeasure. Facebook has a "like" button, in 2016 added a range of other emoji reactions, and more recently added a "care" emoji, but it still has no "dislike" button. Thus, not only can *I* not easily see how much displeasure I've created, but neither can *you* easily see how much displeasure I've created. Scanning through my Facebook, you can see tallies of posts that produced more or less likes, and these and the other reaction-button tallies allow you a vague window into other reactions; but you'd be left with a metric only of relative like, not with solid indicators of dislike. Surely, this is why Facebook has steadfastly avoided adding a "dislike" button, not just so that its many individual users never receive a notification telling them their thoughts have been disliked fifty-nine thousand times but so that their corporate users are free from interacting in an entirely volatile climate. Advertisers can be trolled mercilessly in the comments section, but not only can they delete these if they wish, but the contents don't create a quick, easy, conspicuous metric of dislike: there is no plebiscite on the displeasure they created such that when, for instance, a sponsored post advertising the next Marvel movie pops up on your feed, it announces that two and a half million people have disliked it already.

Facebook is not alone in this matter, as Twitter similarly allows one the capacity to "favorite" a tweet and similarly tabulates these favorites, using a heart icon that communicates favorites as *loves*. But, and as much as Twitter has a reputation for being a hotbed of anger, bile, and villainy, dislike is never quantified and announced. Netflix, Amazon, Hulu, Disney+, Spotify, and many other leading content providers will tell you about content their algorithms believe you might also *like*, and surely they're hiding or burying material that their algorithms believe you'll dislike; but never do they announce potential dislikes. Thus, if I hear about a new television show and search for it in my account, never will Netflix explicitly wave me away, telling me I won't like it; Fandango won't send me a weekly list of movies to avoid; Spotify won't open a pop-up window warning me away from listening to a searched-for artist; and Amazon won't save me from a reckless DVD purchase by mobilizing its algorithm to predict when I'll dislike the item I'm about to order. Occasional smaller start-ups and quirky experiments attempt to harness the power of dislike, such as Paul's Music Wreckommender,[1] which enables you as a user to seed it with music you dislike, before getting further recommendations on music you might also dislike, or such as Hater, a dating app that aims to unite people through common dislikes. Some research even suggests dislikes may be more predictive than likes.[2] But for the most part, the algorithms, platforms, apps, and programs that preside over many of our digital, televisual, gamic, musical, and filmic lives and expeditions strictly privilege like and love.[3]

Like and love are conspicuous, advertised, and openly built into most of the interfaces and logics of our media encounters, even (or especially?) if the joys and pleasures of media are in many cases only anticipatory, driving the market for much entertainment journalism from *Entertainment Weekly* to *Entertainment Tonight*, Apple News' many pages' worth of celebrity reporting to countless listicles of what's new, hot, and about to be released. Comparatively, though, dislike is rarely announced as openly, never completely absent from the picture but often operating in the shadows, unspoken. Our culture regularly tells us how much things have been liked or will be liked, and the algorithms and metrics that increasingly control multiple aspects of popular culture and everyday life heavily favor like and love. In this respect, they follow older, more austere metrics—from Nielsen to Arbitron, box-office stats to Billboard charts—that announce who watched, bought, listened, tuned in. Press and publicity that surround such metrics have often deviously turned mere consumption into liking and loving, moreover, as we're regularly told, for instance, that last week "ten million people fell in love" with a new television show, an assertion based solely on data that suggest ten million people watched. Whether they watched and disliked, left the set on while in another room, watched disinterested, or watched transfixed and enamored, those ten million people are counted as fans by much press and publicity. And especially high numbers are cited in awe as a supposed sign of popular adoration. In a niche-broadcasting era of television, ten million US viewers, for example, would be reported on as a hit—even though, of course, this means that over 320 million Americans variously didn't know about, didn't care, or didn't want to watch. A worldwide box-office haul of $500 million for a popular franchise film will lead to plaudits and the aura of success, even if this number practically means that a clear majority of the globe never watched, some with purpose. Of course, media metrics may cast conspicuous shadows of failure, as when a big-budget film makes "only" $50 million at the box office, but even in such instances, nonviewers are regularly coded as potential fans and lovers whose spark was never ignited, not as those who might actively dislike. Dislike is regularly seen as a failure to like rather than as a productive position and reaction in and of itself.

If the metrics, algorithms, interfaces, press, and publicity of popular culture often favor interest in like over dislike, though, so too has the academic analysis of popular culture shown far more proclivity to analyze like and love and developed many more theoretical tools for the interpretation of likes and loves, while showing far less interest in dislike. Admittedly, much academic analysis is probably motivated by analysts' own disapproval, and when, for example, Mark Crispin Miller can refer to "the great boiling cesspool of daily television,"[4] negative reactions are clearly still represented within the annals of media studies. But when audiences other than the analyst are consulted, invoked, and/or theorized, they are regularly fans or at least casual viewers. One could amass a large collection of books and articles about fans and fandom while finding comparatively little about dislike, annoyance, disinterest, and alienation. Fan studies is a vibrant subfield of media studies with its own journals, conferences, scholarly interest groups, and turf wars, while nothing approaching its apparent opposite exists. As Martin Barker and Kate Brooks note, metaphors of "diet" abound in discussions of reception and "consumption,"⁵ but diets are composed as much by what we choose *not* to eat, by what we spit out in disgust, by allergies and distastes, and by food we eat only because we must (not because we want to) as they are by what we enthusiastically consume. And thus this book begins with the assertion that media studies needs its own dislike button.

Clicking the dislike button repeatedly were the 216 interviewees who talked to my research team. *Dislike-Minded* draws from these interviews to construct an account of what dislike is, what it means, how it works, what it tells us, how it matters, and thus how it should change and nuance our understanding of audiences and of their interactions with media. It also assembles moments when other researchers and/or their audiences have discussed dislike. Far from merely not liking, I'll show, disliking is a complex act. It is also a deeply relational act, one that tells us a lot about the disliker's relations with other people, with other texts, with ethics of media practice, with representational systems, and with other yearnings and needs for the media. At the risk of stating the obvious, dislike is critical. But because it is critical, it is a site of analysis and of reflection, of individual texts but also of media writ large. Dislike can be snobbery and can perform superiority over the disliked object and its presumed audience, but it can also perform identity, self, and community in many more constructive ways too. Dislike is a reaction to those objects that the disliker feels are inescapable and ubiquitous, taunting the disliker with their presence, and thus it tells us about absences that the disliker feels deeply, perhaps painfully. Dislike regularly overflows from single objects to entire genres or types of media and thus offers the audience researcher scripts about generic annoyances and about grander perceived media failures. Regularly, though, dislike operates in the shadows and silences. At times, it can be joyful, pleasurable, and announced, but as or more often, I was told repeatedly, dislikers tense their jaws and say little. However, since, as argued earlier, many of our media aggregators and algorithms do not explicitly ask or talk about dislike and since much of media studies does not explicitly ask or talk about dislike, we know too little about it. Dislike may seem to be a "negative," destructive reaction, but in listening to 216 dislikers talk about and explain their dislike, on the contrary, I was regularly struck by how potentially "positive," instructive and constructive, intricate, and articulative a response it can be, and thus *Dislike-Minded* seeks to share that appreciation and understanding of dislike.

Hate, Dislike, and Antifandom: The Object and Ethics of Analysis

Dislike poses itself as the absence of something ("dis-like"), and while I will argue for its presence and for its constructive, "positive" powers, to define dislike therefore still requires that we start with what it is not. Confusingly, in particular, negative reactions are regularly if problematically conflated—dislike, hate, disgust, and annoyance among them. This book is about engaged, not mundane, dislikes. For instance, I don't especially like most hospital dramas, but I don't care about that dislike and don't feel it speaks any larger truth that I want to share; more accurately, I should say that most hospital dramas *disinterest* me. When someone's response to whether they liked something moves beyond the figurative "meh" or "nah" to a declarative "hell, no," that's when my interests here begin. However, this book is also not about (true) *hate*. Hate is regularly invoked colloquially to mean dislike, as when people utter, "Omigod, I hate that show. It's the absolute worst," and is perhaps especially common when we are trying to distinguish between mundane, disinterested dislikes and impassioned dislikes, wherein the latter attract the word "hate." But true hate is a psychological state, and I am more interested in probing cultural explanations than psychological ones. Just as love, anxiety, depression, and a host of other words describing mental or emotional states confusingly have their colloquial versions, so too does hate, and it's only that colloquial hate that is under analysis in this book.

What is real hate? Hate has been defined in different ways, but most definitions involve the presence of pain, anger, and a desire for elimination. It has also most regularly been understood as "an intense and irrational emotion [and as] a disorder in perception in that it deludes thinking."[6] Hate is usually addressed at groups—indeed Aristotle distinguished it from anger precisely in its direction at groups instead of individuals[7]—and is linked with stereotyping and Othering. Importantly, too, hate requires aggression, a form of anger aimed at eliminating a perceived object of danger and "a complex aggressive affect that is chronic and unstable, unlike rage or anger. Its primary aim is the destruction of the object of hate."[8] The psychologists Robert J. Sternberg and Karin Sternberg note that hate has been hard to study closely from a psychological perspective, in part because potential research subjects are far less likely to admit to hate, while members of hate groups have predictably been slow in presenting themselves as research subjects.[9] Nevertheless, hate groups and hate speech feature prominently in sociological research, and there is even a *Journal of Hate Studies*. As this line of research suggests, hate and its "affective economy" have proven to be key topics of analysis for many scholars precisely because and when hate serves as a precursor to acts of violence including murder, terrorism, torture, and genocide.[10]

While I do not wish to foreclose on instances when dislike and hate *overlap*, hate carries requirements that simply do not exist in dislike by itself. Across over 250 hours of interviews, none of my subjects spoke of legitimately wishing to harm their objects of dislike, and even verbal aggressiveness was remarkably absent from our discussions. The dislike was at times articulated to people and groups but even then was generally directed at texts, stories, and experiences. It was regularly rational, rarely if ever unstable. Largely missing, too, was the fervor of hatred; rather, many reports of dislikes were framed within an acknowledgment that nothing would or (respondents often suggested) could be done about them. Sternberg and Sternberg offer a "triangular hate scale" that examines various forms of hate, variously combining (1) distancing, repulsion, disgust, and disengagement, (2) passion in hate, anger, and/or fear, and (3) commitment,[11] and while this can very loosely be applied as a way of distinguishing some forms of dislike from one another (wherein, for instance, some are based more firmly on revulsion, while some are more passionate, some more committed), by and large the scale's inadequacy and often outright irrelevance for discussing dislike proves a chasm of difference between hate and dislike.

If hate has been well studied and defined by psychologists, though, it has also attracted a fair degree of recent analysis in media studies, largely because in addition to overlapping at times with engaged dislike, it overlaps at other times with engaged like and with fandom. Following critical interventions about fandom's and fan studies' raced and national exclusions,[12] a growing number of scholars in particular are wrestling with the ugly sides of fandom, and both *Television and New Media* and *Participations: Journal of Audience and Reception Studies* have recently published special issues on, respectively, reactionary fandom and toxic fan practices.[13] These publications join a growing body of work on trolling,[14] and specific studies on the racist, sexist, homophobic "swarm" that was and is GamerGate, a period in gaming fandom beginning in 2014 during which many women reviewers and gamers have been attacked, harassed, and doxed for criticizing video games' noninclusivity.[15] Much of this work has underlined Aristotle's point that hate is directed toward groups of people: GamerGaters wanted to remove from gaming at least feminists and antiracists, at most women and people of color in total. Rukmini Pande's discussion of racism in fandom shows how some fans palpably cannot tolerate the presence of nonwhite fans in their midst, while Anastasia Salter and Bridget Blodgett, Suzanne Scott, and Holly Willson Holladay and Melissa Click, for instance, all reveal a strong misogyny coursing through some fan and geek culture that wishes women would just go away so that the boys can play among themselves.[16] These scholars document how various texts and celebrities serve as *proxies* for hated groups of people. Sometimes these hates masquerade as mere dislikes of texts (professing, "I just didn't like *The Last Jedi*") or of particular stars or celebrities (insisting, "Kelly Marie Tran is a bad actress"), but if this textual, personal disagreement gives way to an annoyance and anger with communities of people (where, in some tellings, proclaimed dislike for *The Last Jedi* or for Kelly Marie Tran is in fact hate of women and people of color), we are seeing a manifestation of hate, not engaged dislike.

Hate, then, desires to eliminate people and wishes physical and/or psychological damage and trauma on them, which is why it is regularly the breakfast that feeds war, persecution, murder, and other violence. By contrast, engaged dislike gives voice to a potential wealth of other grievances that are about texts, representational systems, and ethics. Those grievances are not necessarily noble and progressive, but they are not concerned with group elimination or traumatization. Dislike may seek the elimination *of a text*, through cancellation, box-office failure, or so forth, but physical or psychological pain and traumatization cannot be inflicted on a text because—to state the obvious—it is an unfeeling object. Admittedly, celebrities may seem to trouble this distinction, and I will have more to say about this trouble later; but the engaged disliker still only seeks cancellation, not active elimination or an infliction of pain. For example, using the colloquial meaning of "hate," I have told people that I "hate" Céline Dion. Why? Partly because she seemed to be the only Canadian who people knew for a while, and thus her bland warbling seemed too easily to embolden the stereotype of Canadians being bland.[17] I have also claimed to "hate" especially vile contestants in reality television shows. However, I wish no actual harm on either Dion or the reality stars, and while I wish their significant wealth could be substantially redistributed, I don't wish *poverty* and the psychological trauma that poverty would entail on them either. In truth, therefore, I don't legitimately hate Dion or any reality contestant; I dislike them. I don't doubt that some others may legitimately hate them, seeing them as representatives of a feared, loathed group, and thus others may reach the person *through* the text; but at this point they have transitioned out of dislike and into hatred.

Admittedly, distinctions between hate and dislike are not always so easy to disarticulate, especially when analyzing others instead of oneself. Hatred may begin as dislike. The hating subject may have additional reasons for disliking the object of their hate, meaning they hate *and* dislike. Dislike may be a mere performance, perhaps even a self-deceptive one, papering over a truly hateful response. And functionally, especially because "hate" may colloquially mean "dislike," the two can often sound a lot like each other. This is why Emma Jane has rightfully noted a danger with research into "antifans" that ignores at best, or endorses and defends at worst, hate speech, threats of violence, and other traumatization of real individuals. Jane powerfully notes that any study of dislike, hatred, and/or antifandom needs to be based on an ethical sense of audience conduct.[18] Let me therefore pause here to respond to this charge, since the charge is noted in response to my own earlier work on antifandom,[19] where (for instance) I engaged with internet posters' expressions of both dislike and hate for then–*Apprentice* contestant Omarosa Manigault Stallworth (now Manigault Newman) without sufficient attention to the degree to which the commentary of some constituted online harassment. Jane writes, "The fact that human texts are liable to suffer from the circulation of vitriolic antifan discourse in a way that inanimate texts such as films or kilts do not, assists us in beginning to appreciate the ramifications of what Gray describes briefly as antifandom's 'darker dimensions' (2005: 852)."[20] Jane offers an overly kind response herself, allowing that my earlier work was written prior to the explosion in online harassment, but harassment is still harassment even if fewer people are doing it. Here and now, though, I want to distinguish between, for instance, one person worrying that "for many people the image she portrayed is the 'truth' [of what it means to be a Black woman] that the others have been hiding. For them Omarosa will be their opportunity to point and say 'see, I told you so . . . the rest are just pretending,'" and another who emoted, "Bring on the Terminator. This bitch needs to be taken down."[21] The former dislike focuses on Omarosa and *The Apprentice* as texts within representational systems, whereas the latter hatred calls for Omarosa the person (perhaps as stand-in for a larger group) to suffer. Thus, if you've never read my earlier work on "antifandom," great, we can start fresh; if you have, the distinction between dislike and hate for which I am arguing here is missing from that earlier work, as my understanding has evolved, as have my methods for exploring each, as will soon be discussed.

Dislike and Fandom, Dislike beyond Fandom

My thinking has also evolved from earlier publications inasmuch as I no longer see dislike (and hate) as simple opposites of like and love. Writing in a 2003 article, "New Audiences, New Textualities: Anti-fans and Non-fans," an erroneous Jonathan Gray offered a "nuclear" model of affective engagement, likening the fan to the proton, the antifan to the electron.[22] At the time, I was hastily trying to present a visually engaging way of considering how the "physics" of audience studies had been skewed. I like playing with metaphors but sometimes trip over them. Engaging with my data, though, has allowed a more complex and accurate model to materialize, one that allows for like and dislike, fandom and antifandom, to have more intertwined relationships with each other. Indeed, even if fan studies wasn't aware that it was doing so, the field has always been scratching at the itch of dislike, and a study of its scratch marks helps us form a sharper picture of dislike.

Given particularly early fan studies' desire to defend the fan's critical faculties, fan studies scholars have often been most intrigued, ironically, by the moments when fans attack, critique, and write back to their fan objects. Thus, whereas one might perhaps have expected fan studies to gift to media and cultural studies a slate of metaphors about textual care and about feelings of love, the vocabulary they instead offered consists largely of metaphors of violence—fans, we were told, were poachers or semiotic guerrillas,[23] who performed "raids" on and "must struggle with" mass culture.[24] Even Constance Penley's at first seemingly more gentle metaphor of fans offering a text a massage situates that massage as "strenuous [and] deep."[25] To Henry Jenkins, then, "the fans' response typically involves not simply fascination or adoration but also frustration and antagonism, and it is the combination of the two responses which motivates their active engagement with the media,"[26] a postulation that sees fans as already disliking, at least in part. When a decade or so after publishing *Textual Poachers*, Jenkins looked excitedly to what he dubbed "convergence culture" as offering some limited space for realizing a participatory culture that allowed fans into the machine,[27] his optimism was rebuked not just by those who see audience activity as irrelevant but by some within fan studies who insisted that the fan's position is still premised on "frustration and antagonism." A rather stark binary was offered of "affirmative fans," who loved unquestioningly, and "transformative fans," who regularly sought to address disappointments with a text through their actions,[28] and many in fan studies cast their lot with the latter, seeing the field and exploit as one of studying contested fandoms rather than shiny happy, sanctioned, adorational fandoms.[29] Louisa Stein writes that fan love "is almost always in interplay with a spectrum of negative emotions, from ambivalence to frustration to fear to dissatisfaction to hate,"[30] making it clear that fandom and dislike are hardly strangers to each other.

Many fans wrestle with their beloved objects. But whereas a fan has a reason to keep going with that work, to produce more reparative labor, the engaged disliker does not. Fans and engaged dislikers may see eye to eye with their criticism, but whereas other elements of the text beckon the fan closer and reward their poaching and engagement, the engaged disliker either sees too little else on offer or feels the pain of the text's infractions more than does the fan. Thus, for instance, several of my respondents discussed their discomfort with sexual violence in *Game of Thrones*. Some of them were self-professed fans and variously didn't care enough about it, felt the show had enough else on offer, or fatalistically didn't believe one even could escape sexual violence in Hollywood fare. Others actively disliked the show and derided it, feeling annoyed by both the text's and its fans' seeming moral apathy and feeling alienated from a society that held the show up. In coining "antifandom" as a thing, I risked envisioning these two groups as each other's opposite, when in fact they traveled part of their textual road together, diverging at a key point. Fan studies has mapped out part of that road with skill, but my task here is to map the divergent path.

In decamping from "anti-" to "dis-," I am upgrading my prefix. "Anti-" is unequivocal in being opposed, in being "not." "Dis-" may at first seem to be enshrouded by the same haunting air of negativity and negation, and thus it too risks defining the object through an absence, not a presence. Disorder and disbelief, after all, are the absence of order and belief, and to disrespect, dishonor, disbar, disown, disqualify, disband, distrust, disobey, and dismember are all processes characterized by absences. Within this frame, dislike may be seen to be "just" an absence of like. But "dis-" is a versatile prefix and appears in many words as the hero, performing noble work. To disinfect, disentangle, disarm, disrupt, disorient, displace, and discover can be positive and important acts that variously restore, reclaim, improve, or at least clear the path for such improvement. Similarly, I hope to show that dislike is far from a simple failure to like, as instead it can have positive, ameliorative intent and is a reaction and response with its own presence, nature, and value, all of which I use this book to explore.

In this respect, I do not intend *Dislike-Minded* to be a rejoinder to fan studies, for dislike is not simply, necessarily an absence of and opposite to fandom. Precisely because on the one hand no area of media studies has discussed audiences as well as has fan studies and on the other hand dislike and fandom are intricately connected, not Manichean opposites, I will regularly turn to fan studies. I want to avoid overstating the synergy, though, for the dislike-minded audience is not simply and only a subset of fandom. Jenkins notes that fandom's interpretive practices differ "in the types of reading skills it employs, in the ways that fans approach texts,"[31] in ways that demand we examine fandom as its own mode, and we must similarly allow that dislike will have its own reading skills, its own approaches, and its own modes, such that we cannot wholly place it under fan studies' protective wing. To approach dislike only from the direction of fan studies would be limiting, and this book argues for and engages in a broader audit that employs other approaches as well. It is my hope that I can do so without constructing straw fans and in a way that will be of assistance to fan studies scholars but that will also help media, cultural, and audience studies more generally to understand a wider range of perspectives and modes of being that audiences adopt.

The Legacy of Bourdieu

If engaged, passionate dislike isn't hate and isn't either fandom or its mirror opposite, what is it? Media and cultural studies, I posit, have long had their answer to that question, provided by Pierre Bourdieu's *Distinction: A Social Critique of the Judgement of Taste*.[32] Alas, that answer is woefully incomplete. Nevertheless, residing in the field's ür-canon, *Distinction* is widely assumed to have already given us *the* account of what dislike is, why it matters, and how we should approach it. Bourdieu advances the compelling thesis that cultural distinctions are classed by nature, serving the purpose of legitimating a class hierarchy. Taste, Bourdieu argues, allows individuals and groups to perform cultural superiority and to see their classed privilege as a function not of money and power but of a finer palate and regard for culture. As such, "art and cultural consumption are predisposed, consciously and deliberately or not to fulfill a social function of legitimating social differences."[33] In simpler terms, dislikers are elitist snobs. Bourdieu's theory is not "just" theory, no less, as he based his conclusions on social survey research conducted in France in the 1960s. But media and cultural studies scholars were quick to apply this theory to other national contexts. The importance of Bourdieu to media and cultural studies cannot be overstated. The core cultural studies project of discerning what place popular culture has in people's lives often requires a defense of the legitimacy of that project, something *Distinction* helps with par excellence, and *Distinction* opened many doors through which media and cultural studies scholars have fruitfully entered.

Along the way, though, media and cultural studies developed a moral economy of fandom, love, and like that was built in part on Bourdieu's characterization of dislikers as snobs. For many media and cultural studies researchers, dislike was the elitist, hegemonic move of containment and belittlement that preceded their defense of the margins based in like. Witness, therefore, John Fiske's championing of the (always enthusiastic) "active audience," Janice Radway's exploration of why women liked romantic fiction that seemed on its surface so sexist and so trashy, Julie D'Acci's consideration of lesbians whose fandom of *Cagney and Lacey* could not be deterred even by the producers' active disregard of them, or Henry Jenkins's bold initiation of fan studies, for instance.[34]

An odd bifurcation for which we cannot blame Bourdieu occurred in this work, as active audiences were romanticized as fighting hegemony through reclamative acts of like, love, and fandom in ways that associated dislike with hegemony and power, like with the margins and with social justice. David Morley playfully observed of active audience theory, "the sins of the industry (or the message) are somehow seen to be redeemed in the 'after-life' of reception,"[35] thereby alluding to the calcifying cosmology that posited consumers as angels and gods acting through love. Love and like won the day, habitually framed as politically positive and agential, as resisting class, gender, and/or race chauvinisms that called for disdain and disapproval and that aimed to subjugate marginalized groups. Conspicuously absent from this early work are alternative accounts of loves, likes, or fandoms that reinforced and celebrated the status quo (perhaps even by "poaching" on a progressive, "good" text) or of dislikes by marginalized audiences of hegemonic culture. Or, rather, we must dig into accounts to find them unstated—Radway's romance-fiction fans, D'Acci's *Cagney and Lacey* fans, and Fiske's teen-girl Madonna fans surely turned to their respective fan objects because they disliked other masculine culture that offered them less room for semiotic, interpretive movement.[36] While early active-audience work helped our discipline onto its feet and is still vital in its refusal of a determinist notion of identity, interpretation, and media use, alongside its canonization of Bourdieu's *Distinction*, it also willed to us a deep suspicion of dislike and an at times unquestioning defense of like.

Bourdieu was not entirely wrong, for as chapter 4 will detail, dislike can perform superiority. But dislike does other things too, works in other ways, and audiences turn to it for other articulative reasons, reasons that I will explore in these pages. However, and in part because Bourdieu has offered such a strong rebuke of dislike and dislikers, I am particularly interested in examining ways in which dislike may be more progressive. I approached my audience research with an interest in listening to dislikers as more than snobs and in listening to the many critiques they offer of media culture without simply circumscribing those critiques as snobbery. Since Richard Hoggart and Stuart Hall,[37] the cultural studies project has called for us to listen to *how* audiences interact with media as a way of seeing how power, representation, and identity are fashioned in contemporary mediated society, and I contend that this act of listening must be directed toward not only acts of "making do," of poaching, and of creative repurposing of media but also statements of rejection, alienation, disdain, and frustration. Moreover, since our field often envisions the disliking snob as a white, middle-class, heterosexual cis man, as will soon be discussed, I was particularly interested to hear from more marginalized subjects. Inevitably, that choice skews my project in its own way, and I therefore offer no claim to this being the definitive account of all dislike. Where I fail, I hope others will correct me and will add to the record. I have regularly struggled while writing this book, after seeing in society at large all sorts of angry and abusive statements that I in no way wish to endorse, defend, or normalize through my work. Dislike can come from truly awful people for truly awful reasons. But I wanted this book to consider what dislike can do and what it can be for others.

Voyaging into the Upside Down: Chapter Summary

What else is dislike, and what else does it do? By way of piecing together a fuller response, each chapter offers its own answer, cutting its own line through my interviews, through theory, and through others' audience research to make sense of dislike in action.

Chapter 1 begins by arguing for the legitimacy of considering disliked objects as texts, and dislikers as audiences. If dislike and dislikers have been insufficiently studied to date, this is undoubtedly due in part to assumptions that someone who dislikes something isn't engaging closely with it and may not have watched, listened to, or used much of it. Many dislikers have seen only a small portion of a disliked television show, for instance, or may dislike a film without ever having sat down to watch it. Can we therefore fairly say that the unfinished, partial text truly *is* a text or that someone can "count" as an audience member if they have actively resisted being an official audience? Chapter 1 argues that we most certainly can and should, though to do so requires rethinking how we define textuality and audiencehood. If our interests lie in understanding what texts do in culture and society, we must work with a broader, more encompassing theory of textuality that considers all interactions with the text as potentially important and constitutive. To do so therefore ushers dislikers back into the room, for their dislike and their stated reasons for their dislike are as much a part of popular culture, and of the vortex of meaning that surrounds any given text, as are the appreciation of fans or the negotiated readings of casual consumers. I make this case theoretically but also consult audience interviews, noting the near-universal feeling that passionately disliked objects were perceived to be ubiquitous and inescapable. Respondents, in short, regularly felt forced to be audience members, whether because they did not have the power to turn off the television or change the channel, because they had social reasons to keep consuming, or because a text's presence in popular culture made fleeing impossible. Whereas audience studies has usually operated with assumptions of agency, choice, and selection, therefore, respondents reminded me that many acts of consumption are begrudging, annoyed, resentful, or simply required; we probably all consume this way a lot of the time, and thus I attempt to return the voices of such acts of consumption to the overall record of audience studies.

Chapter 2 charts how dislikes were nearly always deemed representatives and banner carriers for qualities of media that respondents disliked in general. First, I turn to "worst violator" discourse, wherein a disliked text was talked of as the worst in class, as especially egregious and awful. In telling my research assistants and me *what* the text was awful at, though, respondents regularly offered a general critique either of media writ large or of a type or practice of media that respondents felt was similarly ubiquitous and inescapable. Here, then, asking about disliked media sent probes deep into respondents' overall reactions to the media landscape in which they lived and into its representational systems, often telling us far more about their understanding of and reaction to that environment than about the specific text per se. Yet, more common in my data were instances in which the object of passionate dislike was not seen as "the worst" but rather had let the respondent down. In many instances, as charted in this chapter, we were told of expectations and hopes that a respondent had for an item of media and then of the palpable sense of betrayal and disappointment when it failed to deliver. Again, though, these moments offered rich commentary on the media environment writ large and on respondents' general senses of what was missing from that environment. If more traditional audience studies have excelled at charting responses to what is there, asking about dislike often focused discussion on what is not there and on the annoyances that attend these absences. Chapter 2 focuses, as such, on the disliked object as synecdochically invoking broad critiques of the media and as something that tells us about the general contexts of and expectations for consumption. Dislike of one text, it shows, nearly always tells us about dislike of many more texts, trends, and patterns. I also consider who might *need* to dislike more than others and what privileges exist in being able to disavow dislike as a response.

Chapter 3 extends this focus on expectation to a specific, if large, category of reactions to adapted, rebooted, and extended media. Whereas chapter 2 focuses on unmet expectations, therefore, chapter 3 turns to instances when an expectation either *was* met at a previous time and by a narrative's or text's previous installment and yet is now perceived to be violated or when its failure to meet expectations festers over time. I begin by examining "deal-breakers" and audiences' moments of turning on a formerly enjoyed text. Then, I study disappointed and disapproving responses to *Gilmore Girls: A Year in the Life*, a Netflix sequel to the popular television show that aired nine years after *Gilmore Girls* ended. My interest in both cases lies in what responses to the text after it has been perceived to cease being good tell us about exactly what audiences "truly" appreciated in the earlier version. I dub this *refractive audience analysis*. I then apply it to critics' discussions of sequels and prequels, offering the case study of reviews of *The Hobbit: An Unexpected Journey*, the critically panned follow-up to the critically lauded *Lord of the Rings* trilogy. And then I apply refractive audience analysis to the recent spate of toxic white-male anger spewed toward sequels or reboots of their beloved fan objects when the sequels aim for more inclusion of women and/or people of color. While serving as a reminder of the more toxic expressions of dislike edging into hate that also populate the world around us and while illustrating how the techniques of analyzing dislike can at times be applied to hate, this case study also shows again how much we can learn about the importance of "the original" to fans through examining their negative reactions to later adaptations. In total, the chapter also seeks to situate dislike as interactive with other responses and reactions—dislikers don't just dislike, and chapter 3 explores moments when like becomes dislike and when dislike becomes hate.

Chapter 4 focuses on expressions of dislike as performances of identity. In doing so, I take my lead from Pierre Bourdieu, whose theories of dislike are—as noted earlier—canonical and widespread. To Bourdieu, dislike performs and reifies class positioning, so I first turn to his statements and to examples of classed performances of identity in my data. I then consider the wider-angle understanding of Bourdieu's work with which some scholars have operated, namely, that dislike performs any form of identity-based superiority, whether that be gendered, raced, nationalized, or other. Again, I see significant purchase here and offer examples from my data. These examples take the form of numerous individual comments, but for a more sustained and shared performance, I turn to a case study of Malawians discussing the film and television they like and dislike. From them, I regularly heard clear articulations of what Malawi was or should be (according to the speaker) embedded in the language of dislike for a particular type of film or television. I thereafter focus on gendered and raced performances by respondents in the United States, working with Bourdieu but also in an attempt to move beyond him to show the limitations of his theory in encompassing the broad range of overlapping, complex performances we construct.

Across chapters 1 to 5, I explore dislike as both a common and a fully legitimate response and reading, insisting that the dislike-minded audience is as important to an understanding of contemporary media as is the fan. I explore dislike as felt when the disliked object is perceived to be ubiquitous and inescapable in ways that invite the analyst to discover what it represents and what that dislike says about the disliker's interactions with the media and social worlds in general. I explore it as a window into what precisely is liked and disliked across the mediasphere. And I explore it as performative of identity. Such is the complexity of dislike, though, that we should regularly expect multiple reasons and/or performances to be operational at any given time, and thus chapter

5 turns to multiplicities of dislike and to these layerings of reasons. The first form of multiplicity I consider is when pleasure and displeasure commingle, when an audience member's dislike of an item of media is variously felt, practiced, or expressed in joyful ways. I focus on the thriving industry of criticism of "awful" films or television shows, wherein a "poetry of putrescence" is employed to describe just how awful something is. Such poetry should tip us off to a conflicted response that mixes dislike with like, that capitalizes on and enjoys dislike. I carry this on to a broader consideration of some viewers' enjoyment of spectacles of failure and consider what pleasures these spectacles—and failure in general—bring. Another form of multiplicity, though, layers various reasons for dislike upon each other, producing not the singular reason to dislike that Bourdieu offers but an intersectional matrix that requires closer study, and I provide several examples from my data to do so. To consider dislike as a performance of sorts, though, is to open the door to another form of multiplicity, produced by deception or self-deception, moments when audiences claim one reason for dislike yet offer evidence in those claims of other reasons. Finally, I consider what multiplicities exist in the socialities of dislike. My project focused on individuals as individuals and thus didn't produce enough discussion or consideration of how one's dislike networks and interacts with another's. However, the deliberations—or lack thereof—that surround disliked media and their communities are the focus of the final section of this chapter.

This book has been motivated by many desires and urges, but one of them rises to the foreground in the conclusion, as I offer some suggestions of how this discussion of dislike of items of media might tell us about dislike more generally. Dislike is notoriously disrespected: critics are regularly waved off with the suggestion that they should "produce something themselves." Tone policing and respectability politics regularly plague any progressive movement, as concerns about "negativity" can shut down many important, vital demands for rights. As a society, I pose, we are disgracefully bad at understanding how dislike works, at listening to it, at knowing what to listen for, and at knowing how it differs from hate. Because we don't talk about dislike enough, we don't understand when and how it differs from other "negative" emotions and don't appreciate when it is in fact largely "positive" in form and intent. This book isn't ultimately about dislike in organized politics with a capital *P*, but in my conclusion, I consider how an understanding of textual, media dislike could inform considerations of dislike, protest, and general grievances about our lot in life, and thus I end with some humble suggestions on how to listen to dislike in the political realm.

Methods for Exploring Unshared Worlds

The relative dearth of audience research on engaged dislike leaves wide swaths of people and reactions un- or underaccounted for. This amounts to a failure of representation, but it is a failure that enables various romanticizations about how media unite, bring together, and include. In Nick Couldry's terms, this failure of representation proffers "the myth of the mediated center": "the belief, or assumption, that there is a centre to the social world, and that, in some sense, the media speak 'for' that centre."[38] The myth is circulated regularly by media narratives that insist mass media such as broadcast television have access to the entire social world and both report to us all that matters and work to bring us to that world. But in talking to my respondents about moments when media narratives alienated them and categorically did not speak either for or to them, I aim to follow Couldry's call "to be sceptical bystanders, not celebrants at contemporary media's ritual feast."[39] Couldry sees the cultural studies scholar's job as one of assisting in the process of demythification, by focusing on moments of rupture, lack, and incompletion, offering the generative metaphor that "grasping the significance of media in the contemporary world is like trying to assess the speed and noise of daily life by standing in the mouth of a motorway tunnel."[40] To get a better sense of what is missing, therefore, "we must also know how to walk—slowly, attentively, with our ears open and not blocked—*away* from the roar of the traffic."[41] We must "listen beyond the echoes of the media process and search for new starting points for critical engagement within everyday practice."[42]

This book aims to listen beyond the echoes by turning away from the success stories to instead focus on moments of failure. Audiences have variously been described by scholars as "nomadic" or "roaming."[43] Offering the latter term, Annette Hill infuses Nordic notions of the right to roam and anchors this "in the tradition of wayfaring, meeting other people roaming the same pathways, and the co-operative endeavour of keeping these pathways open to the public,"[44] while expressing concern about structural limitations. But following Couldry, I ask about those who don't like this path, who want to get off it, who have chosen or been forced onto paths less traveled, and hence whose frustrated journeys have less often been recorded in trail maps or travel narratives. If Nielsen ratings tell us who watched and allow or encourage excited PR about fandom, engagement, and love, I want to listen beyond the echoes for the experiences of those who didn't watch. J. Halberstam and F. Hollis Griffin remind us that one person's failure is another person's success,[45] but concurrently I wish to examine how one person's success is another person's failure. Such a move acknowledges that many of us live in unshared worlds, and many of our interactions with media narratives and characters are structured and characterized by acute reminders of this fact and of the unmet expectations and failed hopes we might have for the media writ large.

To be clear, neither Couldry nor I propose that media narratives *only* fail. I fully acknowledge and regularly feel the experiences of pleasure, happiness, inclusion, and inspiration that media narratives can offer. I hope that media creators continue to try to extend those pleasures to all and to serve a broader range of the world's peoples, communities, and modes of being in their collective work. But my interests here lie in listening to some sounds away from the motorway of media successes and fandoms.

To do this, I set up a large slate of 216 qualitative interviews mostly across three years but including earlier work. More specifically,

1. In 2008 and 2010, I spent time in Malawi researching media distribution and Malawian consumption of foreign media. I conducted interviews myself, while also consuming media with Malawians, and in 2008, I hired a local Malawian research assistant, Stanslous Ngwire, to conduct yet more interviews. Although this project was not about dislike per se, it became one of the inspirations for this book, given how often dislike was discussed in detailed, important ways.
2. In 2014–15, working as a research assistant, Sarah Murray interviewed thirty-two people in one northeastern and two midwestern cities. Some technical issues reduced the tally to twenty-four in-

terviews I use here. We published some findings and commentary previously,[46] from which I draw here (with significant thanks to Murray), while drawing more deeply from her interviewees too.
3. Given the success of the preceding studies, I subsequently hired four additional research assistants in 2015–17 to expand on the project. Taylor Cole Miller interviewed queer respondents. Jacqueline Land interviewed a range of viewer types but including numerous seniors. Caroline Leader was already planning to study parents of small children for her own research but agreed to ask extra questions specifically about dislike. Tony Tran was conducting ethnographic work with Vietnamese Canadians and shared with me ten interviews that included discussion of dislike.
4. In 2016–17, working as a research assistant, Abigail M. Letak conducted interviews with self-identifying feminists about what she dubbed "deal-breakers" in television viewing, or instances when respondents felt that their personal politics required them either to avoid particular shows or to stop watching shows they had previously enjoyed.
5. In 2017, since Nicholas Benson was already intending to run an online survey asking about responses to *Gilmore Girls: A Year in the Life*, I opportunistically hired him as a research assistant to add several questions that plumbed dislike by those who disliked the four new episodes.

In Malawi, we interviewed 62 people as audiences. All were Black Malawians, 32 identifying as men and 30 as women, though ages were not recorded.[47] In the United States, in total Murray, Miller, Land, Leader, Tran, and Letak provided usable interviews with 154 people. They did not all record demographics, but across their interviews, 44 respondents identified as people of color during the interviews (29 percent), 68 identified as white (44 percent); 52 identified as men (34 percent), 102 as women (66 percent); 48 identified as gay, lesbian, bisexual, or pansexual (31 percent), 38 as straight (25 percent); 3 subjects were eighteen or nineteen (2 percent), 58 were in their twenties (38 percent), 42 were in their thirties (27 percent), 23 were in their forties (15 percent), 16 were in their fifties (10 percent), and 12 were sixty or older (8 percent).[48] Since the components in Malawi and the *Gilmore Girls* survey operated quite distinctly, I treat those data individually—in chapters 4 and 3, respectively—but otherwise move freely between the interviews in the rest of the book.

I opted for face-to-face interviews in part to ensure sustained interaction and engagement with subjects and hence in order to better parse between dislike and hate. We heard occasional manifestations of hate but nowhere near enough to allow the same type of careful discussion I feel comfortable offering of dislike. When I did engage hate more specifically, it was online, as in the notable exception of parts of chapter 3. I also opted to focus on shows and films, not on celebrities, in order to similarly focus more on dislike, following Emma Jane's warning about the fungibility of dislike and hatred in talk about celebrities. At times, my interview subjects talked about celebrities and other people involved with the texts they dislike, but almost all of these moments could be understood within context as expressions of dislike. I tried, in short, to heed Jane's call for "an ethics which recognises that the considerable power of new media producers includes the power to do wrong and to cause harm" and which is mindful of audiences' own creations of texts that serve to harass.[49]

All interviewees' names are pseudonyms, except for the *Gilmore Girls* survey, for which no names are offered. We struggled with *how* to name people, in the United States ultimately more often favoring generic names that can be found across racial groups to avoid racially essentializing the respondents,[50] while Malawian subjects were named using a list of popular names provided by a Malawian friend.[51] My concern with essentialism also led to my choice not to list identifying demographics unless a subject nominated aspects of their identity as important to their comments or unless other aspects screamed out their relevance. I realize that this side-steps well-worn social scientific practice of listing someone as, for instance, a thirty-five-year-old gay white man, but I wanted to listen to what aspects of themselves subjects nominated as mattering, rather than deciding on their behalf. A danger with this policy is that at times I may seem to be making whiteness and/or straightness in particular seem "normal" through being unnoted, since many more people of color and queer subjects nominated their race and/or sexual identities as mattering than did white or straight subjects. However, I only note demographics in the moments subjects themselves did, so when an interviewee's race or sexual identity isn't offered, this by no means should imply they are necessarily white or straight. Perhaps this gives the reader less of a chance to "check my homework" and/or to offer their own interpretations based on demographics, but my interpretations are based on access to the full interviews and hence to other, nonquoted yet contextualizing, framing comments, whereas I want to work against offering the false possibility that one quote pulled outside that context, placed against a single demographic piece of datum, should be sufficient to create a new understanding.

None of the interviews were framed as being "about" dislike. Rather, I took inspiration from my data gleaned from work in Malawi, where I had set out to ask many other questions yet dislike kept erupting through the data. Because I had not started those interviews by asking about dislike, I appreciated how much more context I had and how much more wide ranging discussion had been, thereby allowing me to better understand what role dislike played in my/our respondents' media consumption more generally.[52] Thus, I asked my US research assistants to begin their interviews with other questions, about contexts for viewing, about like and fandom, and only as the interview progressed to move toward questions about dislike. Thereafter, the interview "plan" was open. Each interviewer entered with different personal stakes, some hoping to get material for their own research into other topics. I appreciated receiving interview transcripts from different interviewers with different lines of questioning, different strengths as interviewers, and different focal points. I am compelled by Laine Nooney's and Aubrey Anable's proposal of "spelunking" as a method, in which one "grop[es] in the dark," only seeing so much at one time of "a potentially vast space that can be apprehended only a small section at a time," risking some concurrent disorientation,[53] and I liked the idea of sending out a team of explorers, each into their own chamber of dislike's formidably vast cave system. Ultimately, in short, I see variance in style as a feature, not a bug.[54]

Most interviews lasted between thirty and ninety minutes. Only a handful were conducted with two subjects present, as generally we were inquiring into personal reasons for dislike or asking occasionally for reporting on social reasons, rather than observing social constructions in process per se. I would then listen to the interviews via tape and pore over the transcripts.[55] Meanwhile, although the task of analyzing all this data fell officially to me, I benefited considerably from my interviewers' brilliance in noticing patterns, trends, and conspicuous presences or absences. I have conducted audience research myself before but found the ability to cross-check analyses, questioning styles, interview formats, and responses with a team of gifted scholars revelatory and far preferable to the solitary act of interpretation.

Having a diverse team of research assistants also proved helpful inasmuch as it allowed me to access a broader variety of interviewees than I would probably have been able to recruit myself. Some subjects simply wouldn't have felt comfortable talking to me (or even to some of my other interviewers) about certain topics. I regarded my identity—a heterosexual white cis male professor at an elite university—as a potential liability for a project that hoped to recruit a diverse group of interview subjects. Initial chats with random strangers about what they disliked had already made me worry that people with marginalized identities may not feel comfortable opening up to me along certain lines. Audience-based research will always need to work around various obstacles, and while I respect how other researchers have at times worked creatively to overcome the obstacle posed by their own specific bodies, my solution to this obstacle was to remove my body from the scene.

On the topic of bodies, I have come to regret not asking my interviewers to record observations about *how* our respondents were speaking and about their bodily gestures. This regret stems from reading the recent flourishing of academic analysis of affect, much of which carefully considers bodily reactions. Some scholars of affect, Sara Ahmed and Sianne Ngai especially, have written superb theoretical work on what Ngai poetically calls affect studies' "bestiary" of "ugly feelings."[56] My data, however, made a study of affect harder, in part because we collectively did not record bodily reactions, in part because our questions were generally designed to elicit more cognitive, less affective responses. The dislike that respondents discussed—as we will see—situates itself uncomfortably amid the more pronounced and more obviously bodily emotions of love, hate, and revulsion that are more commonly found in affect studies' bestiary.[57] My respondents would at times articulate their dislike as emotional, framing their reactions as truly affective, but not commonly enough for me to find this the most compelling lens through which to examine them. As such, my analysis follows Anable in considering more everyday, mundane affect. Anable begins her book on video games and affect by finding considerable meaning and relevance in the simple act of a commuter playing *Candy Crush*: "She is running out of moves. This is frustrating, but only mildly so. Approaching her stop with no chance of winning, she hastily and disinterestedly matches a couple more pieces and closes the game. She failed the level again, and she has arrived at her destination. She tucks the phone into her pocket, and she does not think about the game again until her next commute."[58] My own approach to affect similarly seeks not the grand affect of hate or revulsion or therefore to find these affective reactions leading to equally grand end products such as politicized activism but instead to focus on what Andre Cavalcante evocatively calls "the microphysics of participants' everyday lives" and on the no less fascinating yet more tame beast that is dislike.[59] This project sits adjacent to affect studies' bestiary of ugly feelings, interacting with it at times, but is ultimately its own creature. I hope others will ameliorate this record with work that is better methodologically designed to analyze the affects of dislike.

Before we continue, readers are reminded that this is qualitative, cultural studies work. My sample was not chosen scientifically, and it regularly relied on whom certain research assistants had access to. I make no claims to representativeness either in the recruiting of subjects or in the selection of whom to quote (with 216 people in a four-foot-tall pile of transcripts, I saw little virtue in citing everyone once, instead privileging more instructive quotes); 216 interviewees is considerably more than is common in qualitative work but is still only a start. Mine is also not ethnographic work and hence represents brief, fleeting encounters and interviews, not discussions that grew across weeks and months. My desire was to solicit a range of responses, such that I could feel comfortable noting some patterns but also some variances. I welcome and actively encourage others to go where my team and I could not, though, and I fully expect that some readers will experience frustration at missing accounts and specificities: I only hope that their response is not simply to furrow their brows but rather to pick up voice recorders and go amend the record.

1

The Audience for Dislike

Media hype regularly tells us that the whole world or at least country loves this or that. "Last week, America fell in love," it might announce, before inviting us to rejoin the country—"See the show that everyone's talking about"—and before quickly rebranding as "America's favorite new show." Entertainment journalism will often assist, promising to keep us in the know by informing us what "everyone" or "we" are talking about, what "the word on the street" is, and hence ultimately what popular culture entails at any given moment in time. Or even when "America," "the globe," "everyone," "we," or "most" aren't invoked directly, media hype frequently works by implying as much, suggesting ubiquitous popularity of the show, film, or other text in question and inexcusable (if quickly rectifiable) failure to participate in the global audience.

As critically aware viewers, we need to resist this rhetoric. There is something in it of the sly teenager who has mastered the art of telling their parents partial truths. A particularly devious word in media hype's arsenal is "most," since one of its meanings suggests a plethora, a majority: if someone ate "most" of the pie, they consumed at least 51 percent. But when the definite article "the" is added to "most," everything is relative, and percentages can drop starkly. Fox News, for instance, crows that it is "the most watched" cable news channel in the United States, a boast that is regularly borne out by Nielsen ratings data. But for 2019, that meant an average of 2.57 million Live+7 viewers,[1] not even 1 percent of the US population. Granted, Fox News' total viewership is surely more than 2.57 million viewers, as some viewers aren't measured by Nielsen's spotty metrics and as some cycle in or out as viewers over time (presumably it's not the same 2.57 million people watching every night). But this number is still worth considering, given the degree to which both Fox News' fans and its detractors assume its centrality to conservative viewers and its cultural impact. And yet precisely because it is spoken of as so central to American life, surely almost every American adult is now aware of its existence and knows what Fox News is. Thus, instead of following the logic of media hype, we could and should just as easily stop and tell its story differently, noting that over 99 percent ("most") of the nation do *not* watch Fox News. We might even note that Nielsen data suggest that most *conservatives* do *not* watch Fox News either. We'd therefore be left with a whole set of important questions about why—questions that should of course also be asked of Fox News' competitors with their even more anemic viewership. Of course many ("most"?) nonviewers may feel ambivalent toward Fox News, their choice not to watch not a determined one, but we might also hypothesize that Fox News is widely disliked, even among conservatives.

Similar questions could and should be asked of a wide range of texts, particularly those whose surrounding hype both boasts a certain level of ubiquitous popularity and ensures that most or all of us have heard of them and know we're supposed to be watching. From 2004 to 2011, for example, *American Idol* sat atop the Nielsen ratings, placing first or second for average viewers each year. The host, Ryan Seacrest, laid the hype on thick when each week, prior to announcing the phoned- and texted-in votes for who should remain on the show, he declared that "America" had voted. Yet during this stretch, the show's weekly audience according to Nielsen was usually between twenty and thirty million, or between 6 and 9 percent of the US population. As with Fox News, it is still impressive, relevant, and worthy of analysis that the show attracted more viewers than any other program, but a whole other set of questions for analysis present themselves, surrounding those who didn't watch. "America" didn't watch *American Idol*, but surely almost everyone in America knew it existed; and thus, amid the 91–94 percent of the population who weekly did *not* watch, many may have been determined nonviewers, not watching for reasons, caring about their choice not to watch as much if not more than those who chose to watch.

These questions should follow all programs, no matter the audience. The Super Bowl has become iconic as a ratings giant, and press and hype surrounding it suggest, in Seacrestian terms, that "America" is watching. Local newscasters report on Super Bowl mania and parties as if the entire nation is glued to the television, and the day after, its Nielsen-measured viewership is reported in amazement. Yet for all the suggestion that "we" are all watching, the largest viewership the show has ever attracted was in 2015, when it averaged 114.44 million viewers.[2] This number is certainly staggering in an era in which, as we saw earlier, the most watched cable news channel garners less than three million viewers, or when *American Idol* can pull in twenty to thirty million. But it also means that about 65 percent of the nation did *not* watch the Super Bowl in 2015. Many nonviewers probably had jobs or needed to sleep or had to take their kids to ballet class or so forth; others, though, surely didn't watch for a determined reason. And those others and their dislike go unmeasured and are buried amid the hype that suggests we "all" watched.

The preceding paragraphs take a US frame, but any calculations of who didn't watch or who didn't listen are even more telling if we adopt a global frame. In 2019, *Avengers: Endgame* grossed $2.794 billion worldwide, while *Star Wars Episode VIII: The Last Jedi* grossed $1.333 worldwide the previous year; and though it is impossible to convert box-office draws into viewer numbers, a stab-in-the-dark assumption that the average ticket price was $10 leaves us only 279.4 million and 133.3 million people watching each respective film in a world of 7.53 billion people. The South Korean boy band BTS topped global album sales in 2018 with 2.7 million sales of *Love Yourself: Answer*,[3] meaning 0.036 percent of the world bought the album. Piracy surely adds to these figures, probably substantively, but once again we're left with globally hyped entities—The Avengers, Star Wars, BTS—whose tales are told as stories of success, fandom, and popularity, even when the numbers dictate that we could *and should* just as easily tell stories of failure and dislike. These latter stories should not *replace* the former, but their relative absence is highly problematic, suggesting that neither media culture generally nor media studies specifically has engaged the true breadth of meaning of popular culture. While any reckoning with the Super Bowl or The Avengers must account for these texts' popularity and for why they are popular, it must also account for the dislike-minded audience, the large number of people who actively dislike them, who refuse to watch or listen, and whose reasons for rejecting them may tell us a great deal about them as entities in popular culture.

More than simply point to a need to ask why people don't like all the things that they don't like, though, the preceding numbers point to a fundamental problem with the way most analyses of the textual universe orient themselves in relation to that universe. I would pose that, to some degree or other, we are all textual analysts, not just the academic experts and professional critics who do more of it but everyone. Part of this is thanks to a universal interest in and engagement with stories and with reading and interpreting these stories communally. However, most of us are taught specific skills for interpreting texts in schools and are taught a specific *mode* of analysis that orients us toward texts in a limited way. The mode and the orientation are innocent enough and are intuitive, but they have limited how we make sense of a wide range of media and their cultural impact, import, and meaning, since they have produced an understanding of texts as entities that exist only or properly for those who engage deeply with them. Behind our collective inability or disinterest in thinking about The Avengers or the Super Bowl as rejected, failed media—not only as wild successes—is a limited understanding of what a media text is, how textuality works, and its place in our lives and cultures. And thus this chapter will expand and correct that notion of textuality.

First, I revisit textual theory to see both how it has directed analysts toward the close reader and how it also offers us the seeds of a theory of "readership" by the dislike-minded audience, even in cases when their dislike involves active avoidance of the work itself. This involves a redefinition of the text and a recentering of media studies on *the text*, not on *the work*, as has often been the case to date. I will then move beyond theory, though, to listen to our interview subjects. I will note how a considerable majority of them perceived the objects of their impassioned dislike to be ubiquitous and inescapable, to the point that they were drawn into the vortex of those texts' audience whether they liked it or not. In examining what these subjects told us, I want in particular to underline that much readership is involuntary. Collectively, we may have convinced ourselves to believe, overoptimistically, that being an audience is always an agential, purposeful decision, and our mode of considering audiences and the audience-text interaction is built on that optimistic approach. By contrast, though, I will argue and illustrate that a great deal of viewing, listening, and use is begrudging, coerced, and involuntary, and I will consider what textual and audience analysis entails if we open the gates to allow all these unhappy viewers into the category we call "the audience."

To do so, however, perhaps inevitably begs the question of whether they are "bad" or "wrong" audience members to whom we shouldn't give full legitimacy and from whom we may have received peculiar accounts of the textual world. Thus, I will close the chapter by addressing this question, armed with a broader, more encompassing theory of textuality and audiences that will allow us to see the complete legitimacy and undiminished importance of "viewers" who haven't actually "viewed" the text they're griping about, for instance. Future chapters will consider the specificities of why and how audiences dislike, but this chapter first engages the important work of arguing that their dislike is every bit as worthy of careful consideration as is a fan's like.

The Text as Object of Dislike

Simply put, most textual analysis proceeds from the understanding that meaning is within a text—by which is meant the work itself (the film, the television show, the song, the app, etc.)—and that we find that meaning by drilling deep into it. More nuanced accounts of textual meaning allow or insist that further meaning will be produced as the text interacts with audiences; they realize, in short, that not all audience members are equal and hence that texts will have different resonances for different audiences. Considerable disagreement exists over the status that should be allotted to these differences, with some people holding onto the notion that texts have a correct, intended meaning and thereby regarding all other interpretations as "wrong," as misinterpretations. Some see all language, and especially poetic language, as having its own slippery power and dispute the notion that meaning can be nailed down so easily, thereby regarding all texts as inherently fuzzy, allowing a range of interpretations. And some adopt a more relativist position, focusing on the audience member as a vital cog in the machine of textuality and expecting the audience's interpretive skills, life experiences, desires for the textual interaction, and social context all to play key roles in the production of meaning. Amid this disagreement, however, all sides regularly hold constant that which is being interacted with, and the audience member—if considered at all—is presumed to have engaged closely with that constant entity. Indeed, I am using the term "audience member," but the literature on textuality regularly prefers the term "reader," a word that conjures up notions of someone sitting with book in hand, carefully engaging with the words on the page. If the entity in question is the Super Bowl, therefore, one critic might look to the broadcast of that event, how it is constructed, how camera angles are used, which lighting and editing choices are used, what commentary is provided, and so on. Another might do this too but allow for a volatility of imagery and meaning, considering the range of interpretations that might attend the entire event. And a third may consult those who watched the Super Bowl, asking them what it meant to them. The entity in question is the same to each. All three may use the word "text" and handily agree, even in the face of disagreement about what to do with it, that they are interacting with the same "text." In truth, though, the text is bigger than any of these critics is allowing, and my task in this chapter is to reclaim that larger text, so that we might consider the meanings and audiences of that larger text.

Roland Barthes's important distinction between "work" and "text" serves as my starting point, since as oft cited as that distinction is, its radical import is too often underplayed. Barthes notes that the work is just an object: the book on the shelf, the digital file, the thing on the screen in front of us. But Barthes was part of a group of intellectuals demanding that we as analysts do more with the textual universe, seeing it as playing a role in the construction, maintenance, and/or contestation and replacement of ideology in the social universe. Books as such weren't just things to look at: they did things. They have meanings, sometimes intended, sometimes not, and they impact culture around them. They move meaning, thought, and ideology. And as much as Barthes was a keen reader of textual mechanics and form, his fascination with texts lay not with what they were, in some objective, clinically sterile, lifeless way, but with what they did and with what role they played in society and culture. Thus, he drew a distinction between that lifeless object—the work—and what it became as it entered culture, as it interacted with readers: the text. The work, he writes, "can be held in the hand, the text is held in language, only exists in the movement of a discourse" and "*is experienced only in an act of production*" that "decants" the work "and gathers it up as play, activity, production, practice," thereby asking "of the reader a practical collaboration."[4]

I contend, though, that while parts of Barthes's distinction were heeded, others were ignored (by Barthes himself, no less). What was heeded, and what inspired many scholars, was the notion that textual studies should be a study of ideology, of how power and meaning worked, how culture operated. Here Barthes's *Mythologies* is more operative and influential, as he offered both a general theory for the way texts produced "mythologies," or deep, ideological meanings, and contributed to scripts about how the world worked, as well as an eclectic collection of readings of various texts (from milk to wrestling) and the role they played in society and culture.[5] Since many of these readings were of everyday items, Barthes played no small role in encouraging textual analysts to realize that texts were everywhere, not just in university libraries and on literature professors' bookshelves, and thus he played a notable role in laying groundwork for media and cultural studies' interest in television, movies, popular music, cereal boxes, and more. In short, the message about what the analyst should do with texts was heeded.

But the distinction between work and text was largely unheeded. For Barthes, the distinction between work and text is not just that the former is on a shelf, lifeless, while the latter is in society; it is that the latter is therefore a larger entity, a "social space" in which language and meaning circulate.[6] As the work becomes a text, in other words, it becomes a vortex that draws all sorts of other meanings and entities into it.

A slate of these entities were characterized by Gérard Genette when he coined the term "paratext."[7] To Genette, paratexts are all those things that surround a work, dependently attached to it, yet that aren't part of the work itself. Genette wrote of books alone, but we can easily apply his terminology to other media. Thus, for instance, any given movie has its trailer, its poster, billboard ads, perhaps radio ads, while later gaining reviews, a DVD release with bonus materials, perhaps merchandise, fan creations and mashups, and so forth. All of these elements are paratexts. Elsewhere, I have written extensively on their importance to the textual universe and have noted the irony that textual studies scholarship still tends to pay disproportionately more (often exclusive) attention to the work, even while media industries regularly direct more money into producing promotional paratexts than into the work itself. Paratexts often occupy considerably more time and space than does the work itself (they may come to us two years before the film, for example; they may pop up on our internet browser or at bus stops; "director's cuts" may follow a film sometimes many years later), and in some cases they're even the whole point, as with the toys that were "paratextually" appended to 1980s kids shows such as *Transformers*, *My Little Pony*, and *G.I. Joe*.[8]

Regrettably, though, Genette makes two key errors in identifying the paratext. First, he is too wedded to the notion of authorial intent and highly problematically suggests that something only counts as a paratext if it originates from the authors. His definition of "author" here is slippery, though, as he clearly allows forewords by people other than the writer of a book, book covers, font and paper choice, and other items over which in most cases a book writer will have little if any control. Thus, while never saying so explicitly, he clearly allows "authorship" to be a broader construct including book-jacket designers, editors, and the publishing house. However, many book covers are designed by people who will never meet the writer of the book, will never discuss intent, and may never even read the book. We cannot assume that book-cover designers have any special relationship to or knowledge of intent. Their relationship to intent should be immaterial to the process of interpretation, though, as this is far less important than the simple fact that the paratext they create—the book cover—could conceivably play a key role in how many audience members interpret and interact with the book. The old saying tells us not to judge a book by its cover precisely because we regularly do judge books by their covers. And if book covers created by graphic designers with perhaps little knowledge of the writer's intent matter, so too do a whole host of other entities that Genette doesn't consider bona fide paratexts. Fan-made trailers or vids, for instance, may prove just as instrumental to an audience member's entry or reentry to a text. When media texts move internationally, the distributor or the new exhibitor may create their own paratexts that locals will watch, read, and listen to instead of or alongside the originals. Any and all paratexts can frame or reframe the interpretive process and hence can prove vital to what that text comes to mean, whether to a single viewer or to popular culture writ large.

Second, therefore, Genette is wrong to envision the paratext as external to and separate from the text. Rather, the paratext is external to *the work* but often becomes a constitutive part of *the text*. Following Barthes, the text is the entity that goes out into the world, that enters culture, that interacts with audience members, but as Genette himself acknowledges,[9] there is no such thing as a text without paratexts. We literally cannot enter a text without paratexts, and as I have argued elsewhere, the paratext is regularly the outpost of interpretation, the thing we encounter first as we move toward interpretation of the text. Genette himself writes that paratexts provide "an airlock that helps the reader pass without too much difficulty from one world to the other, a sometimes delicate operation, especially when the second world is a fictional one."[10] Swirling around any work will always be paratexts. And thus part of the process of a work becoming a text is its accompaniment by paratexts, and texts will always include paratexts. A text, as an entity in popular culture, will always at least potentially carry its paratexts alongside it, making them inseparable. When we talk about Star Wars or The Avengers, BTS or the Super Bowl, we cannot easily escape from the meanings appended to these texts by the ads and trailers, merchandise, discussions, parodies, and so forth that encircle them. Though some texts will have less and/or especially "quiet" paratexts, some more and/or especially "loud" paratexts, as texts become more prominent, famous, and part of popular culture, they produce and attract more paratexts, meaning in turn that any text that we regard as having an impact on culture will by nature be surrounded by many paratexts.

As such, "the text itself" is a theoretical impossibility: it is never just itself. Genette makes this mistake in seeing paratexts as external to "the text itself," but he is by no means alone, as even many scholars who are engaged in the process of expanding how we think about textuality use the term. Tony Bennett and Janet Woollacott, for example, direct Mikhail Bakhtin's, Valentin Volosinov's, and Julia Kristeva's writings on dialogism and intertextuality into one of media studies' smartest engagements with the notion of what a text is.[11] Their *Bond and Beyond* lays down a wonderfully useful theory of intertextuality, arguing for the inescapable interconnection of all texts and hence for all texts' reliance on each other. But they regularly talk about "the text itself," and while they do so largely to posit the dependence of that entity on others, the phrase should be "the work itself," since "the text itself" always includes paratextual and intertextual collisions and transfer. *The work* can be isolated from its social and cultural trappings, but *the text* is per nature a larger, sociocultural entity. Or, to use Nick Couldry's working definition for the text, it is "a complex of interrelated meanings which its readers tend to interpret as a discrete, unified whole,"[12] a postulation that allows for the oscillating size and shape of any given text (as long as we allow that "readers" may include dislikers).

When previously writing about paratexts, I focused on their impact *on the text* and how we think about it,[13] but we should underline what all of this means for an understanding *of audiences*. Namely, if a text consists of a work and paratexts, a work and its social trappings, *its audience consists of all those who have interacted not just with the work but with any of the paratexts and/or the social trappings*. In the case of texts whose impact on popular culture is small, we might therefore expect the audience of the text to be close in size to the audience of the work. But conversely, we should expect that when a text features prominently in popular culture, its audience will eclipse and dwarf the audience of the work. Think here of all the blockbusters you did not watch these past few years. If you saw trailers, heard ads, read reviews or think-pieces on them, read tweets about them, heard friends or colleagues talk about them, you are still part of that textual audience. Or returning to Star Wars and the Super Bowl, surely most Americans know that these entities exist and have some kind of reaction and relationship to them. Moreover, they are long-running texts—Star Wars has been with us since 1977, the Super Bowl since 1967—and thus it stands to reason that many Americans' reactions to and thoughts about these entities will have changed over time. Perhaps those changes will have been influenced by changing, or simply new, paratexts, or perhaps they have calcified. Either way, though, the texts' refusal to die, their continuing presence in popular culture, demands that people have thoughts about them. And so while a subset of Americans will have watched the most recent Super Bowl or the most recent Star Wars film, they are just that—a subset of the texts' larger audiences. When we see that 114.44 million Americans watched the Super Bowl in 2015, we cannot assume that *as a text and sociocultural entity* the Super Bowl only had an audience of 114.44 million; rather, we should assume that its audience is considerably larger and that many other Americans have their own reactions to it. Those other reactions contribute to the Super Bowl's place in American culture and are part of its text. They will frame how others new to the text make sense of it, they will serve as obstacles around which fans will need to steer, and they will play a role in determining what the Super Bowl is, does, and means to the nation.

I do not mean to suggest that each interaction with the Super Bowl will be equally meaningful or that each audience member will care about it similarly. Such is already the case with our (limited) understanding of (the work's) audiences: of those who watched the recent Star Wars films, some will be fans, some not; some may still care about the film many years from now, while others will quickly forget it. So too with the audience as I am conceiving of it: inevitably some people who didn't watch the latest Star Wars film had no real reason for not doing so, as Star Wars means little to them, while others will have adamant, determined reasons and will be sick and tired of this thing called Star Wars or simply of this current iteration. And thus I don't mean to suggest that everyone in the audience will play an equal role in constructing its public image, in determining what work it does in society and culture. Many simply won't care. But many do care. If a text is a work that has come alive for us, Star Wars' detractors are most certainly engaged with a text. Sara Ahmed poses that "to be affected by something is to evaluate that thing,"[14] and when we are affected by an item of media, when we care to evaluate it, something has become a text.

Here, though, I part with Barthes in one key respect, for while Barthes saw the process of meaning-making as one based in play and pleasure, I posit that much meaning-making is based in displeasure. To Barthes, the text is "bound to *jouisance*, that is to pleasure,"[15] and much of media studies' interactions with notions of textuality take this interest in play and pleasure as key. Michel de Certeau's romantic metaphors of the reader as "poacher" and as a mischievous meddler were taken up most prominently by John Fiske and Henry Jenkins.[16] Fiske explicitly merges Certeau and Barthes to offer a theory of "active audiences" that elude official, monologic culture by playing with texts to repurpose them. All of his examples, though, are of audiences having fun with texts, whether by extending and expanding on works they already like or by repurposing and rendering pleasurable a problematic work. Jenkins's model of fans as textual poachers similarly centers on enjoyment; granted, as with Fiske, Jenkins dispels crude postulations of fans as unquestioningly upbeat and reverential, but as with Fiske, his focus lies similarly on acts of play. By contrast, I pose that we must also attend to audiences that engage with texts in meaningful manner but may not be doing so with any sense of pleasure. In doing so, I build off Celeste Condit, who draws from an interview with a young man opposed to abortion watching an episode of *Cagney and Lacey* that defends abortion. Condit notes that the young man is *able* to fight the work but that it is not pleasurable to do so. Condit's aim is quite clearly to throw a bucket of cold water on Fiske's excited suggestion that we are all active audiences and hence that all messages can be and are opposed (and on the implication in Fiske's work that opposition will tend to be progressive, for that matter):[17] "It is not enough to argue that audiences can do the work to decode oppressive texts with some pleasure. We need to investigate how much more this costs them," she writes.[18] In doing so, she also helpfully offers us an example of a reader who engages with a work and its meanings, who (in Barthesian terms) "decants" it into a text yet who does so through displeasure. None of Barthes, Fiske, or Jenkins foreclose on the possibility of displeased reading strategies, but given their centrality in pointing media studies toward readings based on *jouisance*, the field has rarely gone looking for displeasure and thus has rarely interacted with large portions of the audience.

Certeauian/Fiskean notions of use and active audience engagement proved instrumental to opening media studies' door to the investigation of audiences but often privilege a particular type of audience. Fiske helpfully distinguished between "mass culture" as that which is offered by the cultural industries and "popular culture" as that which it becomes when/if taken up by audiences. Rehearsing a similar division between Barthes's work and text, this distinction insists that the *cultural* question to be asked and "the object of analysis, then, and the basis of a theory of everyday life [should] not [be] the products, the system that distributes them, or the consumer information, but the concrete specific uses they are put to, the individual acts of consumption—production, the creativities produced from commodities."[19] So far, so good. But in underlining this point, he also writes, "At the point of sale the commodity exhausts its role in the distribution economy, but begins its work in the cultural,"[20] an artful postulation that insists all texts are cultural resources but one that problematically links the process of use, meaning, and cultural significance to "point of sale," when in fact many of those audiences that don't "buy" the object in question still engage with the text. Sonia Livingstone's own argument for studying audiences insists that "for television to have any effects on its viewers, whether behavioral, attitudinal, or cognitive, programmes must first be perceived and comprehended by the viewers,"[21] and I find her focus on perception and comprehension as preferable, since partial, non-, and aggrieved "viewers" can similarly *perceive* and *comprehend* without ever making a "purchase" (in Fiske's terms) or watching an entire program. Or, in Nicholas Abercrombie and Brian Longhurst's terms, audiences draw "from the endless media stream that passes them by a set of diverse elements out of which they can construct imaginative worlds that suit them."[22] Since we all swim in that stream, though, we should expect audiences to respond not just to those elements in the stream that we're closely watching or listening to but also to the elements and whirlpools we're trying to swim away from and escape.

Ubiquitous and Inescapable

Behind some of the relative disinterest in dislike is a moral or practical judgment, namely, that dislikers could just turn off the television or radio or change the channel, not go to a movie or buy the video game, or so forth. But we're all force-fed a lot of media culture, such that merely not eating it, not uttering some regurgitory resistance, often isn't a realistic option. We may have a preferred media diet, yet social settings and/or available choices may regularly require us to cheat on that diet. I now turn to our interviews to give more empirical heft to that statement. Subsequent chapters will reveal much more about *why* and *how* the audiences consulted for this project disliked what they did, and those reasons and ways varied considerably. Constant across most interviews, though, was the sense that the texts the respondents disliked with passion and purpose were ubiquitous and inescapable. Few respondents were masochistically subjecting themselves to these texts; rather, they didn't feel that they could escape them. They were forced into being audiences. Many brushed off disinterests at speed, meaning that they all dutifully responded to the directive to "just turn it off" or "just change the channel" if they *could*, and in such cases spent little extra time focusing on why and how they didn't like such disinterests. But engaged dislikes were almost universally of texts with which the audiences felt stuck. And as I will show, the ability to "turn it off" regularly required more than the simple act of pressing a button on a remote control, as many of our respondents felt haunted by media that intervened in their daily lives even if they avoided it.

Before I turn to the audiences' commentary, it is worth noting how this consideration of reluctant audiences flies in the face of much of the framing of media consumption as based on personal choices and agential decisions about how, when, and why to watch. Popularly, excited PR rhetoric surrounding new media-delivery technologies aims to convince us that we are only getting more control as time advances, constantly insisting that algorithms cater to the individual, that viewing is "on demand," that delivery systems will filter out what you don't like, respond to your every choice and desire, and thereby give you only what you want, when you want it, and how you want it. Add mobile devices, and it's easy to make the mistake of thinking that each one of us exerts remarkable (*and increasing*) control over our media consumption. But from the outset we should regard such rhetoric skeptically, realizing the degree to which it is premised on a tacit acknowledgment that much media consumption is *not* by choice—the promise to give us what we want, in short, is smart advertising precisely because we regularly do not get what we want.

Academic work on consumption has also risked presenting it as involving more freedom than may honestly be the case. Some of this problematic framing may be an unintended side effect of "uses and gratifications" and "active audience" discourse. These two research traditions helpfully reframe questions of media effects by beginning the tale with the receiver, not the message, and by asking what uses or gratifications such an active viewer was seeking. They thus insist that audiences have agency. But surely agency is relative, always potentially circumscribed and limited by other contextual factors. Ethnographic work on media consumption, for instance, has regularly pointed out that most decisions about consumption are made within power structures, wherein someone holds the remote, owns the television, or so forth and others don't.[23] As David Morley notes of family television viewing, for instance, "As long as there is a main set in the most comfortable room, the question of 'what to watch' will remain a subject fraught with conflict and requiring delicate negotiating skills."[24]

"Negotiations" will at times be external, at times an internalized monologue. Ahmed, for instance, offers her own picture of a domestic scene:

> We begin with a table. Around this table, the family gathers, having polite conversations, where only certain things can be brought up. Someone says something you consider problematic. You are becoming tense; it is becoming tense. How hard to tell the difference between what is you and what is it! You respond, carefully, perhaps. You say why you think what they have said is problematic. . . . In speaking up or speaking out, you upset the situation. That you have described what was said by another as a problem means you have created a problem. You become the problem you create. . . . If you say, or do, or be anything that does not reflect the image of the happy family back to itself, the world becomes distorted. You become the cause of a distortion. You are the distortion you cause. Another dinner, ruined.[25]

Ahmed describes this position as that of the "feminist killjoy," and though her scene doesn't explicitly involve a choice to watch anything on television, nor is the described conversation necessarily about media, we can surely see how choice about what to watch and reactions to what was watched could quickly be pulled into this vortex, whereby the "social order" of the family, "which is protected as a moral order, a happiness order," is one to which some members of the family must either yield and acquiesce or else be willing to challenge at the risk of "caus[ing] unhappiness, even if unhappiness is not your cause."[26]

Or another strand of ethnographic work considers time-shifting and particularly housewives' attempts to control when they consume,[27] but such attempts render clear that for the most part, a lot of media texts aren't offered when we necessarily want them. And yet it's still common for media scholars to frame consumption as agential, chosen, and selected. Roger Silverstone, for instance, offers hopefully, "If we do not like one thing, we can turn to another. If we do not like one thing it will disappear soon anyway. Off the screens, slipping near the edge of the world, like an omelette out of its pan."²⁸ Or John Hartley suggests that "media are more voluntarist and avoidable than, say, school, family and government; all of which I have personally found a good deal more coercive, anti-democratic and manipulative than popular media."²⁹ But what about media's own moments of coercion?

Many of our respondents' most disliked texts were things that family, housemates, or friends inflicted on them. Of *True Blood*, for instance, Alex noted, "I would be at my friends' house when they were watching whatever new episode was on—this was back in college. But I always hated it, always. I thought it was so absurd. I thought the main character was a douchebag. Everything about that show rubbed me the wrong way." Her friends "laughed because they knew [she] hated it. It was a well-known fact," but they wouldn't allow her a reprieve. Or Ilana encountered shows she disliked when watching with her mother: "I don't want to watch this, like on the Health Channel. She also has TLC on a lot, which is the worst. They had this one thing that was like 'unexpected teenager becomes millionaire overnight.' I was like, 'this was the worst.'" Or Blanche disliked *Married at First Sight* but still watched with his partner: "We [I] don't want to leave. . . . We have a house that has multifloors on it. And we [I] could easily go to a different floor, but, um, we'd rather be together. So we'll stay and watch. I'll watch the show even if I don't like it. And it—it's the flip side for him. I mean, I like to watch, um, a lot of uh . . . sitcoms that he really doesn't like to watch."

Workplaces offered their own challenges to avoidance, too, as several respondents noted the steady stream of disliked material in an environment in which they did not have the power to change the channel or turn to another station. Portland, for instance, was a nurse who talked at length about the frustrations of being subjected to patients' media choices. She noted particular approbation to Bill O'Reilly and talked proudly of how she'd mute him whenever she needed to administer tests to patients who were watching him on television, but this was her lone act of rebellion, as she generally had to stomach O'Reilly and countless other objectionable media choices from patients. Sophie, meanwhile, worked at a television station that played *Two and a Half Men* reruns, thereby exposing her to endless episodes: "It's always on at work because in the mornings we always have our station on, so I can always see it. So it's like, ugh, this is like the two hundredth day in a row that I've had to watch this stupid show."

Throughout respondents' discussions of consuming dislikes against their wishes, they often employed the language of fatigue, noting that it is actively tiring and tiresome to sit through things they don't like. And this language of being "tired" offers an explanation, too, of why many of them didn't bother to assert their own preferences more. Erin, for instance, talked of challenging friends on social media about material she found offensive until ultimately, she said, "I started deleting a lot of people because I was just getting tired of educating people. Or at least, I would give them resources to educate themselves. Like, I was tired of searching for people's gaps or, like, searching for resources for people to fill in their own gaps. I was tired of that. So now, I just delete them." Social media provided her with the tools to avoid, through deletion and unfriending, but many others noted various reasons for why they didn't feel socially able to "turn it off" and/or why they felt that as "tired" as consuming disliked media made them, they were variously too tired to push back socially or valued the social togetherness enough to grin and bear it.

Alfred Martin has explored this dynamic in discussing four African American women's strong dislike for Tyler Perry's movies and television. None want to watch Perry, but "consuming Perry's films is rooted in social ties,"[30] Martin notes, and to simply refuse to watch the films—or even to admit to family and friends that they dislike them—would be to risk social isolation. Ultimately, then, they keep watching, since "the desire to be with family members and friend networks structures a reengagement with Perry, even as the experience of watching is not pleasurable."[31] Martin's work thus invites us to consider the displeasures that lie in the shadows of fervid fandoms—when "everyone" seems to like a text, we might be coerced into tolerating that text and into continued consumption. This is, in Martin's words, "the price of admission to maintain strong social ties," for "blood is thicker than Perry."[32]

Our own interviews offered many similar moments of what Martin dubs "quiet anti-fandom,"[33] in which respondents note social costs to tuning out. Melanie, for example, described her home environment this way: "[I will] play on my phone or put in headphones and watch something on my own. That's pretty much how I did handle it even in high school when I would get overwhelmed by what [my family] were into. We don't have internet in our whole house, so I would just kind of sit there with their program on in the background right there and watching something on my own screen in front of me." She described a lonely scenario (and exactly the kind of scenario that Martin's respondents probably feared), and it is no surprise that she then reserved particular, engaged dislike for the shows that isolated her from her family in such moments. Perhaps because of this history, Melanie noted that she became more accepting in college, acquiescing to whatever her friends wanted to watch: "Even if it really sucks, I'll probably grin and bear it, especially if it's something they really enjoy. . . . I usually just put up with them. I'm like, 'Yeah, we can watch this horrible one-hour comedy special,' and I'll fake laugh a few times."

Tellingly, Melanie then articulated this response to the general trials of being one of only a few feminists in an otherwise nonfeminist social group:

> I talk about this with my friends so much. It's like one of the theories that we've come up with is the feminist goggles. So there's certain situations where you have your feminist goggles on, and then sometimes you just want to take them off. So, like, sometimes you might want to see something that you know is violent toward women, and all your friends are going. So that might be a situation where you take your goggles off. And then you leave the theater, and you put them back on. It comes to a point where you have to let yourself enjoy and consume the media, but, like, it's also a scary line to tightrope, because if I'm allowing myself to watch this, I'm literally like an ironic version of myself by doing that. I kind of go out of my way not to watch that stuff on my own. But if a huge group of people were like, "Let's go see this movie where there's, like, one female character and the most interesting thing about her is her boobs"—they probably wouldn't say it like that, of course—but I feel like I can remove myself from my social-justiceness for like an hour, and I'll be like, "Okay, let's just watch this movie."

She claimed to be able, even keen, to remove her "feminist goggles" at times—to not be Ahmed's feminist killjoy—but a sense of the effort ("a scary line to tightrope"), cost ("I'm literally like an ironic version of myself"), and hence eventual backlash toward and amplified resentment of the material she was watching is palpable. And yet if it's hard work not to object in the moment and to "grin and bear" disliked material, Melanie's discussion of this dynamic suggests the degree to which particular people will be asked to perform this work more often, namely, those outside society's norms and comfortable center (as I will return to both later in this chapter and later in the book). A feminist cannot easily avoid sexist media, people of color cannot as easily avoid racist media, and queer consumers cannot as easily avoid heteronormative media. We might, therefore, expect to see heightened levels of engaged dislike amid marginalized individuals and communities, precisely because they are required more regularly to do the hard work of grinning and bearing it.

Sophie even suggested that expressions of dislike might thereby become important precisely because they would speak to the silently hating masses yet also harder to voice because of a social desire not to sound like a squeaky wheel. Her aforementioned dislike of *Two and a Half Men* finally led to her penning a screed against the show on social media. At one level, she thought this valuable, because, she said, "I wonder if some people don't say anything because they think, 'Oh, this is just the way society is,'" but she then quickly explained why she rarely took such a step: "If I say it's degrading, I'm just going to be [regarded dismissively as] another feminist, another person who is putting down some show because I have 'a feminist agenda.' ... It was kind of a unique thing, and so I thought, well, people could definitely relate and think, 'Okay, cool, not all of society thinks the same way, and if I hate it too, yes, there are other people out there who also hate it and agree with me, and I'm not just some 'stupid feminist.' Do you know what I mean?" As with Melanie, Sophie offered a picture of many people needing to sit on their dislikes for all sorts of social reasons, even while they fester and grow in the process. Ahmed poses that "happy objects" are those that we wish to surround ourselves with and that "to have our likes means certain things are gathered around us," which in turn would suggest that "those things we do not like we move away from."[34] But that "moving away" was regularly proven to be functionally impossible for some respondents. As Ahmed surmises, these moments, when one is "out of line with an affective community—when we do not experience pleasure from proximity to objects that are already attributed as being good," are moments of intense alienation,[35] and the objects/texts that actively alienate us will understandably be resented and passionately disliked.

Belabored Consumption: Watching through Gritted Teeth

Sometimes, if viewing is captive, the captivity is nominally self-imposed, inasmuch as nobody holds court in one's living room, holding one's remote controls for ransom, but another form of captivity can still be based on social pressure. Anne Gilbert quotes a critic of *Girls* who complained, "I spent two and a half seasons hate-watching *Girls* because mainstream media told me that as a millennial female I was supposed to like it. I needed to watch it to be part of the cultural conversation and not to like it somehow made me anti-feminist, but it was torture."[36] Similarly, Amy noted trying repeatedly to watch *The West Wing*, given how many of her friends spoke highly of it. She said, "I really want to watch it because it's such an iconic show," yet each viewing reiterated why she disliked it. Or Charlie explained why he watched *Game of Thrones* alone or with his (similarly unimpressed) partner, Trent: "in order to be part of a larger cultural conversation, I think, and conversation among my friends." And TJ noted a general disinterest in and dislike of sports and the Olympics yet reported "feeling more and more pressure only because one doesn't want to be left behind, you know [*laughs nervously*]. For instance, there were people in the office that did not watch the Olympics, and so once it's, like—you know, you're not watching the Olympics—that's what people are talking about, so you—what do you talk about if you're not talking about the Olympics?" As a queer viewer in an otherwise entirely straight workplace, TJ bemoaned always needing to watch "their" shows even when he disliked the shows yet nobody ever feeling compelled to watch his shows, thereby further indicating the degree to which the "labor" of watching can be disproportionately assigned to minorities. TJ suggested that this is even made flagrantly explicit in his workplace: "That's the joke, is that every show I watch they don't watch." TJ offered a sadly touching account of someone who is always watching "other people's" television to please them, even at his grandmother's house, so that he can fit in and have something to talk about, all the while learning to dislike yet more programs.

Tom similarly constantly watched things he didn't like just to please others, though in his case, it was to please partners. He tellingly self-corrected and revised "like" to "I didn't mind" when describing his relationship to such media, as he noted, "It's nice to see. I like to watch the things. I didn't mind watching them with them [partners], because there's an experience in watching it with them and getting to know them in a certain way, like watching them consume the media that they like." Consuming media we don't like can be social labor to fit in, as with TJ, Melanie, and Sophie, but it is also preeminently a form of labor that most intimate, loving relationships probably rely on to some degree, as Tom's case demonstrates. "I wanted to partake in something with him that was more than just me talking about my work all the time," he stated:

> And I wasn't sure what else to do, like, other than, like, go out and do things in [my home city]. And he doesn't really like doing that. Like, he didn't really want to go paddle boarding or kayaking or things like that, and so I'd run out of those sorts of ideas. And this is something that he did actively enjoy that I could just jump into until I thought of more ideas for us to do stuff together—or at least just something that we could do together, because I think that's really important, that you have something that you both—you both like, at least are a little bit invested in. And I can be invested enough in a TV show that I don't like as much in order to have something to talk about that is at least mildly exciting rather than being like, "Oh, yeah, I just worked with bacteria today. That's all I did at work," and then just describing in detail what I did to these bacteria. Like, he doesn't care. He's a computer scientist.

Here, Tom was talking of an ex and later elaborated on his dislike for these shows that he agreed to watch at the time, but his account is probably deeply relatable for many readers and poses the question of how many of us regularly watch or listen to something simply not to be objectionable or because we value the act of watching together more than the content, even if over time that content begins to gnaw away at us and bother us intensely. In this case, bisexual Tom reported similar acquiescence in his relationships with both men and women, but I certainly heard more accounts across our interviews of women performing gendered labor of acquiescing to male partners, especially with older women. Winona, for instance, reported suffering through the Military Channel since her husband liked "reliving the idea of World War II things": "And it's like war's over. It's not entertaining to me, and even in learning things, like maybe once in a while it's interesting to learn about it, and maybe I should want to learn more about this, but to be entertained?" Eventually Winona got a second television.

I'll further consider the possible connections between marginalized positionalities and dislike in future chapters but here will point out that if the labor of consuming other people's favored media in order to keep them happy falls on any particular groups of people with more regularity, a model of audience analysis that doesn't consider such "laborers" as audience members is one that will have built in structural blind spots. This should be troubling to media and cultural studies, a field that has otherwise paid so much attention to disparities of consumption on the basis especially of class, gender, and race. But if collectively we're asking the boss or midlevel manager who gets to decide what the television or radio at work is set to but not the low-level workers who can't stand those decisions, if we're asking the father and husband about his viewing choices but not the wife or children about how they suffer through his choices, or if we're not asking those who are outside society's mainstream how they capitulate and surrender to others' selections and to a mainstream popular culture that may not at all be aligned with their own preferences, then our record of audiences is sorely problematic and limited.

The "gritted teeth" of this section's title were often figurative in my data, but other scholars discuss very real gritted teeth. Bambi Haggins, for instance, begins a book-length account of African American comedy that refuses to sit back and be quiet by noting how often African Americans have had to endure racist bullshit, listening without responding. Haggins notes herself being struck by hearing Richard Pryor and her own father share the phrase "My jaw was tight" to allude to the affective, embodied experience of suffering as a listener, as an audience to someone else's racism, and she asks, "How does one respond to the African American legacy of enforced silence"?[37] While I heard more examples of the gendered labor of consumption in our interviews, Haggins reminds us of how often the labor of listening and watching against one's will can be foisted on racial minorities, who similarly may too often feel as though they can direct their resistance to their jaw alone. The rest of Haggins's book studies African American comics who use their comedy to speak back, but it is this affective position—of being forced (or feeling like one is forced) to "grin and bear it"—that is too often required of marginalized viewers.

Ahmed encapsulates this position in her notion of the feminist killjoy, complete with other affective, bodily analogues. "You might be speaking quietly," she notes, "but you are beginning to feel 'wound up,' recognising with frustration that you are being wound up by someone who is winding you up."[38] Ahmed's feminist killjoy ultimately decides to release her jaw, to speak, to disturb, but our interviews are full of those who felt compelled instead to stay silent. "Does the feminist," Ahmed asks, "kill other people's joy by pointing out moments of sexism? Or does she expose the bad feelings that get hidden, displaced, or negated under public signs of joy?"[39] Implicit in her rhetorical questions is the acknowledgment of a perpetual, returning dilemma and a replicating, repeating labor, wherein sometimes the feminist killjoy will answer yes but other times she will simply be wound up, grit her teeth, tense her jaw, and say no more.

Andre Cavalcante documents similar responses in his work with transgender audiences. Powerfully noting that media and cultural studies has privileged resistive reception at the expense of properly considering "resilient reception,"[40] he notes how often his interview subjects were forced to endure demeaning media representations and how often this materialized in bodily responses. "I'm tired, tired, tired of seeing movies that I feel have done violence against me by making me sit there and watch," one respondent noted, and Cavalcante adds, "As Sebastian spoke to me, his body communicated the sheer force of the viewing experience. His voice rose, his body became tense, his eyes swelled, and his hands collapsed into tightly clenched fists."[41] Sebastian also shared, "I feel like I am getting assaulted every time I have to sit in a room with 300 people and watch another trans body be destroyed and violated for everyone to watch. I'm tired of it. I had a total meltdown after that movie,"[42] and Cavalcante observes this to be a common experience of his subjects who "squirmed in their chairs, gazed downward, tightened their jaws, and exhaled heavily. They rolled their eyes, puffed their chests, and vigorously shook their heads. A few welled up with tears."[43] Cavalcante acutely notes, therefore, that viewing for many of his subjects required a form of emotional labor and "affective resilience" even as it took a heavy toll on them.[44] Another of his respondents shared, "It takes a lot of energy to convince myself to go see a movie," more directly showing the labor/energy required to do so.[45] Our white patriarchal society regularly requires people of color, women, and queer subjects to perform the emotional labor of enduring offensive commentary and suffering it quietly, not speaking up and disrupting others' enjoyment,[46] to a point that we should be unsurprised to see the "work" of resilient media reception added to this list of required labor for many marginalized subjects.

Another viewing labor, once again gendered, was evident in parents and especially mothers. On the one hand, parents regularly reported needing to watch media that their kids adored and that they might even acknowledge as beneficial or at least acceptable for their kids but that they disliked. Herman Bausinger's and David Morley's classic accounts of family viewing of television provide multiple examples here, as with a mother who Bausinger notes watched football with her son simply to connect or as with the many other mothers who reported having little to no control over what was watched, as they instead surrendered or sacrificed time and interest to husbands and children.[47] Among our own respondents, mothers of little children in particular often reported watching media they gradually grew to dislike. As Abra noted, a text's ubiquity—and the labor required to watch it anyway—also extended to repetitive viewing and reading: "I mean, I've seen these things a thousand times," she noted. "It's like the books that we read to him at night. I love them, but again I'm like, 'Ugh, I can't read this book one more time.'" She "loves" these programs and books in theory, but repetition produces dislike.

On the other hand, the fear of media on the horizon loomed large for parents, as they often reflected on media they wanted either to protect their children from or to avoid themselves yet that they feared would prove unavoidable. Many parents to whom we spoke felt overwhelmed by the prospect of needing to "prescreen" media to check their appropriateness and hence ultimately had to throw up their hands and allow that their kids would encounter things they disliked. Jacob and Aida, for instance, reserved particular ire for YouTube Kids, given its inability to effectively screen out objectionable material. Parents of young children also worried about the future more generally, happy that their kids were into innocuous material right now but speaking of future media as an approaching tidal wave. Marta noted with great resignation of her son, "Eventually he's going to get into Star Wars or Spider-Man or Superman or whatever. It's just going to be unavoidable at some point," later stating, "I kind of feel like we have this precious amount of time when we can shield him from that. . . . It is unavoidable."

All the Space and All the Time

We also heard about how many disliked shows commanded so much space on television, such that respondents were "always" happening upon them, seeing snippets here and there. Amelia detested *South Park* and *Family Guy*, for instance, yet, she said, "I've randomly stumbled upon them, like if someone else is watching an episode I've caught part of or sat through an episode or two. But I don't seek it out. I've never chosen myself to watch it. It's more situational." Or Jim noted that he can't avoid *Two and a Half Men*: "I probably have seen, like, one hundred episodes. . . . I've never once chosen to watch the show, but it has been on everywhere. The [*sings tune:*] 'me-e-e-e-n' in the background, when you hear that intro song, I—that whole song, I'll—it'll happen sometimes, I'll be walking around in public, and I'd never, ever once put that show on. It's just been on so much. And it seems like pointless shit to me." Or Simone noted that she had indeed watched some of *How I Met Your Mother*, a show she claimed to despise, because "you can't miss it if you're sitting in front of a television ever."

Music can mount even more of an all-out assault on public space. Thus, for instance, Carl Wilson, in introducing his own impassioned dislike for Céline Dion in *Let's Talk about Love: A Journey to the End of Taste*, situates Dion's inescapability and "*Titanic*'s musical attack" as exacerbated for him as a resident of Montreal, Quebec (Dion's home province).[48] When *Titanic* was released, I was living on the other side of Canada, in Vancouver, but this experience was key to my own impassioned dislike of Dion: "CanCon" (Canadian Content) rules required Canadian radio stations to play a certain percentage of Canadian music, and in the wake of *Titanic*, cynically every second station seemed for two years to be using exclusively Dion to fill its quota.

Many audience members, though, were clear in noting that a text's ubiquity extended to its presence in media talk and popular culture. As Andrew talked of media he didn't want his kids watching, he quite explicitly observed, "I'm actually less concerned about the media than about the Pandora's box that is the media universe," reflecting on the degree to which the multiple toys, games, and products that surrounded shows were what truly bother him. Chelsea, too, spoke passionately against Disney princess films, even while amusingly allowing the films themselves off the hook, since it was the paratextual surround that she intensely disliked:

> I do enjoy Disney movies. I think they're great, but the whole—every item, it was like everywhere. And that was all that you would get. And it was also, like, the wastefulness of it, too. There'd be tiaras and plastic earrings and silk gloves and cheap shit, and she would get piles of it from relatives because that's what people do. "Oh, you have a little girl, and she likes pink and princesses. Look at this! It's so cute!" And it would break immediately, and we would have to throw it out or recycle it. You know, it's just gross. It's too much. It's just too much.

She liked *the work* but disliked *the text* because "it's just the way it's so shoved." Rachel, too, disliked *Frozen* intensely but, when asked why, went straight to its merchandise: "They love *Frozen*, so every single holiday, they get a huge box full of *Frozen* shit. And it's the lunchbox and the backpack and everything, pens and art kits and stickers and—and last Christmas, his sister got one of those Jeeps with *Frozen* stickers everywhere. And we didn't put the decals on it, but it's still like the pink and the blue. And it sings. You push the button, and it's like, 'Let it go!!!!' It's what the radio spurts out. And that's what pisses me off." Candice disliked *Keeping Up with the Kardashians* yet openly admitted to having watched only one episode, "and it was ages ago," but she quickly insisted, "It's really more, I think, just their portrayal in the media," as the (to her) constant reporting on the show and family render it inescapable. In this respect, she was joined by several older respondents, who shared a strong dislike for the show, all admitting to watching little to none of it yet locating the object of their dislike in the program's wider paratextual existence.

Undoubtedly we all have our media culture bêtes noires that seem to be ever present, but in positing the existence of "forced fandoms," Abigail De Kosnik once again reminds us how commonplace this experience must be for those who belong to groups that don't get to decide what is popular, mainstream, and worthy of ubiquity. De Kosnik focuses on the experience of Filipinos forced into a fandom of *The Daily Show* and *Desperate Housewives*, and she defines forced fandoms as "primarily imposed from without, in circumstances of political, economic, social, and/or cultural subjugation, rather than emerging from within the user."[49] But the "fandom" here seems superficial and performed alone, as she instead posits a deep-seated dislike of the shows. If dislikes are perceived to be ubiquitous, a disliker's conflicted relationship with them may stem precisely from the continual reminders that they therefore deliver that the disliking subject is outside society's mainstream, unable to influence what is or isn't popular.

Discussion of disliked shows also has a clear and present amplificatory effect, moreover, wherein "bad" material can become actively irksome and deserving of attack not because it exists per se but because people around one regularly talk about it. Annie, for example, professed dislike for "stupid, multicam shows that are usually on CBS": "I can't, I can't do it. I can't do like the bland humor, and I especially cannot deal with people being like, 'Did you see that? It was so funny!' and me being like, 'I just—no, no I didn't watch *The Big Bang Theory* last night, Aunt Judy.' I just couldn't." Mark strongly disliked the YouTube star PewDiePie, in part because he couldn't avoid PewDiePie's "Nazi or Hitler jokes," instead encountering them secondhand via comments on the blogs and discussion groups he frequented. Or Jim talked of the challenges of being a bartender who was expected to know results for prominent sports matches, even though he didn't like sports: "I had to know who had won, whether I liked it or not. And people came in, if I didn't know that, it was like [a] detriment to my job."

Kyle self-reflexively noted that the things he "hated" were therefore exactly those things that he couldn't avoid and that, concurrently, when he could avoid something, there was no need or desire to "hate on" it:

> I get so annoyed by the way that some of these—well, a lot of these—things dominate the conversation. Like, I'm on Twitter all the time. But

every Sunday, it's just all *Game of Thrones*, or I guess there's *Twin Peaks* too. But I get so annoyed by how these things that I don't think are all that great really get a lot of attention, so it just makes it very easy for me to be like, "No, it's just a piece of shit. No, I don't like it. It's bad." Because, if nobody were talking about it, like nobody's talking about *Gilmore Girls* right now, like if I hated that, I wouldn't be like, "Guys, *Gilmore Girls* sucks." That would just be mean to pull this thing out of obscurity to shit on it. But because people worship it, I'm like, "Guys, this is bad. It's bad." It's a way to maintain my sanity almost. This sounds a little intense and unbalanced, but, yeah, I don't know. It's like my life is an act of resistance almost.

Kyle provides an interesting example of someone disliking things precisely (and at times solely) because of their popularity, rather than merely finding their popularity and ubiquity an irksome amplifier of alternatively motivated dislike. His thoughts are especially relevant here, though, since he goes beyond self-reflexivity in acknowledging that *he* need not dislike things if they are not ubiquitous to challenging the logic of press fascination with shows that are not legitimately ubiquitous. "Like, you and I might watch a lot, but objectively no one saw *The Beguiled*. So talking about it a bunch and every news media outlet talking about it, that's kind of a waste. . . . Or like *Girls*. . . . Twelve people watch *Girls*. There's a lack of perspective about what matters in our media." Kyle is brash, elitist, and dismissive in how he voices this point, but he echoes a sentiment expressed in one way or another by many of our respondents, that actively disliking something is only "worth it" or required if that text's presence serves as an obstacle to one, if it is unavoidable. Thus, while he offers quick critiques of *Gilmore Girls* and *Girls*, even his own criticisms disinterest him, since he sees neither text as unavoidable or particularly impactful.

Many other respondents, though, disliked particular media and found it inescapable because they felt directly impacted by what it was doing to others. Personally, in other words, some respondents felt they could and would "just turn it off," but they worried about or directly witnessed third-person effects. Sometimes this dislike was of the media writ large, as with Greta, who was "concerned about the impact of the sort of saturation with media and entertainment and entertainment that is fairly mindless": "because I think it revs everybody, it overstimulates everybody, and it distracts people from having actual face-to-face relationships with each other and from settling in to calm when they're at leisure, so . . . it's impacting our daily life and our relationships."

Elsewhere, the concern was about specific shows' inordinate (perceived) power. Talking of *Basketball Wives*, for instance, Deanna thumped her hand on the table as she insisted,

> [It] is something that directly [thud] impacts [thud] me as an African American [thud] woman. And it impacts me on a daily basis. I feel like, especially, we live in [place name], which is a pretty much all white or Asian Indian—a lot of Asian Indians live around here—suburb. So I alwaysfeel myself feeling very self-conscious. Are these people consuming these images, and are they reflecting those images on me? And I find that's something I struggle with on a daily basis: What do people see when they see me? Do they see those images that they're consuming from those *Basketball Wives* franchises? . . . It only takes one interaction with someone who doesn't know that I'm [a professor]—that's all they know about African American women—to impact me in a way. And so I see that as a very real image that can impact the way that people perceive and see me, and that drives me nuts.

Boyd, an immigrant from Ethiopia, strongly disliked how American news programs reported on Ethiopia, mostly because this led to ignorant questions and presumptions about Ethiopia expressed to him by the people around him: "People, when they see on the news and they ask me where I'm from, when I tell them, they'll be like, 'Ohhh, poor thing.' . . . [And] you'll be pissed. You'll be like, 'Don't believe whatever you see,' you know? I'm from there, grew up there, and it never happened, never seen [it] in my life." Boyd's initial adaptive response was to turn it off, and he reported watching very little television—and no television news—and yet with pained frustration, he acknowledged that watching it himself or not ultimately made little difference, since *others were still watching*, still learning erroneous information, and still Othering him as a result.

I will return to Deanna and Boyd in chapter 2 and to the concern that certain texts' *impact* is inescapable, and I will consider other viewers whose various levels of privilege allowed them more easily to "just turn it off" more successfully. Suffice it to note here that ubiquity was registered in many different ways. Something need only be *perceived* to be ubiquitous to usher in dislike. Deanna, we might note, told no tale of encountering someone else who had actually watched *Basketball Wives*, so perhaps her neighbors were oblivious to the show. But perceived ubiquity proved central and was in almost all cases *an active requisite* to engaged dislike. This should remind us that media consumption involves all sorts of acts of capitulation and resignation—we're regularly watching and listening to media we don't want to. We often can't control the music we hear in public spaces or even in our workplace; we may have little to no control over what gets watched on the (private or public) televisions around us; we don't always get to pick which movie we're going to see; sometimes our choices of music on local radio are between one disliked song and another disliked song; book groups force disliked books on each other; and so on. However, it would be ludicrous to pose that we're not responding to and interpreting these texts, even through grit teeth. Rather, all of us are regularly engaging with disliked media, some more than others, in ways that should require media studies to revise its understanding of two of its key terms: the audience (which includes, as I have argued, dislikers) and the text (which includes, as I have argued, the broader imprint of media culture, not just the work itself).

Even when all machines are off, all books closed, we might still be subjected to the toys, the games, the posters, and other accoutrements of media culture, especially for popular texts with large footprints; indeed, we should entirely expect that texts with large footprints will attract more dislikers since they are likely to be the most objectively ubiquitous. Ironically, then, the more popular a text gets, the more unpopular it probably gets, too. Aja Romano refers to this amusingly as Tumblr's Newton's Law: "For every great fandom, there's an equally vocal antifandom, bringing it down a peg or three."[50] Long-running texts might also be expected to draw particular ire, given their inescapability and resilience across time. To some audiences, they may become akin to the interminable dripping sound from a leaky faucet: tolerable in the short term but eventually annoying. And the story of that faucet is a story not just of a single object or event but of something that keeps happening, in ways that explain why its dislikers can't simply ignore it or switch off its sound.

Simon Frith notes the stakes of such otherwise seemingly petty discussions of "noise" in his essay "What Is Bad Music?" The problem of noise, he argues, often tellingly leads to concerns about music being "too loud," but "the problem is not volume as such (measured by decibels) but the feeling that someone else's music is invading our space."[51] Noise, he continues, "refers to people's sense of spatial integrity, and the question becomes how music works to include and exclude people from this kind of aural space, and when and why other people's music is felt to invade."[52] We might extend this observation beyond just sound, to realize that much of what is being voiced through impassioned dislike is an objection to how a text fills our lived environments. The elements of perceived inclusion and exclusion that Frith notes are vital components of this discussion, and hence I will return to them in chapter 4 especially; but Frith also notes how the disliker's objection is often precisely to a text's perceived control over space.

Shifting from music to television, David Morley has written of how much is at stake in battles over disliked media when it is perceived to violate spatial boundaries. Morley cites both Philip Batty's work on Australian Aboriginal communities' concerns about satellite allowing "hundreds of whitefellas [to] visit without permits, everyday"[53] and Aniko Bodroghkozy's archival work that unearthed letters of complaints to NBC about *Julia*, the first major network sitcom with a Black female lead that some viewers felt forcibly integrated their otherwise aggressively white living rooms.[54] In both cases, dislikes represent challenges to control over what is perceived to be sovereign and/or personal space. Again, we might expect especially popular texts to be especially unpopular too, therefore, for these texts' advertising and merchandising footprints might render them especially *invasive*—a stain on public space, finding their way into one's workplace and car, taking over one's social media feed, plastering themselves on one's food, sitting down uninvited in one's home. Impassioned dislikes, as such, do not "just" violate our space and force us into being their audiences; in doing so, they serve as perpetual reminders that we have less control over our "personal" space than we would like. They don't just ignore choice; they threaten its existence, which may be why Sianne Ngai notes that negative affects regularly result from "a state of obstructed agency."[55]

"Obstructed agency" was an oft-described position of our respondents. Or, rather, our subjects' situations and descriptions of them made it clear that choices to watch or not watch, to engage with popular culture or not, were not easy. Many needed to choose between a desire to turn off the set and a desire to please their viewing partner, and they performed a form of relational agency wherein they chose to be a loving partner, parent, or child, a good friend or officemate. They reminded us that choices to consume are often framed by, and subject to, other choices and desires that may win out over whether one truly wants to consume.

Genres of Dislike

I have been writing of *texts* as the object of dislike, but we should also expect and allow that some dislike is appended more accurately to a cluster of texts, to the genre, and to an overarching "type" of media. Thus, for instance, earlier I quoted dislikes of Tyler Perry films, military television, and children's books when none are individual texts. Undoubtedly these dislikes will be focused on specific texts and specific times, for many dislikes move quite easily from textual host to textual host over time. The singer I dislike right now may be, to my mind, the current iteration of a type of singer I've long disliked. Wait three years, in such a case, and one could expect my dislike of this singer to have transferred to someone else: I will probably still note dislike of that original singer if asked, but their current gestalt will bear the emotional brunt of my dislike, given their primacy of place in popular culture.

Kyle is telling here, for his previously quoted commentary on not "needing" to voice dislike for less popular texts such as *Gilmore Girls*, while contrastingly wanting to save his criticisms for more popular texts, is a reflection on some texts as interchangeable to a degree. Kyle offered long, involved criticisms of media and contemporary life in general and appreciated the chance to attach these to specific texts; but at times, the texts appeared incidental to the critique, and his insistence that, for instance, *Gilmore Girls* wasn't a good "host" for his criticisms was less ethical than strategic. Like a speech writer who knew what he wanted to say but went searching for a pithy quote or parable to aid in communicating his point, Kyle's criticisms preceded the *texts* he attacked, and he used them to help him communicate *genres* and issues he more profoundly disliked.

Some such dislikes are predictable and follow obvious logics: witness some people's dislike of any popular media directed at young women that allows them sexual agency, for instance, or witness other people's dislike of any and all boy bands. Others will require slightly more sleuthing to determine the true object of dislike, the genre in formation, and its related iterations. Procedurally, therefore, we need to be prepared to regard any particular text as a stand-in for the genre. To take a hypothetical dislike for *Game of Thrones* as example, if our disliker has had minimal engagement with the work, we might expect the "textual" interaction *in some cases* to be more properly an interaction with genre. The individual disliker, here, may have a bone to pick with fantasy, less than with anything specific to *Game of Thrones*, yet its prominence in popular culture, linked with its inescapability, variously allows or demands that public professions and performances of dislike *of fantasy* be directed (in 2019) at *Game of Thrones*. In such a case, the text as an entity of meaning with which an audience member interacts may exist almost wholly within and fused to its genre. In this case, therefore, as analysts we would be fishing for a red herring if we looked deeper and deeper into the work of *Game of Thrones* rather than considering this "textual" interaction as largely an interaction with genre.

How We Are All "Bad," "Wrong," and "Ill-Informed" Audiences

Impassioned dislikers are audiences too, I hope by now to have shown, and I will spend the rest of this book examining why and how they engage with their disliked texts. But perhaps some readers remain skeptical, thinking, "Okay, but they're *bad* readers and not at all reliable or even helpful informants." Granted, some impassioned dislikers are forced to watch all of a work, but should we bother to listen to or care about dislikers who instead operate with limited knowledge? Before we can move forward, I must address these critiques. Let me start with a curt and practical answer, that if a text impacts an audience in some way—*if it becomes a text for them*—even if that audience has misunderstood it, the impact is real. Think here of the 1938 radio broadcast of Orson Welles's *War of the Worlds* on *Mercury Theatre on the Air*: many listeners tuned in late after listening to Edgar Burgen on another channel, thereby missing the radio drama's opening frame that made it clear that the following program was fictional. Some of these listeners in turn panicked, thinking that the world was actually under attack by aliens. They were wrong, yes, and they were operating with limited knowledge; but their reaction is a large part of why this text is still (in)famous today.

As analysts, we can always consult the work, employ our close-reading skills, and argue for its correct meaning, but that is just the work. Once it interacts with others and takes on meaning for them, it is a text, and though both audiences themselves and we as analysts may find tactically important reasons to argue for its correct meaning, we must also be able to ascertain what meanings now surround and accompany the text, regardless of whether we consider them to be "right" or "wrong." Much of the world and its actions are built on bad readings, but we abdicate our role as analysts of popular culture if we refuse to engage with such readings. As Justin Lewis writes, "whether a reading is partial or exhaustive, vague or informed, it is still a reading. Meaning is being constructed and solidified."[56] Or, embracing a similar (self-nominated) "pragmatism," Richard Rorty responds to Umberto Eco's insistence that, yes, there are bad readings, "For us pragmatists, the notion that there is something a given text is *really* about, something which rigorous application of a method will reveal, is as bad as the Aristotelian idea that there is something which a substance really, intrinsically, *is* as opposed to what it only apparently or accidentally or relationally is."[57] Rorty implores us to move beyond such "occultist" desires to detect "What Is *Really* Going On," and since audience studies was always meant to be precisely about avoiding the imposition of essentialist readings, at a certain point, we must be willing to engage as closely with readings with which we might disagree as with our favored ones.

However, while I therefore insist that all readings matter, regardless of whether they are based on "close" or "proper" interaction with a text or on "distant" or "incomplete" interaction, as all the quotation marks in this sentence should suggest, I also wish to problematize a distinction between readings that would create a hierarchy of interpretative value based on how much of a text one has interacted with in the first place.

Paratexts are key to my argument here, but first let us place them to the side and consider just "the work itself." While a minority of works are entirely self-contained and singular, most works are in some way messy, sprawling beyond their current form, offering up multiple versions, and/or spread out over the textual universe in ways that guarantee no necessary synthesis.

For a stark example, take a long-running television show such as *Law and Order*. Over the twenty-year run from 1990 to 2010, NBC Universal produced 456 episodes of *Law and Order*. I don't doubt that some fans have seen every episode, but its ratings and viewership relied on many others to dip in and out. And surely we would not limit a discussion of *Law and Order* to only those who had seen every single episode. Even if we did, would the original show suffice? Or perhaps we would also need to consider its spin-offs part of the work proper, in which case we'd need to add over 450 episodes of *Law and Order: SVU* from over twenty seasons, 195 episodes from ten seasons of *Law and Order: Criminal Intent*, 13 episodes from the lone season of *Law and Order: Trial by Jury*, 22 episodes of the lone season of *Law and Order: LA*, 8 episodes of *Law and Order: True Crime* (currently "on hiatus" and hence perhaps never to return for subsequent episodes or perhaps with more to go), the 1998 made-for-television film *Exiled: A Law and Order Movie*, and 241 episodes from four foreign extensions in England, France, and Russia. At the time of writing, *SVU* is ongoing, moreover, so would we consider any discussion of the franchise's meaning premature, given that the franchise has not finished? In sum, with at least 496 episodes of television to consider as part of "*Law and Order*" and as many as 2,000 or more episodes and a television film, there is simply too much *Law and Order* to feasibly expect someone to watch it all before hazarding an interpretation of the series or to make a comment on what it's doing.

Granted, not all texts are as vast as *Law and Order*. But most media works enjoy some level of structural complexity, whether through serialization; through distribution and release over prolonged time (as with many radio and television shows, comic series, movie and video-game franchises, podcasts, and so forth), such that the audience must interpret in fits and spurts; or through nominal or intricate connection with other media works via sequels, spin-offs, and such. Another complicating factor with many media works is the proliferation of various versions. Each time *Law and Order* is syndicated, it may be shown out of order, specific episodes may be cut slightly to allow for varying programming blocks, and ad breaks may be inserted or subtracted in ways that affect the program's flow. Similarly, films may be rereleased on DVD or a new streaming platform with extra scenes; comics may be compiled into a graphic novel with slight or major changes; video games may be remastered in ways that change the aesthetics of the game; podcasts may have ads and preliminary, situating chatter removed; and so forth. As media works move across the globe, moreover, translation may introduce subtitles that will inevitably miss some nuances and take other liberties with the original script, or dubbing that introduces new voices and performances to the work. Different regulatory environments, too, may see certain content removed from a work. And technical differences at the point of exhibition will further change the work, as grand Christopher Nolan blockbusters intended for an IMAX screen are played on tiny old televisions, as pirated copies introduce scratches to a work or fail to copy sounds and images, as aspect ratios change, as pixilation differs, and as thousands of other small or large technical differences bend and augment the work. In short, few if any media works themselves reach all audience members in the same state, as instead it is the nature of media works to vibrate and oscillate, thereby requiring audiences to interpret and talk across differences.

Most media works take *time* to come together, too. Writing of literary analysis, Stanley Fish astutely notes that a great mistake is made when analysts arrive at the work after it's over and assume that audiences respond only to that finished work, when in fact they were of course responding to it as it happened: "in an utterance of any length," he writes, "there is a point at which the reader has taken in only the first word, and then the second, and then the third, and so on, and the report of what happens to the reader is always a report of what has happened *to that point*."[58] Fish therefore states of a literary work that "what it does is what it means,"[59] thereby joining Wolfgang Iser in seeing the work as a *phenomenological* entity, not simply an *ontological* one, and in seeing meaning as something subject to "a process of continual modification."[60] Many media works are perpetually in the process of happening, and they may mean the most to us in the middle of this process. But whereas Fish and Iser seem to assume a well-behaved, disciplined reader who reads the entire literary work closely, any theory of media textuality that requires total viewership or listenership is woefully naïve, as we might all miss episodes, a segment when our partner stops in to ask who is making dinner tomorrow, installments of a franchise, the last half of the song as we park our car and turn off the radio, and so on. Thus, to apply Fish and Iser's phenomenological approach to media works, we should allow for audiences constantly to be interacting with "incomplete" entities.

If this is true of the work, it is even more the case with the text, due not only to differing social contexts but to differing paratextual entourages and assemblages. Earlier I noted that people who dislike a text may be interacting largely with its paratexts, but even its fans, and even the viewers of the work itself, will be interacting with different paratexts. Whereas I might watch a trailer for a new film, hear a review on the radio, and flip through an article about it in *Entertainment Weekly*, you might read a fan discussion board's careful discussion of it, encounter an army of its merchandise already lining the shelves at Target, and see snarky tweets about it. Each of these paratexts will play its own role in framing and transfiguring the text. Even those who watch or listen to the same work, therefore, will experience different versions of its text. How, then, can we have discussions about that text? In short, each text is a discursive entity, meaning that it is constructed through discussion, where some of that discussion is with other people directly and some of it is with paratexts, which are of course statements about the text made by particular people with particular interests and/or beliefs about that text.

In both of these regards (the text's variability and it mattering as a social entity as much or more than as an aesthetic, ontological one), the text is comparable to what we (should) already know about genre, such that a brief comparison is illustrative. Genre is variable. We could write a list of all the possible component parts of a genre, yet any given work that exhibits that genre will have a different assortment of those parts. Thus, for instance, some components of "the cop show" are a partner team looking for the perpetrator of a crime, tension between those partners engendered by their being from different walks of life, a wise older cop who has learned how to work around "the system," a naïve and/or hotheaded younger cop, a fondness for dark lighting, an urban setting, scenes filmed in alleyways, a red-herring suspect, and a narrative structure that keeps the audience guessing "whodunit." Each one of these is probably recognizable, yet we could think of examples of cop shows without some of them: think, for instance, of *Fargo*'s rural, not urban, setting and of its fondness for bright white, snowy scenes, not dark alleyways. And yet, in spite of all this chronic and inherent variability, the cop show is a legible entity—I suspect that most of us have a good idea of what it is and could probably recognize one in little more than a few seconds if surfing through channels with a remote control.

To draw this comparison to the text may seem somewhat problematic, given that one might expect the work to hold particular pride of place within the variability of work and paratexts. But genres provide us with an analogue, as surely some characteristics of genres would seem important and central. As the films of Star Wars are to the Star Wars text, we might expect humor and laughter to be to the comedy, for instance. And yet there are comedies that regularly don't even try to be funny. *Transparent* is one such example, a show that has won Emmys as a comedy yet that often eschews humor. A key reason why *Transparent* can still be a comedy, why cop shows without crime can be cop shows, and why Star Wars or any other text doesn't need the work to be present is due to the other structuring mechanism of genre and textuality, namely, that they exist as much if not more as social entities. Or, reworded, they are discursive. Jason Mittell has made this argument powerfully about genre, noting that the way a genre is classified by its regulators, by the industry that produces it, and by the audiences who talk about it plays a decisive role in determining how it is classified and what it means. Mittell is clear to note that "bad" viewers get to play this discursive game too: "Genre categories are often made culturally salient and manifest by people who are not viewers of the genre, but rather use 'bad objects' to define their own *habitus* and viewing practices. Evaluative discourses constituting generic categories often come from voices who would be excluded only in listening to actual viewers, and thus an analysis of the genre's cultural circulation would be incomplete without these nonviewers' opinions."[61] If we substitute "text" for "genre," though, this is no less true. Star Wars is talked about, exists as an entity—a text—in popular culture, and whether the person talking about it, listening to that talk, or thinking about it has watched a single Star Wars film does not stop it becoming a text; nor does it make its existence as a text any less legitimate, real, or potentially impactful for them. To repeat Couldry's definition of the text, it is "a complex of interrelated meanings which its readers tend to interpret as a discrete, unified whole."[62]

This understanding of the text may disturb academics and analysts. But once again the analogy and comparison to genre is illustrative, for just as an academic's well-meaning construction of a genre means little socially and culturally unless it gains popular discursive traction, so too are we working against cultural reality if we stomp a foot down and insist that someone needs to have watched *The Empire Strikes Back* to "count" as someone worth listening to on the topic of Star Wars. I empathize with the frustration: as a fan of Star Wars, I want the world to see *The Empire Strikes Back*, certainly before weighing in on what Star Wars is. I am not advocating here that we throw our hands up entirely, for there are still questions about form and aesthetics that do not require us to consult the discursive record (this is why I can insist that we define "text" differently, for instance, even when I feel that the discursive record has it "wrong"). But if we want to know what Star Wars means popularly, academics and analysts aren't the arbiters of what Star Wars is popularly, and thus we must be willing to engage that entity on popular culture's terms. We must be willing, therefore, to give up on the work's holding any necessary, primary role in determining what the text is and to realize that many—and at times even *most*—people in the text's audience will be "bad," "wrong," or "ill-informed" audiences of the work or of a small part of that work.

Conclusion

In this chapter, I have argued that texts may have a rich abundance of meaning for their detractors. To do so, I've focused on the ubiquity and inescapability of much popular culture and on the prevalence of coerced, involuntary consumption. That said, the disliked object's ubiquity does not only make it an imposition (though it definitely remains an imposition): it also renders the disliked object a discursive resource or tool for opportunistically articulating why and how it is disliked and for potentially articulating the pains that undergird and determine that dislike. Precisely what is being articulated is the topic of chapter 2. The task of this present chapter has been to insist on the textuality and audiencehood of dislike. We all engage with many texts and genres through close viewing, fandom, and choice, but we also spend a great deal of our media-consuming hours yielding the remote control, choice of film, or radio dial to others, perhaps unable to challenge their control, perhaps unwilling to do so, or perhaps instantly regretting our own decisions yet feeling compelled to stick with them. At the moment that our interest turns to dislike, though, we do not cease to be audiences, nor does the text disappear from our heads. I use "we" here, too, to insist that our dislikes are a part of all of us as media consumers—dislike is not just something for others to do. Annette Hill offers a spectrum of engagement from arrangement to enragement and estrangement,[63] but we will all slide along that spectrum in our textual and consumptive journeys, requiring a critically enabled media and cultural studies to follow us along that spectrum, not to limit its focus to moments of excited enthusiasm and approval. In short, along the way, I've argued that audience studies needs to spend a lot more time focusing on why, when, and how people don't consume or don't consume what they want to consume. If many scholars have looked to the media for its ability to operationalize a public sphere,[64] cultural forum,[65] and hence cultural and political citizenship,[66] that sphere, forum, and citizenship exist as much for us when we dislike as when we love. What we use our dislike to say about us, the media, and the world around us are topics for the rest of this book.

2

What's Wrong and What's Missing

In arguing for a close connection and interweaving of television and everyday life, Roger Silverstone notes, "We take television for granted in a way similar to how we take everyday life for granted. We want more of it (some of us); we complain about it (but we watch it anyway). . . . Our experience of television is of a piece with our experience of the world: we do not expect it to be, nor can we imagine it to be, significantly otherwise."[1] I read those words as a graduate student at Goldsmiths College, and when Professor James Curran asked my MA class first to read about the American, British, and Dutch media systems and then to create our own, new media system, the challenge seemed so daunting to us all and embarrassingly underlined for me Silverstone's words: "we do not expect it to be, nor can we imagine it to be, significantly otherwise." However, I refused and still refuse to acquiesce so easily. Do we really not expect changes from the structure of television? Do our complaints never rise to the level of asking for something more, something different? This chapter wrestles with that question, asking how dislikes may be an advance guard of sorts that, if we learn how to listen to them, might have a great deal to say about what audiences perceive to be wrong with media, what is missing, what media could and should instead be and do.

In chapter 1, I worked with theories of textuality to suggest that texts are larger, more complex conceptual entities than textual analysis often allows, thereby entailing that any given text's audience is similarly a larger, more complex collective than is usually allowed by audience analysis. However, precisely because texts have often been imagined to be more contained, simpler beings, discussions of the text have also regularly treated it as a self-sufficient unit and audience interactions with the text as reactions to that unit. Textual analysis is thereby regularly about what one particular text means in and of itself. By contrast, in this chapter, I will instead focus on the object of dislike as a social being, in conversation with other texts, and will use audience commentary to make sense of those texts' social networks rather than just the text in question. In short, I will consider the object of dislike as relational and dislike itself as regularly telling us things about a larger media field of play and about representational systems, not "just" a single disliked text.

Such an approach was required by our interviewees' commentary, given how often their disdain and displeasure at least alluded to, and often explicitly invoked, larger genres of dislike. The tale of their dislike, and the reason they disliked, was as much if not more about other dislikes, other presences and absences in the media as a whole, as about this specific text.[2] This chapter, then, is about perceptions of excessive presence and of glaring absence and argues that discussions about dislike offer a rich space for hearing articulations of what is too much with us and of what is worryingly missing. It thus also focuses on instances when impassioned dislike stems from the experience of exclusion. Much has been made about the converse, about media's powers to include, to become as Roger Silverstone suggests "a member of the family in a metaphorical sense."[3] "Where 'arts' exclude," Paul Willis writes in a moment of excess, "'culture' includes," while Joke Hermes suggests that "popular culture makes us welcome and offers belonging."[4] And for sure, media and popular culture will nearly always be joining *someone's* family, including and welcoming *someone*, for as John Hartley and Jason Potts state in their sweeping approach to storytelling, "all storytelling is political, constituting the 'we'-community, seeking to create politics of trust, to expound the costs of cooperation for characters and deliver its symbolic rewards."[5] But as Hartley and Potts's postulation signals, if there are "we"-communities, there will always be "they"-communities. This chapter turns especially to the failures of representation and to those who feel left out, who arrive at particular texts whose failures and exclusions anger them in particular and invite commentary on the general patterns of exclusion to which the impassioned disliker sees the texts adhering.

I begin by examining cases where the disliked object was seen as worthy of scorn because it was the worst violator against a value or norm held dear to audiences. The existence of this form of dislike is predictable and should not surprise us—just as we would expect a fan to love something that they consider to be the best in class, we would expect engaged dislike to be directed toward the worst in class. But I then turn to a formulation that was far more prevalent in our interviews, namely, a discourse of unmet expectations, in which the object of scorn was something from which the audience member desperately hoped for more. Something about the text promised or teased the prospect of a rare reprieve from a dispiriting, alienating norm—and yet it failed and let down the audience member. That failure hurt and regularly resulted in engaged dislike. As I'll note, though, in both cases—of the worst violator and of the unmet expectation—engaged dislikes tell us about the values or norms that audiences hold. As documented in chapter 1, engaged dislikes are habitually seen as ubiquitous and inescapable in some way. Elaboration on "worst violator" and "unmet expectation" dislikes tells us about a general class, genre, or mode of media that the audience member finds to be problematically ubiquitous and popular and often grapples with exactly what is so bad about that class, genre, or mode. Thus, in both cases, the object of dislike gestures outward, since it represents a whole field of play and a slew of texts and/or ways of being. In talking about these texts, audiences articulate preferences, sadnesses, hopes, and frustrations directed toward the entire media system.

Worst Violators

Our interviewers were generally careful not to ask what was "the worst," instead asking what audience members especially disliked, but numerous subjects were keen to answer by telling us their worst in class. Simone, for example, "hated" *The Newsroom* and told us about this while trying to articulate something she appreciated about the media and wanted more of:

> There is this trend of pretty kick-ass, hardcore chicks in a lot of these shows, now that I'm looking at it. Like, I don't identify a lot or won't stay watching shows where I feel like women are misrepresented—I can't stand that about—what is it?—*The Newsroom.* All right. And basically Aaron what's-his-face [Sorkin]. . . . He writes the worst female characters, like, unbelievably bad. Everything they say is so unreal, like, stuff like that, I mean, that bothers me. . . . I just don't like them. I don't like the women. I don't want to be around them. I don't want to spend my time with them. So I don't have that much free time to watch TV. I don't want to hang out with all these bitches that I think suck.

Simone highly values strong female characters with whom she can identify. To tell us what that should look like, though, she finds it ultimately easier to do so through alterity—she wants characters *not* like the women in *The Newsroom*. Interestingly, although she begins this comment by noting a "trend" of stronger women "in a lot of these shows," first, "these shows" refers to a curated list of shows often written of as feminist in the popular press that one of my interviewers presented to her interview subjects, but second, her comment suggests that *The Newsroom* is representative of an even larger collection of shows without strong women. Simone yearns for such characters precisely because they are actually few and far between, and the rest of her interview suggests as much, regularly returning to her intense frustration with finding so few "relatable" or "identifiable" women or simply calling them "unreal." *The Newsroom*, in short, is the tip of a very large iceberg, albeit a particularly sharp and jagged tip in Simone's telling.

Sophie's worst violator was *Two and a Half Men*, a show that she found deeply misogynist:

> You know what? This is the worst. People shouldn't settle for this. We can do better. I guess, like, women on *Two and a Half Men* could be "hot," but they need a personality. Like, be funny, be smart, be interesting, be an engineer. But don't be dumb and hot. Like, don't spread that stereotype. Let them do something. Let them be someone. Let them call the shots. Don't let Charlie or whoever run the show. Like, I think women can do better. And they should do better and aspire to do better, and I think television should show that.

This closing comment, that "television should show that," implicates more than just Charlie Sheen, creator Chuck Lorre, or broadcaster CBS, though, suggesting that television in general is *not* "showing that." Thus, Sophie hit boiling point with *Two and a Half Men*, but the temperature was turned up by countless other shows with a similar ethic and approach to depicting and using women. *Two and a Half Men* may be "the worst," but to Sophie, the competition is, sadly, quite open and contested; and *Two and a Half Men* only warrants mention precisely because it has so much competition.

Mark bounced a disliked object off a beloved one, as he talked about favorite and least favorite musicians: "One of my favorite bands, Rise Against, is really proactivist, so for me, the lyrics and what they mean are almost just as important as how the song sounds. Which brings me back to Ariana Grande—like, yeah, 'I'm going to make a song ["Side to Side"] about getting fucked so hard I can't walk straight.' That's dumb. I'm not going to listen to that." The depths of Ariana Grande do not matter to him. To him, she is "dumb," and as he alludes to, he had already shared his dislike of her earlier in his interview. But he claims to dislike her so strongly because of what she represents—music without a political, civic message. His criticisms are also enshrouded in sexism, suggesting multiple reasons for his dislike, even though (as cited in chapter 4) he also professed love for romcoms and pivoted from that to a screed against toxic masculinity. Thus, I'll return to Mark and his complexities in chapter 5—but he still nominates Grande in particular as "the worst," using her to moor one end of a spectrum. This is a classic move in discussions, as we all regularly state opinions in the negative, voicing favor for something by articulating disfavor for something else. Here, Mark is clear to note he's listened to much more Rise Against, and more closely, than Ariana Grande, but she exists as a pivot and switcher to him, anchoring what music should not be, inviting discussion of what it should be instead—namely, to him, politically charged and "proactivist." Marvin offered a similar dislike of the Kardashians:

> Any celebrity who isn't doing something worthwhile with their power kind of annoys me. Whether it's, you know, saving puppies or orphan children or veterans or whatever it is, you've been given this gift to—or just giving money to some worthwhile organization. . . . Even the celebrities that speak for politicians on the right, I admire them for at least trying to do something for what they believe in. But I find that—here, it's a little annoying to me that you've been given this position of celebrity and stardom, and why not do something good with it? Right? Or why not try to make the world a better place?

As with Mark's dislike of Ariana Grande, Marvin uses the Kardashians to offer commentary on what celebrities *should* do but anchors that commentary in a sense of the nadir of possibility, which to him is the Kardashians.

Boyd spent much of the first half of the interview seeming disinterested and offering short, curt answers to questions about dislike. As his interviewer became aware of how little he cared for the media and asked him more questions about this, though, he had more to say and became more engaged with the interview. As noted in chapter 1, Boyd found American media derogatory toward and ignorant of Ethiopia, where he had grown up before emigrating to the United States. US media simply didn't speak to him and didn't understand his world. And yet he nominated the news as the worst violator. Boyd seemed almost willing to allow fiction a break, but he gave news no such excuse: of all genres, the news should present accurate, informative, truthful information about Ethiopia when discussing the country, but instead he felt it lied and Othered, thereby feeding the people around him with misinformation and stereotypes and giving him nothing of use. Talking about news became a way for him to talk about what media *should* do and to talk about a common failing that he saw across US media.

We heard a great deal of discussion of respondents' personal ethical codes, preferences, and dislikes through hearing about their impassioned dislikes. Boyd yearned for a more globally aware media and United States. Eric wanted a media system that presented options and ideas but that never tried to proffer particular opinions, and thus even though his own politics leaned more clearly conservative, he reserved particular vitriol for several right-wing pundits, Rush Limbaugh in particular. "I don't like it," he insisted, "when people force opinions about people, and you really don't know much about them, and then stir up a bunch of nonsense. I just don't like that stuff. The media just creates a bunch of chaos. . . . It's just so sad. It's so sad what's going on in the world, the violence, deviance, the hatred. It's ridiculous. Even in the sports world, the media will just bash somebody's character and their family. It's crazy. So, yeah, that kind of stuff I just don't care about." To Eric, Limbaugh was the worst violator of this ethic. Karen had no particular bone to pick with Limbaugh but instead focused her general dismay at current culture's "negativity" and incessant criticism with a specific and strong dislike of the news:

You probably think of media and you think of the news, and I feel like for me, when I talk to people at work, media is usually the news. . . . And I feel like—because all we do as a culture is stream negativity, negativity, negativity. What's wrong with the world? How much hate is out there, instead of putting out what's actually the good things that are happening? There are these people who are doing really great things that are really trying to help, but we don't talk about that. We talk about all the bad stuff that's happening. And I think after a while you can only take so much of it. . . . And then, when you watch kids' shows, it's in there to some degree: the hate, the bigotry. It's everywhere.

Jenna, for her part, couldn't stand violence, especially violence with intent to harm, a position that led her to quickly nominate, "I absolutely despise boxing. It is so angry." At length, she explained that she couldn't understand why people would hurt each other so brazenly, as sport. She insisted that blood and physicality didn't bother her per se, and she defensively presented her love of medical dramas as evidence, but she simply couldn't countenance violence or the media's celebration of it. Boxing, as such, was a worst violator. Charlie (interviewed separately) concurred, telling us how angry he got at *Marvel's Daredevil* because of its parade of violence: "I just dropped *Daredevil* in the middle of the first season, right around the moment when he—or Kingpin, I think it is—bashes someone's head in with a car door. For me, my political stance with media is often surrounding violence. I just find that . . . there's enough of it going on in various other media forms that I need to consume in order to be a good citizen, and so if I can avoid it in fictional television, I try [to do] it."

Julie at first responded to a question about dislikes quite playfully, noting, "There's one show that I *absolutely* hate. It's actually kind of a strange one, but that show *Undercover Boss*." Her playfulness quickly eroded as she talked further about it, though, betraying how adamant she was about her principled dislike. She described being forced to watch it at a friend's house. The premise, she offered,

> is that the boss of some huge company—you know, multimillionaire—goes undercover like a low-level worker. And at the end of the show—she

made me watch like three episodes, and they're all the same; it was like some kind of marathon—and at the end of the show, the boss reveals himself, and he's crying, and he gives them some kind of monetary reward, the guys he's, like, working with. And it's just, like, all so scripted and, like, this postcard for corporate America. This is the worst thing I've ever seen. . . . It's really fake. And usually that doesn't bother me, since I do like some reality TV for that terrible, not-real, dramatic stuff. But for some reason, that one just got under my skin. . . . What bothered me about this one is that they tell these people, like, they're on a show where a guy is trying to get a job, and tell them it's about "oh, it's a bad economy, and this guy is gonna see if he can do this job that he's not qualified for," when he's actually their boss or boss's boss's boss. And they don't know who it is. And then the crying. The crying bothers me. In my mind, he's not really sorry that he doesn't know about all these things that are happening, and it feels really fake, for the camera, like they're trying to make their corporate appeal go up.

Though her critique (which extends beyond the quoted passage) regularly returns to the show's "fakeness," a common knee-jerk complaint about reality TV, Julie is careful to protect reality TV in general from her criticisms, which are not about the fakeness of the genre and are instead about a show masquerading as caring about the working classes when in fact it is just shilling for CEOs or, in her own memorable term, is "a postcard for corporate America." As a working-class viewer herself, Julie is angered by the PR feat represented by this show, and the change in tone of her interview is stark, from playful and chatty to obviously angry. But as bad as it is for her, it can only irk her so much because it is one of what she regards as a large group.

The parents to whom we spoke, meanwhile, regularly peppered their discussion of engaged dislikes with superlatives, making it clear that the shows they especially despised were those whose sins were first in class. Andrew, for instance, dismissed princess culture in general, asking rhetorically, "Could something be more perfectly mutually gendered and hypercommercialized?" Chelsea shared a displeasure for princess culture, singling out its overproduction of stuff and "the wastefulness of it" (see chapter 1 for the full quotation). Molly, too, disliked princesses in particular, though when asked why immediately pivoted to a broader critique, saying, "Just because there's a brand. Because it's branded. For myself, I don't like anything with a brand on it, whether it's Princess or just other stuff. I just like plain clothes. So the way [my kids] dress probably reflects my own taste. I like patterns—stripes, polka dots, solids." Worth quoting at some length, Rachel explained why she "hates" Barbies:

> The whole doll thing makes me so angry because we don't have Barbies in our house. And [my daughter] would love—we go shopping a lot in thrift stores, and we'll go to Goodwill. And there are a lot of dolls, and the way they're painted just makes me sick. Bratz dolls—I just want to go into Target and rip all their heads off and be like, "We are better than this, society." These Bratz dolls are just bratty little bitches, the absolute antithesis of what I want to teach my girls. . . . That's what gets me mad too, is when I try—it's so porous when you're trying to create a boundary, and then suddenly someone gives you a Barbie doll, and then, what do you do? "Thank you so much, but no thank you"? Do you take it and then hide it or throw it away? Do you just relax your boundaries and say, "She has it now"—a *Frozen* backpack and lunchbox that I never would have bought her in a million years? But now Grandma bought it for her. Now I'm the asshole who takes it away. So that's some of the stuff that happens. Media in some ways is wonderful. But it's shifted to become this monster, this megacapitalistic, conglomerate corporation of "I'm gonna make a great movie, and then I'm going to force-feed you merchandise for the next ten years." And I don't like that.

Barbies open a pathway into concerns about children's behavior, hypercommercialism, and franchising that quickly leaves Barbie far behind.

Jacob was more bothered by children's media that approached his child with traditional, "normative" moralism, a position that led to his particular annoyance at and dislike of *Thomas the Tank Engine*, which he saw as "this crazy moralistic, preachy kind of show": "And what it's trying to do with the messages—it's this Victorian-style nursery rhyme kind of thing, like, you know, very normative. I'm not a big fan of *Thomas the Tank Engine*. I wanted to put that on the record." Rebecca's frustrations, in turn, were directed toward apps that seemingly required constant play. "One of the things I don't like," she said, "are the games that you feel pressure to play every day. Like, you lose something or you lose points if you don't log on every single day. So they're constantly asking you to log in, or they'll lose points. Those I don't like because they just make [my son] want to play more and more, and it punished them for not doing it. And *Clash of Clans* is one of those games."

In scanning these critiques, though, the attentive reader will have noticed how most of them "spill over" into other media. Sometimes this spillover is explicitly stated. Boyd's and Karen's dislike of the news extends to multiple media. Karen insists, "Then, when you watch kids' shows, it's in there to some degree: the hate, the bigotry. It's everywhere." Eric strongly dislikes Limbaugh for always "bashing" other people, yet the sins of Limbaugh are everywhere, he suggests, "even in the sports world." And Rachel's nominated dislike of Barbie morphs into Bratz, then into *Frozen*. But even when the spillover is not stated directly, in all instances it is still clearly happening. Simone and Sophie don't think that *The Newsroom* and *Two and a Half Men*, respectively, are the only prominent shows with poorly written women and misogynist men. Mark and Marvin don't see Ariana Grande or the Kardashians, in each of their respective cases, as uniquely apolitical: they are representative of a mode of musician and celebrity that bugs them. Jenna and Charlie don't dislike boxing and *Marvel's Daredevil*, respectively, because they alone are violent; they dislike them because they see violence all over the place, are annoyed by it, and find it to be particularly concentrated in these texts. Charlie's comments on *Marvel's Daredevil*, indeed, suggest that his tolerance for violence is already tested by "various other media forms" that he "need[s] to consume in order to be a good citizen." Behind Julie's attack on *Undercover Boss* is a clear sense of dismay at television as being corporatized in general and at the medium's habitually ignoring the actual struggles of the working classes. And each of the parents who nominate particularly disliked children's texts do so with an acknowledgment that they are especially egregious yet by no means alone—Andrew, Chelsea, and Molly know that princesses could be wiped from the Earth and hypercommercialism would still exist, just as Jacob knows that *Thomas the Tank Engine* is but one carriage in a long train of shows espousing "normalized," "Victorian" values to his and other children and just as Rebecca knows that *Clash of the Clans* is but one in an even larger army.

These worst violators, in short, are not unique, and they are intensely disliked not because these shows alone violate respondents' personal sense of ethics but because they are perceived to be sites of concentration and amplification for those ethical violations. Zoey, for instance, strongly disliked *The Bachelor* but, in describing why, soon reflected that it was by no means alone in its sins. She stated, "I feel like it puts forth this, like—or not even puts—continues what has already been an unrealistic expectation for what, like, women should expect from men they're dating and what men should expect from women they're dating." In listening to critiques like these, we can hear values the respondents have for the media as a whole, and in many ways that is the communicative point—talking about worst violators allows a shorthand to talking about personal ethical systems and to engaging in a much broader critique of media culture writ large. Talking about worst violators is a way to highlight an issue that, in Zoey's term, "continues" and to offer up a plea for better media in general.

Unhappy Objects

In the case of worst violators, the text takes on special significance because it comes to stand in for and represent an entire class of disliked media. Given the projection involved in such a process, object relations theory may help us to explain what is going on. Object relations theory was profitably introduced to media studies first by Roger Silverstone's application of the child psychologist D. W. Winnicott's writings on transitional objects to rituals of viewing.[6] Winnicott saw transitional objects as key to children coming to terms with the ontological insecurity of being apart from their mothers or caregivers; to reestablish a sense of ontological security, they might invest their feelings of comfort and safety into a now-beloved blanket, teddy, pacifier, or other transitional object. Silverstone observed how media rituals may work in comparable ways for adults coming to terms with a world that is fundamentally full of risk and insecurity. Thus, for instance, after a long day of work and after reading or hearing news of the world's latest horrors, we might appreciate the role played by certain late-night television shows in finding humor in that horror, in keeping a tone of general levity and optimism, and hence in assuring us that everything is all right. Matt

Hills then applies Winnicott directly to fandom, arguing that fan objects become primary transitional objects—a fan's happy place, reminder of better times, and so forth—and that they may in time become shared objects, open to an entire community.[7] Speaking personally, for example, Star Wars is imbricated with memories of playing with the toys with my brother and best friends, of my dad's excitement at returning from a business trip from Hong Kong with hot-off-the-conveyor-belt figures, of the general feeling of joy, power, and freedom in imagining I was a Jedi or Han Solo, thereby making Star Wars a powerful transitional object for me.

However, if we project ontological security, safety, and warmth onto some texts, we also project trauma and exclusion onto other texts, as both individuals and communities. Sara Ahmed writes of "happy objects," noting that affect "sticks" to objects, since in this case, "to be made happy by this or that is to recognize that happiness starts from somewhere other than the subject who may use the word to describe a situation," and thus "if objects provide a means for making us happy, then in directing ourselves toward this or that object we are aiming somewhere else: toward a happiness that is presumed to follow."[8] We should expect that unhappy objects will also be "sticky," wearing our anxieties and experiences of alienation, and the mere memory or thought of them might conversely direct us toward feelings of unhappiness, pain, frustration. Texts may often exist in perpetuity as reminders of a pain inflicted on us. Sometimes these pains will have come from within the work itself and its messages, as when a work gives voice to odious prejudices. Sometimes the pains will come from incidental interaction with the work, as for instance when a certain piece of music was playing in the background when something horrible happened to one. Sometimes they may stem from the cultural context of the text, as for instance when one knows a text to be especially adored by a group of people whom one cannot abide. Sometimes, too, the genre may be the true culprit. If, following Michael Ryan and Douglas Kellner, genres tend to give voice to particular worldviews, "establishing and enforcing a sense of propriety, of proper boundaries which demarcate appropriate thought, feeling, and behaviors and which provide frames, codes, and signs for constructing a shared social reality,"[9] we should expect the victims and opponents of such worldviews to identify powerfully against such genres.

Projections of pain may even slide back and forth between texts within a genre—especially as, per chapter 1, the texts' relative fame, ubiquity, and inescapability ebb and flow: just as transitional object status can be transferred, from a teddy to another plush toy and so forth, a particular pain may also transfer from text to text across its life.

Another type of object relation is discussed by Cornel Sandvoss when he posits that fan objects can at times become narcissistic mirrors. Sandvoss draws from audience research in which fans offer a wide range of understandings and interpretations of what a text is and of why they love it, suggesting that in such cases they render the text "neutrosemic," or neutral of meaning. He points, for instance, to Star Wars fans who variously read the franchise as pro- or antiwar and to Chelsea Football Club fans whose readings of the club vary wildly. In such cases, Sandvoss suggests, fans turn the fan text into a mirror that reflects back their own image and values so that "the object of fandom becomes part of the self."[10] If this is the case with some fandom, though, with "acknowledgment of the object of fandom as an external object disappear[ing]" and becoming a symbol of home, Heimat, we, I, and belonging,[11] we might expect that engaged dislike may be based on a desire to create an Other, opposed to the self, and that the disliked object may serve as a perpetual reminder of Otherness and exclusion. Our interview subject Cindy comes to mind here, as she stated with pride that she "does not have an open mind" and proceeded to illustrate this through noting a slew of strongly held dislikes against anything more progressive with regard to queer identities, race relations, politics, or religion. Thus, just as Sandvoss notes a concern that some fans will refuse all difference through only consuming more of the same, Cindy stands out as a clear example of how strong dislikes can similarly be used to shut out a world of difference, for Cindy policed her worldview more through her dislikes than through her fandoms.

Object relations theory draws from psychology and hence often points to *individual* relations, but just as Hills notes the prospect for transitional objects to be shared, so might communities have shared traumas, pains, and exclusions that lead to communal dislikes. Admittedly, precisely *what* a text represents will range from the petty and banal to deep, searing pains, but amid these, worst violators become particularly important objects because of the spectrum of pain, dislike, and exclusion that they not only represent but also focus into one or a limited few specific texts.

Unmet Expectations

When embarking on this project, I fully expected to hear about worst violators. What surprised me, though, was that many respondents' most disliked texts were *not* those that they regarded as categorically "worst" but instead were those that had *disappointed* them the most. When respondents had hoped for more, had seen a text's potential to do something for them that other texts weren't doing at all or as well as they'd like, and yet the text had failed to hit the mark: this is when many respondents were most likely to nominate that text as especially worthy of criticism and dislike and when their dislikes meant the most to many of them. The rest of this chapter will explore this dynamic in depth.

In talking about worst violators, respondents regularly told me a great deal about the aspects of media culture that they found most insidious and dispiriting, but so too when respondents described texts that failed them. Whereas discussion of worst violators generally turned to what was "wrong" with the media, a discussion of disappointments became more specifically one of what was *missing* from the media. Discussions of contemporary mass media can often be pervaded by notions that there is "something for everyone." As yet more technologies and content providers bring us yet more television, music, games, apps, movies, podcasts, and so on, it is easy to fall into the trap of thinking that "everything" is out there in the media world and that every taste, desire, individual, and community can be catered to if only the right choices are made. But dislikes targeted at unmet expectations challenge this excited rhetoric. Certainly, the past few years have provided a significantly broader slate of media options than even one decade ago: one cannot imagine television shows such as *Transparent, The Leftovers, Atlanta, Pose, This Close,* or *Random Acts of Flyness* running the gauntlet of network-era programming executives; podcasts address many more taste and identity communities than most media before them; and so forth. But more is not all, and just because we can name exceptions does not mean the fundamental rules have changed. Herein lies a challenge for audience studies, though, since if we predominantly or solely ask for reactions to material that exists, how do we hear about what *else* audiences want or need? In what follows, I propose that an examination of dislikes, especially of texts that disappointed, helps answer this question, offering us glimpses of audiences variously imagining or yearning for more.

As elsewhere in this book, though, I am particularly interested in what marginalized viewers', listeners', and users' dislikes tell us. As Martin Barker and Kate Brooks note, in an early examination of expectation and disappointment surrounding *Judge Dredd*, "We don't believe there is anyone who hasn't experienced going to the cinema and having their hopes and expectations disappointed—and disappointment is an obvious mark of the presence of an ideal. But we are arguing that to identify ideals is to identify some key organising principles in people's ways of responding to films and cinema."[12] This chapter aims to access some of those organizing principles, not just for film and cinema but for multiple media. Echoing Barker and Brooks and Ahmed's positing of objects "directing" us toward feelings we presume will follow, Roger Silverstone points out that all media consumption is driven by hope: "We are drawn to these otherwise mundane and trivial texts and performances by a transcendent hope, a hope and a desire that something will touch us."[13] But what happens when that hope is deflated?

When Shit Is Just Shit: Beyond the Active Audience

In part, I am trying to move beyond an audience studies that searches for such audiences and their voices solely through "active audiences" "making do" and "poaching." Such scholarship has proven both monumentally important in complicating how we think about contemporary media and its relationships to audiences and vital as a tool for exploring marginalized individuals' and communities' relationships in particular. Certeau argued that everyday life is full of acts of "making do," wherein people face structures not of their creation that they cannot replace but with which they can inventively work.[14] Taking the lead from Certeau's example of reading as one such terrain wherein such "poaching" can occur, John Fiske suggests that our interactions and engagements with media similarly involve acts of poaching, domestication, play, and repurposing. Popular culture presents itself not as "a completed object to be accepted passively, but as a cultural resource to be used," and "the art of the people is the art of 'making do.' The culture of everyday life lies in the creative, discriminating use of the resources that capitalism provides."[15]

Neither Certeau nor Fiske performed much audience research of their own, but Janice Radway's *Reading the Romance* offers a clear instance of this creative appropriation. Beginning her book with a reading of romance fiction's sexist, demeaning messages, Radway then turns to actual readers and therein finds women who use those books in more empowering ways.[16] Julie D'Acci documents how *Cagney and Lacey*'s producers and network actively worked to "straighten" their titular characters' relationship, yet she finds lesbian fans who refused such efforts and read them as a couple nonetheless.[17] Or Henry Jenkins examines fans as "textual poachers," arguing that "consumers are selective users of a vast media culture whose treasures, though corrupt, hold wealth that can be mined and refined for alternative uses," later suggesting that in doing so, these miners also become alchemists turning shit into gold.[18]

Fiske, Radway, D'Acci, Jenkins, and their various cohort mates and followers regularly focus on marginalized audiences, arguing that such audiences are especially required to "make do" and "poach." White, middle-class, American, het-cis men have long been the imagined audience of many media industries and creators, and such viewers do not lack representation, characters with whom they can identify, or stories situated in their world and experiences that care about their desires, hopes, fears, and interests. By contrast, Fiske, Radway, D'Acci, Jenkins, and other active audience researchers note that marginalized viewers have less media directed toward them and their desires, hopes, fears, and interests, forcing them to repurpose, refashion, and redirect those texts through the act of consumption. Jenkins poses that "the school girl required to read a boy's book, the teenager dragged to see her date's favorite slasher film, the housewife forced to watch her husband's cop show rather than her soap" are all faced with a greater need to poach than the school boy, the teenage boy, or the husband in those scenarios.[19] Echoing this sentiment, other researchers have noted fannish repurposing by Black women,[20] queer viewers,[21] young people,[22] non-Americans,[23] immigrant communities,[24] and other nonhegemonic audiences. Later fan studies scholars would propose a binary of "transformative" fans and "affirmative" fans,[25] wherein the latter can engage more unquestioningly with the fan objects, allowing their fannish practices to be affirmative, celebratory, and "sanctioned" by the industry, whereas the former's "nonsanctioned" fandom requires and is based around acts of repurposing.

However, "affirmation" and "transformation" are not opposing ends of a binary; instead, they are both points on a spectrum of engagement that also extends outside the realm of fandom. Jenkins's quote about school girls, teenagers on dates, and housewives suggests that these various women might turn to poaching, but we might expect that some would simply disengage, feeling alienated and ignored. His miners, too, will surely sometimes judge land to be polluted, its shit just shit, not able to be turned into gold. Or one may simply be unable to work with one's fellow miners: as Rukmini Pande's recent work underlines, fan communities themselves can be toxic, hostile spaces to fans of color (or to women, as Suzanne Scott's work details).[26] Pande focuses on fans who labor onward, but in reading her discussion of the strategies they must develop to do so, of the continued abuse, "erasure," "alienation," and "loneliness" they face,[27] one can easily imagine them instead giving up on the dig altogether.

To poach, one must still find something to hold onto, something redemptive or more likely beautiful and inspiring about a text (and/or fandom). Thus, if we want to connect an interest in privilege to an interest in modes of fandom, we need to extend this spectrum outside fandom to consider the cases of audiences who don't have anything to hold onto, who cannot find (enough) redeeming qualities in a text or genre, who find not beauty but ugliness, not inspiration but alienation. Of course, this will not be all minority audiences—as Adrienne Shaw reminds us, identification is a complex process.[28] But if fan studies has either explicitly or implicitly posed that underprivileged audiences are more likely to need to be "transformative" fans, we should expect that other underprivileged audiences, or even especially underprivileged audiences, are more likely to be alienated ones, who will relate to the media with dislike and disappointment more or as often as with fandom.

Constance Penley proposes that "there is no better critic than a fan. No one knows the object better than a fan and no one is more critical," while Louisa Stein suggests that "it is precisely fans who have the vested interest and thus reason to hate."[29] I propose, though, that at best these are unempirical hypotheses to be tested; at worst, they are wrong. As noted in my introduction, dislike is as open to fans as it is to others, and both Stein and Richard McCulloch (in addition to Radway, D'Acci, and Jenkins) document well how disappointment is rife within fandom. As McCulloch playfully quips, "to concentrate on anti-fandom is to ignore negative emotions where they are most prevalent."[30] But it strikes me as dangerous to suggest that fans dislike best and most completely, that "no one is more critical than a fan," or that only fans have the "vested interest" that others do not. Poaching is a common response to media and is one that always involves some disappointment and displeasure. But outright disengagement, disaffection, and alienation are also common responses, and we cannot dismiss the disliker's ability to criticize, their reasons for criticizing, or their own stakes as either lesser than the fan's or mere subcategories of the fan's criticisms, and we must be willing to ask how their own disappointments happen. If, per Fiske, all texts are cultural resources or tools, what is entailed by the choice to throw a tool to the side? How do dislikers' disappointments work, and how were they discussed?

Great Expectations

Before I turn to my own data, I turn first to Andre Cavalcante, who provides the stark example of transgender audiences watching a history of dismissive, ridiculing, demeaning representations, unable to turn such shit into gold. If media images "franchise what is and is not possible," Cavalcante notes, his respondents looked eagerly to the scant few representations of transgender lives, hoping to be offered possibilities. Instead, though, they saw representations of transgender characters positing "gender variance [as] impossible and nonsensical."[31] One respondent, Kate, shared of the media images she saw of trans characters, "[They] all left a horrible memory and made me feel confused and weird about who I was. I sort of refused to take myself seriously."[32] She and others singled out *To Wong Foo, Thanks for Everything! Julie Newmar*, *Silence of the Lambs*, *Ugly Betty*, *Nip/Tuck*, numerous documentaries, episodes of *CSI*, and *The Jerry Springer Show*, reflecting on how some lured them in with the promise of a more humanizing depiction, only to fall back on the same delegitimizing tropes always applied to transgender. Shows such as *Jerry Springer*, therefore, might be "the worst"—respondent Remi asked, "Why would Jerry Springer, the audience, the TV show do that to trans people? And why would it continue?"[33] "I watched it," she further stated, "and felt really angry and disturbed, upset, and sad."[34] But some of the other shows raised expectations, only to fail. When these texts left Remi repeatedly describing her experience as one of complete "alienation,"[35] exacerbated by being a trans woman of color, which left her feeling rejected in total by media representations, clearly there was nothing to poach on.

Robin R. Means Coleman similarly documents numerous African American audiences finding Black-cast sitcoms deeply disappointing. Coleman recounts how several of her respondents appreciated Black-cast sitcoms, variously enjoying them without caveat or negotiating a response. But as much as several other respondents wanted to like the shows and were keenly aware of the representative capacities of television, they strongly disliked what they saw. Speaking of the entire genre, D.R. noted African Americans were made to look "like fools. Like clowns. Buffoons. . . . Everything is just negative," while B.B. bemoaned their bad representations of Black women, "always puttin' women down and talking about their butts, even when it's a decent little comedy or something, they make fun of each other so bad, and I hate that."[36] Several of Coleman's respondents, though, were especially disappointed with, and hence reserved considerable ire for, Black performers in these shows. Hoping for more from African Americans, the respondents felt particular dismay when they seemed complicit in these representations. For example, L.E. said, "It's really disappointing to see an intelligent Black person looking at trying to have a successful acting career and only fitting this type of role. . . . You don't have to play that role. And I cannot accept that, I do *not* accept the excuse that the actors give about, 'well if I want to be an actor.' You have to have some dignity, and you have to remember that you're representing the race, even if you don't want to, you are still a role model."[37] Nancy Cornwell and Mark Orbe heard similar responses from African American dislikers of *The Boondocks*, who were particularly disturbed that the comic strip's creator, Aaron McGruder, would peddle such images as a Black man himself.[38] These respondents leave little room for creative reappropriation in their reading, instead generating strong dislike for the shows—and in some cases the cast and/or creators—having wanted and needed something more from them yet having been let down.

From my own respondents, Bob nominated *Modern Family* as an especially frustrating, annoying text because of its portrayal of gay men. Bob cared deeply about such portrayals, and thus *Modern Family* held great potential for him, to show a gay couple and one that was part of a larger family at that. And yet that depiction was, he felt, fraught with problems. Of Cameron and Mitchell, the show's gay couple, he noted, "Those two—I can't picture how those two have ever stayed together, let alone haven't murdered each other in their sleep by now. They just fight and they fight and they fight, and it's just like, have you two not met?! [*Laughs*] I know for the other couples it's nice and evenhanded and all that, but . . . they really just kind of pick the fight-of-the-week format." He also found the characters forever in pursuit of heteronormative respectability and complained of this and other contemporary shows with gay characters:

> The idea is that you can't be "too gay." . . . Every character now has to have an arc about a romance and has to be searching for "the one" and be looking for a wedding ring, and that doesn't really represent me at all. I've never really—I've been single *mostly* by choice but most of my life, and I haven't really been out there boy-crazy hunting for a husband, like apparently now we're supposed to do. . . . They're all doing the exactly same life. They're all looking for the exact same thing. They're all either married or looking to get married. Nobody is just there as the crazy gay neighbor anymore. I guess that's just unacceptable. . . . Everybody is looking to be normalized and to prove that, . . . and it just feels like we want to be accepted, and in order to do that, we're willing to just roll over and do the roles that everybody else is doing. I don't know how to explain it, it's just—it seems in the quest for acceptance, we've just moved to a different stereotype, which is the fabulous gentrifying gays that come in with their biracial children and live happily ever after [*laughs*]. *Not that there's anything wrong with that!* But there's a lot more to my community than that.

Bob categorically did not see *Modern Family* and its other (unnamed) peers as "the worst violators" in terms of depicting gay life. He reflected on how worst depictions exist or existed, whether through being limited or outright offensive. And he could of course have also nominated countless shows that ignore gay life altogether. Instead, though, *Modern Family* was especially disappointing to Bob because it promised to depict the everyday, familial lives of a gay couple—something he desperately wanted and welcomed—and yet ultimately offered a couple that didn't resonate with his own experience of gay life. Anne Gilbert quotes the television critic Alan Sepinwall's coinage of "hope-watching," wherein we watch owing to a "belief, founded or not, that there is a good show hiding inside the bad one,"[39] and Bob had clearly hope-watched *Modern Family*.

Similarly, Ilana spoke at length of how much she disliked Lena Dunham and *Girls* and why:

> Whereas a lot of other people worked super hard to get to the same place—I mean, like, the *Broad City* girls and Issa Rae all had their own shows [web series] and stuff.... But she just got super lucky to get her voice out there. The other thing is, like, well, a lot of people hate her because she's a white feminist. And I'm, like, they're not wrong. Like, even if it's not intentional, like, she is a white feminist, [but] she's given a lot more representation to white women than women of color.... She just doesn't understand. She does need to kind of stop pretending she does. Like, she kind of needs to admit that this is just her life. I mean, like, that's so shitty. New York City is a really diverse place, and she did not represent that at all.... I think it was supposed to be a feminist show the whole time though, because she was like—like, she always talks about that, that she's a feminist. She, you know, playfully called herself the voice of a generation, and she took that up as a kind of like—well, I think she was trying to make a statement about our generation, like we are feminist, we are women. And then, like, she in interviews and stuff, which I've watched, says things like, "I just wanted to make a space for women," like that was her intention. But why only white women though?

Ilana made quick and offhand remarks throughout her interview about more actively misogynist television shows but really hit her discursive stride when talking about Lena Dunham, not because Dunham's *Girls* was categorically *worse* than those many other shows but because, to Ilana, Dunham and *Girls* were meant to be so much better. Dunham "playfully called herself the voice of a generation" and "says things like 'I just wanted to make a space for women,'" promises that Ilana clearly found compelling. But Ilana never saw Dunham follow through on those promises and deliver on that vision, instead focusing solely on relatively privileged white women.

Dunham and *Girls* had many detractors for similar reasons. Simone said, "I know all those girls and I don't like them in my real life," while Wes quipped of the show, "It's supposed to be feminist, but ... it's run by Lena Dunham, which is, like, the most problematic white feminist we have in this country." Patricia said, "There's not a lot of diversity in terms of—there's really no women of color on the show. They're all pretty wealthy and privileged. And it just doesn't seem like it's—I don't know—representative of women. And I know it's like you can't expect a show to be completely representative of everybody, but it just seems like it's showing one very narrow viewpoint. Which I don't really, I don't know, I don't really like." Amy Schumer proved similarly unpopular, especially in the sample of respondents interviewed about feminist deal-breakers. Of Schumer, Sasha explained, "I listened to a lot of her interviews. And her Twitter is problematic for me, where she's just, like—one time she was at a benefit dinner, and she sat next to a Black man and was, like, talking about how she was offended that he *didn't* hit on her. I think her and Lena Dunham are just *not good* in terms of that!" Or for similar reasons, Melanie's own bête noire was Taylor Swift, who "preaches about being this feminist icon but her feminism isn't intersectional," while Olivia couldn't stand *Gilmore Girls* for posing itself as feminist yet being filled with stereotypes of Asian parents and being, ultimately to her, "a pretty racist show." Across many of my interviews with feminists, the elusiveness of an *intersectional* feminist show looms large,[40] as the feminists of color and many of the more sensitive white feminists directed particular ire and disdain not toward the sea of misogynist or male-centered media that many acknowledged as existing but toward the few avowedly feminist shows that had the potential to be intersectional but that squandered that potential in their eyes. Or as Patricia summarized reflexively after discussing her dislike of *Girls*, "I feel like shows [that] are marketed as, like, feminist shows—I don't know if this is, like, fair of me, but I feel like I hold them to a higher standard. And so when they don't meet that expectation, I, like, hate them."

Other feminists saw a more general dearth of legitimately feminist texts and stars. For instance, Samantha noted that she didn't like Dunham, Schumer, or Swift, and her white friends would insist that she, as an African American woman, just didn't like white feminists. But stepping away from the charges of their being insufficiently intersectional feminists, Samantha said, "They just happen to suck" in general. "Taylor Swift is such a weak woman," she continued. "She, like, represents weakness to me. And I feel like her strength is like a farce. I would never be, like, 'Oh, that's a strong woman who I, like, want my daughter to see as a role model.' I feel like she seems really weak. And I think her weakness—you're probably like, 'Oh, well, why do you think she's weak?'—I would say because she, like, demands the affirmation and attention of men *constantly*."

Laura, for her part, quickly noted her dislike of *Mad Men*'s Betty Draper (January Jones) and of *The Way We Were*'s Katie Morosky (Barbara Streisand), because both the hype and the shows themselves presented the characters as strong women, yet she found them anything but. Of Draper, she complained,

> She's the epitome of the type of female that I don't like. She's very passive. Uh, she's the stereotypical trophy wife, so she's passive. She seems to be unhappy all the time. She doesn't seem to take ownership of her own happiness—which pisses me off. . . . I want her to try and manifest her own happiness, and I don't think she does a very good job of that. So, um, she's a sad character. I feel like part of the reason that she can't do that is because this show's set in the 1950s, and she's emblematic of a type of female at that time or maybe emblematic of life at that time for many women. So on some level, I'm not blaming Betty. I just don't like her, and it's probably because I would never wanna be that person. I would rather be one of the other ladies. But she seems like a bird in a cage, and I wouldn't want to be that.

As small consolation, she playfully concluded, "But I don't hate her with all my being," leading my research assistant to ask whom she *did* "hate with all her being," to which the response was Streisand's Morosky: "Yeah, I hated her with all my being. I remember watching that film, and then afterwards, I sobbed for several hours just thinking how much

I hated this woman. She was so pathetic. . . . She didn't like herself, and she was looking to Robert Redford to provide her with her own sense of affirmation, and she was just basically pathetic as a female. She didn't like herself. She didn't love herself. She didn't seem to have any respect for herself. She was looking at this man to fulfill her sense of satisfaction." Laura wanted strong women to look up to, to admire, and to engage with in more positive terms, but each text failed her, all the more because they offered the semblance of delivering a much-wanted entity, only to renege on that offer, in her opinion.

Michelle Rivera documents another form of this disappointment, when she explores Latinx dislikers of reggaetón. Here, Rivera notes that the dislikers are well aware of the advertising pitch that the musical genre is *supposedly* designed with urban, globally minded Latinx audiences in mind, but she details how many dislikers expressed "*frustration and ardently resist[ed] interpellation as the target audience for this Latin urban branded and ethnically and racially commodified form.*"[41] The music does not so much ignore them, therefore, as it imagines them to be a homogeneous, undifferentiated mass, leading to Rivera's suggestion that "anti-fandom, dislike, and/or hate for a text or genre can also serve as a means to reject the ways fans/anti-fans are constructed and interpellated as audiences or target markets—particularly for those constructed in ethnically and racially marked, coded, classed, and gendered ways."[42] In this respect, her subjects are not unlike Bob, all uncomfortable with media texts that nominally are for and about them but in such a way that flattens who "they" are.

Adrienne Shaw's audience-based explorations of what sorts of representations queer gamers want is duly sophisticated in reminding us that people don't just want more "good" representations and less "bad" representations. Rather, she offers, what many want from representation is a broad collection of images of what's possible and what could be.[43] Many of our own respondents, indeed, objected less to a "bad" representation and more to a paucity and a limit of possibilities. The representations and the texts that irked many of them the most were those that at least seemed to embark on a journey of representational possibility yet that didn't go far enough for their own liking. Many objects of dislike, as such, were not the truly awful representations weighing down the status quo on a spectrum of possibilities; they were instead those texts that went further but not enough. Respondents could envision more beyond them, but since they acted as representational limit points and fences restricting further travel, they could easily become symbols and painful reminders—unhappy objects—of the limits of representational possibilities.

Vocabularies of Engagement: Deanna

In chapter 1, I quoted from Deanna's lengthy exposition on what is wrong with *Basketball Wives*, a show that she actively worried about because she thought its popularity was likely to make it a resource for her non-Black neighbors trying to understand what she and her family were like. It is worth quoting further her disdain for the show, however, since her dislike stemmed from her concern about the paucity of depiction of African American women in general and hence from her intense annoyance that a show with multiple African American women characters, framed as "reality," would fail so monumentally at living up to her hopes and needs for such programs, rare that they are. First, though, Deanna's interview is stark for the degree to which she hardly mentioned race in the first half of that interview, when she was being asked about fandoms. When the discussion focused on things she liked and/or loved, Deanna spoke as a woman, about characters with whom she could identity as a woman and shows that she enjoyed as a woman. But when asked about dislike, she shifted to speaking at length and eloquently about her frustrations at the state of representations of African American women. Fandom and like, in other words, quite simply couldn't provide the grounds or vocabulary for an adequate discussion of race, with no text offering her enough to "poach" on. But when she was asked about alienation and dislike, we reached the point where her viewing as a woman intersected with her viewing specifically as a Black woman, and she then found the resources with which she could talk about race at length. Her case, in short, highlights how some discussions about wants and desires for the media will only take place when talking about dislikes.

Echoing some of Coleman's and Cornwell and Orbe's respondents' particular dislike for African American casts or creators engaged in such projects,[44] Deanna announced with considerable, if playful, relish, "I want to find and maim Shauni O'Neal. She is Shaquille O'Neal's ex-wife, the creator and founder of the *Basketball Wives* franchise. I want to find her and run her over with the car." Why? "That show is—it has set all women, Black women, in particular, back about thirty years. It is the worst mess on television. It is horrible, horrible, horrible. And I've only watched a couple episodes here and there, but just the things that I read about it online—these grown, adult women throwing drinks at each other, fighting—it's just ridiculous, and it's like of all the things to be doing on television when we're trying to combat stereotypes about ourselves, they are just pandering to every possible stereotype about African American women possible." Her lengthy discussion of this show (of which I quote only a small portion) constructs the show as a doorway to her feelings about televisual depictions of African American women writ large. In its wake, she struggled to nominate any better, preferred depictions: "I mean *Girlfriends* has been canceled for years, and I can't think of when was the last time there was some good representation of African Americans on TV," she said. Or later she decried Niecy Nash's Deputy Raineesha Williams on *Reno 911*: "I felt like she was every single stereotype. Like, the outfit that she wore, her cop outfit, her bottom was like these really small pants, and she has a large behind." *Basketball Wives* was singled out, therefore, but for it to have the status of threat suggests that Deanna sees television as always already failing, or barely succeeding, at offering fair and just depictions of African American women.

In this regard, again we see how dislikes are often tips of icebergs, reflecting not just a blip in reception but a general sense of the mediascape. Deanna strongly dislikes *Basketball Wives*, but to state that it is setting "all women, Black women, in particular, back about thirty years" posits a fragile line of development, wherein, according to her, progress in representation has been occurring but precariously and languidly enough that single shows can undo many years' worth of work. This image suggests no confidence in the success of the supposed "progress," coding it as tenuous. Moreover, Deanna sees the work as an ongoing battle, not a finished one: "We're trying to combat stereotypes about ourselves," she says. And in suggesting that *Basketball Wives* is "pandering to every possible stereotype about African American women possible," she further posits a widespread *desire* (by other viewers) for stereotypes that the show satiates. Her comments, therefore, tell us a great deal about her sense of disillusionment and weak faith in televised representation *in general*. They also repeat Kristen Warner's observation that "black female representation on television and in film is so scarce that any woman cast in these roles is believed to have the power to stunt the progress black women have made in society."[45]

Certainly, later in her interview, Deanna posited a special responsibility for O'Neal, *Basketball Wives*, and its cast, holding them quite explicitly to a higher standard than other producers, media, and casts. "Generally speaking," she said,

> I don't think that these shows have a responsibility. If I don't want [my child] seeing something, I shouldn't let her watch it. And it's my responsibility as a parent. . . . That's the decision that we have to make as parents. But I do feel as a woman, particularly as an African American woman, a certain kind of way about the *Basketball Wives* franchise. I think that it was very irresponsible of Shauni O'Neal to put this on the air—especially, and then go and say, well, she wants to empower African American women. How are you empowering us? And then you're having this show? Those two don't match. The two don't match. What you're saying and what you're doing don't match, and I think that our history as African American women in this country is already troubling; we already have a very hard time. And then you have the masses consuming these images of us. I feel like I'm constantly defending myself as an African American woman. So I take issue with that show in particular because of who I am.

After herself invoking the directive to "just turn it off" if you don't like something and after even applying that to the often-especially-touchy realm of children's television, she creates a special case for African American women, alluding to a long, troubled history in the United States at large, not just in the media. Given this history, she sees a particular, special, heightened need for media at the least not to exacerbate an environment of stereotypical representation but more ideally to be part of the solution, not the problem. Racquel Gates's work suggests that Deanna is not alone, as she details how *Basketball Wives* serves as a bad object for many African American women. In writing that "this focus on the alleged impact of reality TV on young people is a coping mechanism aimed at alleviating feelings of helplessness or frustration in a world where structural racism still has material and political effects,"[46] Gates similarly reflects on how this dislike is the tip of a much larger iceberg, by no means just about one show.

Following Deanna's, Warner's, and Gates's comments and taking further cues from other scholarly accounts of media representations of African Americans that collectively suggest a lot more to dislike than to like,[47] we might speculate that engaged dislike may be an especially common response for some viewers in a context in which they have historically been so poorly represented that an understandable anxiety hangs over the viewing of many texts. Of course, other Black women may appreciate and enjoy characters who directly eschew the politics of "respectability,"[48] as both Warner and Gates write of the "ratchet" depictions of *Basketball Wives*, *Real Housewives of Atlanta*, and *Love & Hip Hop* as significantly more complex. To Gates, they serve as "a type of virtual reality" allowing for "collective catharsis" and "an opportunity to linger in the emotional messiness that characterizes everyday life,"[49] and Melissa Click and Sarah Smith-Frigerio also document considerable engagement with and pleasure in *Empire*'s Cookie Lyon in their study of Black women audiences of *Empire*.[50] I do not mean, reductively, to suggest an inevitability. But Deanna displays how a heightened need from a text may easily lead to a heightened dislike when it fails.

Basketball Wives, to Deanna, could have been so much better, at offering role models to her daughter, at educating her neighbors about African American women, and at combating the country's racist and sexist history. To her, it failed spectacularly, leading to her particular approbation but also opening a doorway for us as analysts into understanding one of her foremost desires of the media and one that was closed to us when we talked only of her fandoms. That section of the interview on her fandoms was quite light and jaunty, showing the degree to which she could enjoy shows on other levels and for other reasons. Just as Melanie (quoted in chapter 1) could remove her "feminist goggles" to enjoy a text, Deanna didn't sound at all unhappy about the media when talking about shows she liked, but as soon as the frame changed to dislike, we heard her greater hopes, desires, and wishes for the media.

In discussing housewives' creative readings of romance fiction, Janice Radway wisely offers the rejoinder that "the act of purchase, then, does not always signify approval of the product selected; with a mass-production system it can just as easily testify to the existence of an ongoing, still only partially met, need."[51] Radway was part of a cohort of audience researchers who examined fannish repurposings and transformative readings as a way to clarify that "need." But her comment should serve as a reminder that articulating needs can be hard, and we should not expect all audience members to articulate their own needs through poached readings. Instead, many needs go unarticulated. This is the theme of Nina Eliasoph's book *Avoiding Politics: How Americans Produce Apathy in Everyday Life*, which draws on extensive ethnographic fieldwork to examine how Americans do—or, rather, don't—talk about politics.[52] Eliasoph refuses the easy (and demeaning) answer that her subjects didn't care about politics, instead asking, "Can people possess values, just as they possess other objects that may lie in the closet gathering dust?"[53] What, in short, goes unsaid, even if felt, and what yearnings go unspoken? So many of Eliasoph's subjects, she states, "were worried about the wider world, and yet so few were able to express their broader desires and concerns in public," thereby keeping "their enormous, overflowing reservoir of concern and empathy, compassion and altruism, out of circulation, limiting its contribution to the common good."[54] Fan studies has offered a wonderful way of listening to those concerns and those needs and has regularly proved a helpful "back door" into discussions of politics and political communication. Deanna's case, however, offers an example of how not all subjects will articulate their concerns, needs, and political convictions through the vocabulary of fandom, even transformative fandom; instead, some employ the vocabulary of dislike, requiring us to add that vocabulary to our critical repertoire.

Other Yearnings and Articulations

Great yet unmet expectations for representations of sexuality, gender, and race were commonly voiced by our respondents, but we heard of many other types of media failure too. Ilana, for instance, not only yearned for a more intersectional feminism on television but also decried the state of media discussions of depression and mental health issues. After sharing her engaged dislike of Lena Dunham and *Girls*, therefore, she pivoted quickly to state, "I am offended by *13 Reasons Why*." "I think that it super-glamorizes depression and suicide," she continued. "I remember reading the book and just being, like, 'Oh, this is so freaking stupid.' But in addition to that, you can't blame people for your suicide. Like, there's no reason for your suicide other than you're depressed and had a sickness. You know what I mean?" She then discussed the dearth of other prominent depictions of depression, noting that most were limited to "indie movies where they can show things better because it's not super commercialized." And thus *13 Reasons Why* bugged her because of its relative prominence. "Like, that's what we're teaching kids?" she asked incredulously, pained that a topic that she found important, since she knew several people who had died by suicide, and that she wanted talked about more and better would be championed in the public sphere by a show that, to her, dropped the ball entirely. "I wish less people were watching it," she stated. "I really do. I think it's super messed up. It's just renewed for another season because people are watching it, but I don't think it should be."

Unmet expectations could also overlap with a sense of *missed opportunity*, even from texts that weren't primarily "there" to deal with a particular issue. Andrea, for example, talked of a strong dislike for *Breaking Bad* because of its poor and simplistic representations of disability. She reflected on knowing that the show was by no means "about" disability in the same way that, by contrast, *13 Reasons Why* is about suicide and depression or *Girls* is about young Millennial women's lives and is articulated to notions of feminism, but she felt teased and disappointed by its potential to deal with disability. She described seeing that the show's central character has a son with cerebral palsy: "I was like, 'Oh, it would be interesting if the show was just about, like, his relationship and parenting a child with special needs and not, like, drugs.' So it almost opened up for me, like, 'Oh, this would be a better way of doing this show.' Like, you don't need the cancer or the drugs." Andrea knows that this would result in a profoundly different show; indeed, Andrea's alternate premise for the show to some degree "poaches" on *Breaking Bad*, offering something akin to fanfic, albeit very briefly, and yet it is based not in fandom and continued viewing but in dislike and tuning out. She has little critique of what *Breaking Bad* did but uses it to note a prominent absence in media of meaningful, popular stories about people with disabilities. She is scrambling for something about disability, and her act of lunging for *Breaking Bad* tells us as more about her freefall and lack of options than about *Breaking Bad* per se.

Ellen spoke of *The Tonight Show with Jimmy Fallon* in somewhat similar terms. Ellen was deeply dispirited by the state of politics and reporting on television, finding politics toxic and reporting largely feckless. But, drawn in by the likes of Stephen Colbert, she saw great potential in late-night television to be a rare space for what she saw as a much-needed critique of the inanities of politics. Since Jimmy Fallon failed to provide that, she found him "terrible" and clearly articulated the (unmet) expectations she had of him:

> I think that people in the position where they have a late-night show have a lot of responsibility because they have a lot of eyes on them, and they should use that to inform people and care about the time that they're giving to them, to give them something of value. Jimmy Fallon just showing celebrities playing board games is . . . not original. It's not. People will do it because it's easy to digest, and you can get it—like, it's a very surface-level type of entertainment. I just think that Jimmy Fallon doesn't care about the responsibilities that he should have. He's very much just, like, I don't know, "I just want to make money. I just want to do whatever. I don't want to think about things. I just want to be the likeable, fun guy." . . . I'm glad that Stephen Colbert has overtaken his ratings because I think Stephen Colbert really takes that responsibility seriously and does a great job of it, whereas Jimmy Fallon is just like, "We'll talk about Chris Christie's weight and move on." But there's like serious things happening. It's not like I want him to come down with a heavy hand, but I think he should at least try to educate people or create content that is worthy of their time.

Ellen's critique here is interesting, in that it is framed within the realm of political television broadly and late-night talk shows specifically, yet her demand for Fallon to "educate people or create content that is worthy of their time" appears to point outward to television as a whole and to her felt sense that television provides too little of this (or else why would she object to one lone program failing?).

Ellen's comment also offers an example of a respondent connecting a dislike to a like, showing the degree to which fan objects and disliked objects regularly work together: she likes Colbert in part because he isn't Fallon, and she dislikes Fallon in part because he isn't Colbert, each providing meaning to the other. This was a common move among our respondents, as they would quite often situate their fandoms in relation to a disliked text, or vice versa, in turn suggesting that we as analysts might be wise to extend discussions of fandom and dislike into each other, rather than treat them as distinct. Vivi Theodoropoulou observes a similar process within sports fandom, where support of one team practically requires engaged dislike of other teams.[55] What I have elsewhere,[56] building on Theodoropoulou, called "competitive anti-fandoms" are prevalent within the framework of sports, wherein wins must always come at another team's expense, but we should not underestimate the savvy of viewers in realizing how many media texts are similarly engaged in some form of "competition" with one another. The popular press regularly employs a framework of competition to report on ratings data, for instance, with some shows "winning" their time slot, the week, or the year. Late-night talk show hosts are often seen to be engaged in a "ratings war," inviting discussions such as Ellen's. Or, for films, box-office revenues tell us who "won" the summer or an opening weekend; "console wars" are regularly invoked in video-game reporting; and so forth. Even in an era of plentiful media options, such framing reminds us that space is still restricted and that one show's, film's, or video game's budget and existence was granted it instead of another's. Thus, we should not be surprised to see audience members adopt a competitive framework that results in them variously resisting texts whose existence might threaten the livelihood of a beloved fan object or seeing any and all texts as occupying space on the television, movie screen, or console that they wish could be vacated to make room for a preferred *type* of programming, filmmaking, or game. Certainly, Yiyi Yin offers a particularly revealing look at recent developments in idol fandom in China, wherein fan groups organize their postings on the social media site Weibo not only to ensure that their beloved idols are recorded by Weibo's metrics to be succeeding but also to attack other idols and to deflate their own relative metrics.[57]

These dislikes and the respondents' elaborations on them should also help us understand another reason why so many dislikes coalesce around popular texts. As examined in chapter 1, on the one hand, popularity translates to a level of ubiquity and inescapability: we do not "need" to passionately dislike a small indie film with a tiny release or an obscure program on an obscure channel, because both will be easy to ignore or "turn off" (unless of course our particular social context renders them peculiarly ubiquitous), but we cannot easily escape the Star Wars episodes and superhero movies of the world. On the other hand, though, popularity raises the stakes for unmet expectations and/or can offer tantalizing opportunities. All of the aforementioned dislikes have in common a popularity that *could*, in the eyes of their dislikers, have made them superb vehicles for, variously, offering a broader depiction of gay life, a more intersectional vision of feminism, a slate of stronger women characters, a rare image of African American women being more than stereotypes, a more accurate and sensitive depiction of depression, a large step forward in representations of people with cerebral palsy, and a more critically engaged, informationally rich late-night television. Countless other texts, some popular and some not, had failed to meet our respondents' expectations, and their comments gesture as much if not far more to those failures as to the nominated text of dislike. And yet because these texts could have been better, could have been exceptional, in many cases promised to be better *and were popular*—meaning that they would have been better *for many people*, not just for the respondents—they were disliked and singled out as "terrible," "pathetic," and "horrible, horrible, horrible." We can see why such texts would, like worst violators, also become objects that encapsulate and contain within them pains and disappointments from many other texts.

Those who "hate on" popular texts can often be pegged as contrarians by nature, and we will turn to such motivations in chapter 5; but just as fandom has been described within media and cultural studies as regularly "transformative," directed toward the amelioration of a text, so too do these respondents' comments illustrate how often dislike can be similarly motivated. Dislike is regularly born when a popular text lures us into thinking it will challenge the status quo, doing something better and different, going somewhere better, only to fail us. Sometimes those dislikes will be based on close viewing (as with "hatewatching"), sometimes on fleeting interaction, but across the board, dislikes can be wonderfully helpful in telling us what a respondent wants from the media writ large, what their dream and vision of a better media is, and hence of a systematic failure in the system.

The Privilege Not to Dislike

Earlier I posed that one's relative level of privilege will play a role in deciding what strategies of engagement are more or less available or difficult to mobilize, in turn meaning that we could expect to see certain forms of dislike as more common among audiences with lesser privilege. The preceding examples are drawn from the many cases among our interviews in which queer audiences, women, women of color, people with disabilities, and their allies felt anger and/or disappointment toward texts that failed them and their communities. But this dynamic of privilege was also evident in numerous cases when other respondents' privilege allowed them *not* to be too bothered by media.

While Ilana, Melanie, Olivia, and several others yearned for more intersectional feminism, the interviews about feminist deal-breakers revealed as many respondents—all self-identifying feminists—who were unbothered by such media failures. These respondents regularly framed their ambivalent level of concern with some degree of guilt, noting that perhaps they *should* dislike and cease watching a show, even though they had in the final analysis decided to keep watching. Charlotte noted of *Family Guy*, for instance, "I hate myself for watching *Family Guy*. It's so bad, and it, like, it's so racist and sexist and just horrible," but offered an excuse that her tone betrayed as only halfhearted: "The only way that I can, like, accept myself for watching it is because they pretty much make fun of everyone." So, in spite of the fact that, she said, "every time I watch it, I just feel like this horrible person, like a bad feminist or something, . . . yeah, I just, like, can't resist sometimes." Ivy similarly discussed her ambivalence toward *Supernatural*. Earlier in the interview, Ivy had credited feminist media analysis and criticism on Tumblr, and especially of *Supernatural*, with introducing her to feminism and honing her critical skills. Yet even in the face of her own sense that the show's sexism and homophobia were problematic and of her familiarity with many feminist and queer critiques of the show, she sheepishly admitted, "I really like the show because of the story, and I think the characters are interesting and funny. . . . So I think the show and the characters are interesting, and I guess, personally, I guess I'm just not *so* strong in my feelings about I should only watch shows that are like this or that are feminist or whatever."

Kelly, meanwhile, insisted that criticisms of a show's politics might stop her from watching a show before it began but honestly admitted that she would be unlikely to stop watching a show if she was already watching and then heard these criticisms:

> So I think with some shows, if there is a big controversy or a group of people of color who say this show is kind of trash, before I even start watching it, like, I just won't start watching it, kind of like with *Girls*. *Girls* has always been, like, you know, not a lot of racial representation.... So that's probably one of the reasons I never started watching it—I was just, like, "eh." Yeah, sometimes I think it's a little bit harder, though, if you do start watching something, and it's like, "Oh, this is messed up." Then it's like, "I kind of want to see where it goes."

Kelly alluded to sometimes feeling like "a bad feminist" and, when asked further about this, clarified, honestly, that perhaps more accurately she was "a bad *intersectional* feminist" or a bad ally, noting that she still watched and enjoyed *Unbreakable Kimmy Schmidt* in spite of critiques of its racial politics. She asked, rhetorically at first, "I guess I don't know what I could do about it?" before somewhat sheepishly realizing an answer: "Stop watching it. But, like, I am, like, addicted to television." Patricia was similarly honest in noting her privilege as being central to not needing to stop watching. The interviewer asked, "About a couple of the shows that we've talked about, you've talked about them being really white. Is that something that would ever bug you so much that you'd stop watching?" and Patricia was frank in replying, "I don't know. To be honest, probably just—it probably wouldn't be a sole reason why I would stop watching something. Which is probably because I am white, so I can still find representation in a show that doesn't have a lot of diversity in the cast." Heather reflected,

> You feel bad because you think, like, you know, "If I'm a feminist, then I should be, like, actively doing things to promote feminism, more than just saying, 'I'm a feminist.'" Um, and, and maybe you do, except I make little exceptions, like, "Oh, except for this one show I really like" or whatever it is. Like, ... those little things start to add up after a while, and it's like, "Oh, I actually watch a lot of TV that ... on paper I think I should

find offensive or . . . should turn off or send a letter to the writers or something." And you don't. Uh, it—it's really, um—I'm, like, I'm—after talking about these shows, I feel very conflicted. I don't know.

And even Kyra joking about how she'd react to a show's reputation for being intersectionally problematic by probably analyzing it involved reflection on the privilege not to feel implicated and to step to the side to treat it academically.

My interest here lies not in calling out these interviewees. On the contrary, each one of these women called themselves out, noting their white privilege in not feeling implicated by texts' treatment of nonwhite characters. On the one hand, they might even offer us another viewing position—that of disliking one's like, even if such a position is more often glossed over as simple "ambivalence." Taking their nomination of their white privilege at face value, they all suggested that overlooking a text's problematic representations and racial politics may be categorically easier for them than for women of color, but their reporting of it made it sound hard nonetheless. Whether that difficulty was created solely due to being *confronted* with the contradictions of their viewing position or whether it attended their everyday viewing, I do not know. I would also want to note that their contradictory, complex viewing positions are hardly unique and sound entirely similar to the fannish positions of critique found abundantly within the annals of fan studies. Yet all variously insisted or suggested that being white came with the privilege of not needing to get as riled up about as much media, because it meant not feeling implicated in as many texts' problematic racial representations, which they acknowledged to be commonplace.

On the other hand, many other audiences were not so reflective about their privilege, even if it was evident to my research assistants and me. We saw this especially when some respondents criticized anyone else who would care to dislike anything, holding fast to a "just change the channel" or "just calm down" rhetoric, sometimes even casting shade on their disliking counterparts for "choosing" that path instead of their own, supposedly more enlightened, more cheerful path. Winona, for example, claimed rarely to care enough about dislikes to bother sharing them: "In my mind, maybe when people are talking about something, I'll think, 'Oh, I didn't like that or care for it,' and in my mind, I'll move on. But I won't say anything. I don't feel like I need to talk about something I don't care for. I just let it go on. I'm not trying to stir up any problems." Nicole, for her part, fell back on a defense of creativity, arguing, "Behind every piece of media, there's a human being, and somebody put their effort into it and their creativity and their heart into it. So I think it's like anything else. There's good and there's good." Nicole was unwilling to engage in dislike, or so she claimed, because to her, the importance of the creator being able to say what they wanted trumped any ethic of caring about effect or reception. Dorothy was clearly upset by the suggestion that she might find *anything* worth disliking, explaining that she only watched things that made her feel good and happy, a category that was clearly plentiful for this middle-class white woman. Celise, too, came close to suggesting that only lesser, weak viewers would need to feel dislike or to be truly bothered by something. By contrast, she boasted, "I'm able to recognize the values that a lot of people on the show hold don't align with mine, and, like, rather than letting that influence me, it's more just you can kind of laugh at that. . . . I think I'm less easily influenced than others and that sort of thing. I know what I believe, and I know my values, that sort of thing. And I can watch it and take it at face value. I'm not going to let it dig deeper and change my life." Zelda concurred that since media's "not the center of [her] life," she was personally able to overlook infractions, while implying that others who could not "just change the channel" were, by contrast, unhealthily and excessively centered on the media. And Quinn framed dislike in terms of maturity, seeing it as "childish" to care enough to launch into a tirade about anything that is "just entertainment."

And yet if this section began with an intersectional awareness on behalf of several feminists that their viewing was racially situated, we might also note a gendered context for some of the preceding comments that failed to see privileges of whiteness and straightness. After all, readers may well have picked up on the conspicuousness of all of these comments, save for Quinn's, coming from women. In quoting them, I certainly do not mean, stupidly, to suggest that only women had privilege, whether acknowledged or not. Rather, the fact that many women felt that criticism and dislike were in some way problematic and that they needed to be either explained and apologized for or clearly disavowed might indicate the degree to which women have often been encouraged not to dislike or at least not to full-throatedly share their dislikes. Evelyn Brooks Higginbotham's respectability politics are as much about societal expectations of women as they are about societal expectations of African Americans.[58] Women are too often supposed to like things or at least to profess apathy. Angela McRobbie notes that "the new female subject is, despite her freedom, called upon to be silent, to withhold critique in order to count as a modern sophisticated girl. Indeed this withholding of critique is a condition of her freedom."[59] Sara Ahmed powerfully reclaims the mantle of "killjoy" for feminists of color, to "give the killjoy back her voice,"[60] but of course, "killjoy's" more regular usage is as critique of those who "won't stop complaining," who "must always cause a scene," and whose dislikes are thereby framed as tedious, bad-tempered, and disruptive for the sake of chaos alone. Serving as premise to Ahmed's reclamation of the term, then, is this expectation that women shouldn't disrupt or "be so negative." Thus, I found it interesting and telling that this discussion of when one could dislike, and by what degree, was one conducted almost solely by women respondents, while many of the men less self-reflexively enjoyed the privilege of not needing to apologize for, frame, or disavow their own dislikes.

Ultimately, then, as much as some marginalized and underrepresented viewers found a position of engaged dislike as the one best suited to communicating their feelings about and hopes for not just individual texts but the whole media system, and thus as much as I hope we can, as a field, think about how marginalized viewers may be especially directed to dislike, we must also think about who needs to dislike and who doesn't and about who is more easily allowed to dislike boldly or who may need to step carefully with their dislike, frame it, and hedge it. If dislike has gotten a bad name, this is in part because of the respectability politics and tone policing that regularly delegitimize marginalized people's voices when they're angry, upset, and focused on grievances, not pleasures, or that stop them from complaining in the first place. What we have to say about dislike, therefore, and about one's freedom to dislike seemingly mundane media texts may have significant import to our understanding of what it means "to complain," to criticize, and to dislike in society more generally, a reason I will return to this point in the book's conclusion.

For now, though, I note that privilege also seemed at play in relation to whether people nominated worst-in-class dislikes or disappointed dislikes. Across our many interviews, I was struck by how often many marginalized and less privileged viewers turned first, mostly, and/or most vociferously to disappointments, whereas less marginalized and more privileged viewers tended more often to luxuriate in discussing worst violators. And thus we find the oddity that Lena Dunham's or Amy Schumer's flawed feminisms drew as much collective ire across our interviews with feminists as did *Two and a Half Men*'s more forthright misogyny. Many marginalized viewers, in short, had often already come to expect a mass media system full of more sexist, racist, homophobic material and had written it off but simultaneously found it more strategically useful and worthwhile to focus their concern, efforts, and public denunciations on media that they believed could have been better. As Patricia was quoted earlier as saying about *Girls*, many viewers held their expectations to higher standards. At the individual level, such a choice is entirely rational—if nothing about *Two and a Half Men* suggests a desire on its producers' behalf to listen to feminists, why not instead direct one's complaints toward the likes of Dunham and Schumer, whose claims to feminism *might* make them or at least their fans more receptive listeners? Or if nothing about many white-cast shows suggests a cast and crew either interested in or capable of offering thoughtful depiction of African Americans, why not instead focus on *Basketball Wives*? At a societal level, though, the likes of Dunham, Schumer, and the cast of *Basketball Wives* are already being pilloried from regressive angles for being "unruly women" who are "too loud," "too ugly," "too rude," and generally violating hegemonic expectations of women.[61] The addition of a progressive attack makes them veritable Bad Objects and explains why we can hear so much volume to complaints about Dunham, Schumer, and reality television's more "ratchet" African American cast members yet not far more about more ostensibly and flagrantly sexist and racist performers and material.[62] At a societal level, it also enacts another, if unintended, form of respectability politics wherein the worst violators at times can escape with far less criticism, far fewer attacks, than disappointments can. A centrifugal force is applied herein, pushing dislike away from hegemonic norms and centers to their outskirts. Again, I will return to this centrifugal force in the book's conclusion.

Conclusion

If I began this chapter with the mission of finding scripts of change and improvement on the media, I both succeeded and failed in offering them. Interviewees' comments about worst violators and unmet expectations succeed in articulating dissatisfaction with the media as it is, with articulating needs, hopes, and pains that undergird their dislike. One might find it extravagant, though, to consider these enough to amount to a full-fledged revision of the media system, and in this regard, they fail. Only a tiny handful of my respondents reported taking their concerns about representation, for instance, to activist ends, and thus generally I cannot bridge respondents' accounts to a tale of collective action.[63] Still, I am reticent to set the evaluative bar too high and to require that all demands for change be bold and full-throated in order for them to count as legitimate. We should expect that many "demands" for change will instead be humbler requests. Scholars of representation have continually shown how marginalized subjects in particular have systematically had voice and legitimacy denied to them. Audience scholars have a rich opportunity, though, to hear these voices, albeit quiet at times, albeit restricted to the discussions of which show is good, bad, or worst. In our respondents' discussion of the shows, films, music, and other media that they disliked, they regularly offered us broader critiques of a wider range of media and of their hopes and expectations for media's representational systems. In doing so, they showed us how transformative a deeper exploration of dislike could be for our field's understanding of representation and of people's everyday expectations of representation. In chapter 3, I hold focus on expectations but shift to considering expectations of a subsequent text in a series. What, I ask, can we learn about what a text really means and represents to its audience by listening to their complaints about its sequels, adaptations, and extensions?

3

Fallen from Grace, or, When Sequels Attack

Many of our respondents, as we have seen, were actively disappointed by their dislikes. But a particular type of disappointment was especially prevalent, thereby warranting separate consideration. This was the disappointment in the latest iteration of a once-loved text or franchise. Certainly, popular discussion of media is replete with insistences that adaptations, sequels, spin-offs, and remakes are both plentiful and bad. While I do not mean to foreclose on questions about lazy industrial practices, in this chapter I step back from the broader questions of whether more of a story and/or its characters really *is* so bad to instead ask what it means that we're regularly talking about adaptations as bad, as "letting down" a noble original. Such discussion requires separate treatment in a book on dislike since it represents a major genre of talk about dislike, one that cuts across popular, press, and academic treatments alike and one that unites a great many expressions of disappointment. In chapter 2, I argued that articulations of unmet expectations regularly gesture to systemic critiques of the media, precisely because they invoke the alluring presence of a missing ideal, but what of instances when the ideal was seemingly achieved and has now been perverted? How does talk about disappointment in adaptations, remakes, reboots, sequels, prequels, spin-offs, franchise development, and/or falls from grace help to tell us exactly what it was about "the original" that was so valued and about the way love and fandom can quickly morph into dislike?

Admittedly, if we heard so much about such disappointments in our interviews, that is in part because we actively went looking for them, hoping to better understand the mobility between positions of like and dislike. By contrast, the extant literature on audiences regularly arrives on the scene when one is already a fan, sometimes backing up to ask how the fandom began but rarely continuing the story into decline. Even the abundance of scholarly work examining resistance to established texts or franchises tends to frame those acts of resistance as fannish by nature. I wanted to go further, though, and see when the respondent approaches a state of disavowal and rejection and/or feels betrayed or abandoned by the formerly beloved text. I did so in part to work against an essentialist notion of fandom or dislike wherein one simply *is* a lover or a disliker, to instead regard love and dislike as stages through which many of us progress. As more and more texts are rebooted, revived, and prolonged over multiple decades, the possibilities for enduring fandoms increase, but so too does the likelihood that some texts will lose fans and lovers along the way, sometimes to mere casual appreciation or apathy, sometimes to active dislike. I turn to adaptations, sequels, and the changing tides of their audience's loyalties, therefore, to begin to construct an apparatus for understanding audiences as more than "just" liking or disliking and as my own contribution to an audience studies that focuses as much on transitions, becomings, departures, and changes in status. Such an audience studies would avoid placing dislike and like on different, far-flung islands, instead focusing on the interchanges, mingling, and thoroughfare between them.

I begin by consulting the feminist "deal-breaker" interviews specifically, exploring how, why, and when self-identifying feminists decided that they could no longer endure a text. This exploration segues easily into the following section on *Gilmore Girls* fans reacting to its belated Netflix sequel, *Gilmore Girls: A Year in the Life*, for many of their objections focused on a perceived weakening of the formerly strong Rory Gilmore. Here, I propose a *refractive audience analysis* technique of using commentary on an adaptation or continuance to study audiences' responses to the original, and I then apply this technique to reviews of *The Hobbit: An Unexpected Journey* to offer another study focused on a single text. To discuss fan disavowals, though, requires that we also look at the spewing beast of dissatisfaction that is white-male "fanboy" rage at franchises that add women and/or people of color to their next chapters. Thus, the final section of the chapter shifts to white-male rage at *Star Wars Episode VII: The Force Awakens* and *Star Wars Episode VIII: The Last Jedi*. In doing so, I aim to explore another complex transition or overlap of reactive positions, between fandom, engaged dislike, and hate. I hope to show that some of the tools and approaches I've used for analyzing dislike—refractive analysis in particular—can also be used to tell us of the ground rules some fans established for continued positive engagement and thus what triggers existed to create a spiral into dislike and hate.

The Love Stops Here: Deal-Breakers

As noted earlier, a preponderance of work on fandom begins and ends with the fans in question already ensconced in fandom, perhaps gesturing obliquely to fans trying to convert friends but rarely focusing on how one becomes a fan or ceases to become a fan. A prominent exception, CarrieLynn Reinhard's *Fractured Fandoms*, collects stories and analyzes cases of "fractures" within fandoms, which Reinhard defines as "a communication problem that arises out of a tension between communication participants within a fan collective or between different ones. The gaps involve tensions, struggles, and problems when people interact with others. Fractured fandom, then, occurs any time communication between fans, within anti-fans or non-fans, within fan communities, between fan communities and/or between fandoms breaks down."[1] However, this interest focuses entirely on fractures between people, not between people and texts: Reinhard examines a variety of reasons for fracture, but all cases in her book of fans leaving a fandom are thus catalyzed by interpersonal disputes. The book contributes a great deal to the burgeoning literature on "fantagonisms"[2] and on "toxic," "reactionary," and racist fandom,[3] all of which provide an abundance of reasons for why one might leave a fandom for interpersonal reasons. Reinhard's work, though, and the wealth of this literature in general, risks presupposing that the natural destiny for a fandom should be to continue and thus leaves unanswered (since, in all fairness, these were not the research questions of these scholars) questions about when fans leave a fandom due to a fracture with the text, not the fan community.

Nevertheless, a few other examples of fans leaving their fandom exist across fan studies. For instance, Henry Jenkins considers *Beauty and the Beast* fans who united first around a love of the television show, mobilizing to save it in the face of its cancellation, and then in finding the new version of the show—changed to, in theory, make it more commercially viable—a pale shadow of its former self.[4] As Jenkins recounts, though, their fandom never seemed truly to be in question, as instead they collectively rallied around their mutual feelings for the earlier version. The text left the fandom, we might say, rather than the fandom leaving the text. Meanwhile, Matt Hills posits the existence of "cyclical fandom,"[5] wherein the fan is not committed to any given fandom and instead experiences their passion in bursts, enthusiastically consuming a text and engaging in its fandom for a while, before roaming onward to another text. Absent from Hills's account, though, is any sense of the fan leaving through a sense of betrayal or dislike: cyclical fans don't move to dislike, simply onward to the next fandom.

Rebecca Williams's book *Post-object Fandom: Television, Identity, and Self-Narrative* offers the richest account to date of fans dealing with the "end" of their beloved text. Many of the cases she studies are of television shows that have finished, hence necessitating the fan to "move on" in some way, and her focus is more on how fans "renegotiate" their relationship to a fan object that is in many cases still loved dearly but that must now be loved differently. Nevertheless, she also considers some instances in which a show's conclusion angers fans, leading to a more acrimonious rejection. Williams helpfully writes of the "loveshock" that occurs at such moments, of an ensuing "period of mourning" when a formerly happy object loses its ability to represent ontological security, and of the renegotiation not simply of a relationship with a text but of its role in one's construction of self-identity.[6] She primes us to expect a quick swing of the affective pendulum in some such cases, as loveshock turns to embitterment and as the audience member in question must quickly reconstitute their self in relation to the text. Williams's work inspired me to look for more cases of loveshock where the text continues but the fan walks away, no longer able to abide it.

I turn first, then, to the "deal-breakers," as my research assistant Abigail M. Letak called them, and to instances when self-proclaimed feminists turned against a show that they already liked. Some had no deal-breakers, as was discussed in chapter 2, which is not to say "they didn't care," but many respondents reflected on the slim pickings of truly feminist work out there and hence clearly felt able (or resigned) to keep watching imperfectly feminist shows, albeit with a critical eye. But others recounted instances when they left a television show. Their reasons tended to focus on texts' wavering or unrealized feminism, as we'll see, but I remind the reader that this is because of the framing of the interviews—surely a broader range of reasons to "break up with" a text exist, but these particular interviews were designed in ways that elicited reasons based primarily on a text's gender politics and performances.

Rape and sexual violence were often listed as reasons why subjects could not continue with a show. In a few cases, the objection was framed as less of a critique and more as a statement of being personally triggered and unwilling to continue. Amelia, for example, said of *13 Reasons Why*, "When it first started, I liked it a lot. I was really into it." However, toward the end of the show's first season, she found the sexual violence overwhelming. She did not see the sexual violence as filmed or written offensively but had personal experiences with sexual violence that made it too uncomfortable to continue. By contrast, though, *Game of Thrones* was roundly criticized by numerous viewers for relishing its sexual violence; some of these viewers decided to keep watching, albeit with some ambivalence, while others turned it off. Annie, for example, noted how she struggled with the show's first two seasons, on balance enjoying them but uncomfortable with what the writers inflicted on its female characters, until that changed:

> The third season I kind of fell off it because of even more of these changes. Like, slowly they just kept reducing female characters as actual decisions and then also then somehow increasing the, like, torture porn and sexy rape, which is awful. And then in season 4, which is the real breaking point, which is I *love* the character Circe—that's a deeply unpopular opinion. I love her. I think she's amazing. I think she is an extremely interesting female character. I think that's great. And then they had, uh, Jamie, her brother/lover, rape her in the show, which does not happen in the book—that scene was extremely consensual in the books—and then the showrunners were like, "It wasn't a rape scene!" and that's when I really had to quit, because it was like, if she was sobbing and saying, "No, no, please no!" and I was like—I can't watch a show made by people who don't think that a woman sobbing and saying "No, no, please no!" as someone has sex with her is not rape—like, I can't. So that's when I was like, "No more! I can't do it. I can't watch this show anymore. Enough is enough."

Rayanne, too, insisted,

It was just too much rape. I couldn't really—I didn't feel good watching anymore. I don't get paid to write about television or review television, and so it felt like I wasn't getting a lot out of it anymore. And so it was no longer, like, a pleasurable viewing activity. It had become instead a kind of endurance test of how long can I watch this show that I really didn't enjoy anymore to prove that I was like, I don't know, "a discerning consumer." And I was like, "No, it's just that I don't want to watch rape and gore!" I don't care if people think it's well made; it's no longer a pleasant experience for me.

Marina similarly reached a breaking point with *Game of Thrones*, wherein after watching an especially graphic rape scene, not only could she not countenance watching it any longer herself, but she also became actively concerned with why anyone else could watch it:

It's just frustrating because when I'm watching a show like this, there's others that don't quite see that as a problem. They think that's part of, like, the era and the history of medieval times, so that's appropriate. So then when I'm frustrated or weeping, I'm having a really bad reaction because it's very sensitive and traumatizing in a way to see stuff like that on TV, and others are like, "So, whatever?" Others are not agreeing with me, and my reaction to that sort of thing is worse than another kind of crime or whatever. That has become something that I really hate, seeing something like that on TV, especially when it's graphic and you can see.

The scene was clearly personally difficult to watch for Marina, but her horror at the scene and show stems from the unflappability with which others around her approach it.

Game of Thrones poses an especially interesting case study, since whereas—as we'll see—it is common for fans of any text to complain about new developments, (perceived-to-be) profound changes in characterization, and/or other tonal, stylistic, or political shifts, all of these (and several other unquoted) former viewers or fans of *Game of Thrones* reflected on how the show had always contained sexual violence. Even its pilot episode contains numerous instances of sexual violence. And thus these viewers' eventual acts of leaving the show indicate the degree to which fandoms often contain wounds and sores that may fester or inflame over time, either because the fan object keeps prodding the wound and making it worse or because the sustained, constant pain inflicted by the wound eventually becomes too much for the fan to countenance continuing with the text. More common in the academic literature are tales of fans treating their wounds through productive, creative outlets such as fanfic, and more common in the journalistic literature are tales of fans justifying and/or ignoring all wounds; but these former viewers of *Game of Thrones* render clear that fans often wrestle with their fan objects in more conflicted, less playful or less oblivious ways.

Accounts of deal-breakers also showed how social the turn to dislike could be. Of *Family Guy*, Sasha noted that although "in high school it was cool to stay up at ten o'clock with your friends and watch *Family Guy*," after moving to college, her new group of friends were feminists, in front of whom she would feel ashamed watching it. Now, she has "a huge problem with *Family Guy* and the way they treat Meg": "Because, you know, not only does she show signs of, you know, chronic mental illness, but they make fun of her, and they don't support women the way they should. Even the mother is that. I won't watch *Family Guy*."

Violet similarly noted that a single class presentation made her realize all sorts of problems with *Unbreakable Kimmy Schmidt*:

> Someone in a class I took last semester did a whole presentation about how Tina Fey is kind of racist by breaking down the movie *Mean Girls*, and then they also started talking about *Unbreakable Kimmy Schmidt* since that's a show that she produces. I never, like, really realized that before, and I used to really like *Unbreakable Kimmy Schmidt*. But as I continued watching it and noticed more things, it kind of turned me off of it. Like, the representations—there's, like, one Black character who is flamboyantly gay and how that is a representation of the Black community and the gay community that is not very accurate and is very stereotypical. Some of the jokes can be really off-putting too, and so they reminded me of that girl's [from her class] project.... I had already watched all of it [to date], and then they just came out with a new season on Netflix. So I started watching the third one, I think. I just really couldn't get into it. I watched like a handful of them, and then I was like, "ehh." I just kind of lost interest.... I think it was the presentation. I don't think it has changed that much, but I'm just more aware of it now.

Fans don't just speak to other fans and must continually interact with nonfans and with dislikers. Just as fans may proselytize and convert nonfans and dislikers, so too can dislikers convert fans. Violet's case offers a clear instance of how hearing from another disliker caused a reappraisal of the fan object and a concurrent defection and falling out of love.

Amusingly, Sophie offered another reason for disavowal, namely, that the act of binge-watching might lead to an otherwise mildly problematic show being perceived as more clearly and objectionably problematic. Of *The Mindy Project*, she said,

> I'll, like, binge-watch a bunch of TV shows at a time, and it gets to a point where you watch a certain show so much that you start noticing things you wish you weren't noticing—certain stereotypes and things like that. . . . Like, recently I was watching *The Mindy Project* exclusively. Like, I pretty much watched the whole first season, and then I got halfway through the second season, and I almost got sick of it. It just felt like the same thing over and over. I just felt like it got really stereotypical and kind of annoying. So I was like, "You know what? I should take a break, because I really liked this, but now I'm hating it. I'm going to take a break until I don't quite hate it anymore, so I can go back with more of fresh view of it and then enjoy it more."

As she closes off, here, Sophie offers the prospect that not only did she go from fan to "hating" it, but she may return to fandom in the future, if she can first get some needed distance.

As noted in chapter 2, these disappointments speak to expectations the subjects had of media, and especially of their beloved media, and of moments when either they themselves or assisted by others decided that the shows' payoff no longer justified continued viewing, that their expectations had been violated. Or, as in Sasha's and Violet's cases, they also point to developing expectations and to the regular "checkups" we might perform on our fandoms and their general health or lack thereof. These are especially interesting moments, therefore, since they crystallize key expectations: it is one thing to hear from afar of a new show that is guilty of a particular sin and to decide, with no skin in the game, not to watch it. But when fans turn on their texts, we see the expectations that matter most. And we see how fan object disavowal may prove to be a momentous performative act for some, amounting to declaring, both to themselves and to others, "I will no longer accept this." I will thus return to some of these performances of identity in chapter 4; for my current focus in this chapter, though, they remind us that expectations change, and changing fan identifications can be a rich site for exploring negotiations of expectations and demands. Our own interviews only truly show these negotiations as personal or occasionally brokered between small groups, but broader culture offers us plenty of examples of how such negotiations can be communal or cultural, as we might, for instance, consider the #metoo movement's tentative successes in rendering some stars' past or present behavior potentially disqualifying for fandom with them or the texts in which they appear to a degree that previously was less the case. As such, one can use a timeline of fan expectations—personal or communal—to tell a tale of changing investments in various causes or principled beliefs.

What's Wrong with Rory Gilmore? When "Good" Characters Go "Bad"

Throughout this and chapter 2, I've been arguing that a study of expectations is a study of what matters, and thus it is also helpful to focus an examination of expectations and disappointment on a discussion of adaptations, sequels, and reboots. It is on this note that we can turn to the survey responses to Netflix's revival of *Gilmore Girls*: 718 people responded to the survey, most of them reporting that they were fans of the original series, yet a healthy portion of them strongly disliked the revival, claiming now to be "done" with the text. Why?

This question opens a doorway to adaptation and franchise studies and to the age-old response that an adaptation, remake, or sequel isn't as good as the original. Adaptation studies as a field has tired of endless discussions of fidelity and infidelity. Noting how an adaptation, remake, or sequel differs from the original has long been one of the lowest-hanging fruit for uninspired criticism, and thus adaptation studies has understandably moved beyond discussing (in)fidelity to ask a wider range of questions about the textual, industrial, and even political processes of adaptation and remaking.[7] For the most part, I celebrate this move. But some nagging questions about (in)fidelity remain, for most of the literature on (in)fidelity is written with only the critic in mind or sometimes erases the critic altogether and dubiously claims an objective Archimedean vantage point. Missing from this literature is much discussion of what the original meant to its audience, how and why it mattered, and hence what the audience wants fidelity to. And yet in popular cultural discussion at large, (in)fidelity discourse is pervasive and a key lens through which many audiences claim to be interacting with adaptations, remakes, and sequels. Thus, I follow Liam Burke here, who calls for the fidelity debate to be reopened "as a means of productively addressing how fan discourses . . . can be a vibrant part of the many relations that shape an adaptation."[8] Few audiences seem to want complete repetition (and charges of unoriginality and laziness abound when insufficient changes are perceived to have been made), but *some* things from the original matter. Therefore, as much as adaptation studies' foray into a broader range of issues across textual, industrial, and political analysis is opening up the field, greater attention to audiences would open it up yet further. In particular, greater attention to asking audiences precisely *what* they want fidelity to—and what they don't care about—could allow us to use adaptations, remakes, and sequels to better ascertain precisely what value and importance various ("original") texts have to their audiences. Sometimes we can read value and importance from audiences' *own* adaptations and fan productions, and thus in fairness, I'll note that fan studies has long been doing this work; but there is more work left to be done in using the dynamic of adapting, remaking, or continuing a story to ask questions about the meanings of its various parts to its audience.

A superb exception to the textual-formalist tradition of analyzing adaptation, offering a promising foray into how audiences engage issues of adaptation, can be found in Martin Barker and Kate Brooks's *Knowing Audiences: Judge Dredd, Its Friends, Fans and Foes*. Though Barker and Brooks are rarely cited within adaptation studies literature, their book stands out for its inventive methodology of asking viewers and intended viewers of the 1995 *Judge Dredd* for their reactions to the film. They delineate six different orientations to the film, or five SPACEs (Sites for the Production of Active Cinematic Experience), each of which effectively acknowledges that the film is a continuation of other ongoing texts or textual experiences. While two of these are genre specific (action-adventure, future-fantastic), one star specific (based on followers of Sylvester Stallone), and two general film-follower and culture-belonging SPACEs, a sixth pertained to *2000 AD* readers and fans, and those intended viewers within this SPACE are charted as reacting to *2000 AD*, their structures of viewing imported from their responses to and readings of the source comic series.[9] Barker's subsequent work on *Crash* with Jane Arthurs and Ramaswami Harindranath further develops some of these concepts in examining the furor that preceded and engulfed the British release of David Cronenberg's film (and adaptation of J. G. Ballard's novel) about people who get sexually aroused by car accidents. Barker, Arthurs, and Harindranath offer the helpful rallying call for an audience analysis based around dislike in noting that "there may be some methodological virtues in attending to the unsettled because, in the course of thinking out loud about their uncertainties or complications, they may disclose the wider orientations" the unsettled viewer or nonviewer takes to society and media interactions more broadly.[10]

Inspired by *Knowing Audiences*, Bertha Chin and I conducted audience research in 2000–2001, when news of Peter Jackson's big-budget adaptation of *Lord of the Rings* had hit. We set out with the task of asking people how they were responding to a set of films that did not yet exist, for fan boards were alive with discussion and careful parsing of details, prerelease. Perhaps predictably, most such discussants were more properly fans *of the books*, and their discussions of what they feared, hoped for, anticipated, and dreaded about the filmic adaptations were in many ways continued commentary about the books.[11] As with Barker and Brooks, we did not primarily (or even secondarily) frame this as a study of adaptation per se and hence didn't focus our analysis on what their commentary told us about what the books meant to them—our key point was more simply and observationally that audiences can react to texts before they seemingly exist. However, in returning to this data, I see all sorts of declarations about what Jackson's trilogy "needed" to do that are statements about the enduring value that Tolkien's books had for these audiences. Those declarations tend to be fragments, though, and tantalizingly have long called to me to do more, to ask a different slate of questions.

Adaptations offer the audience analyst the prospect for wonderful insight. If fidelity to an original matters so much to so many viewers (and one need only open an internet browser to find that it does), audience research could allow us to ask precisely *what* about the original matters. I therefore propose what we might call a *refractive audience analysis*, wherein asking about responses to the adaptation tells us about responses to the original.

A clear pattern of dislike emerged in the survey data on *Gilmore Girls*, as many respondents repeated a similar tale of loving the original show because of the character Rory (Alexis Bledel) yet feeling that she was the worst thing about the sequel, *A Year in the Life* (*AYITL*) and was horribly mishandled. A common concern with Rory was that she had lost integrity and decency. One respondent wrote,

> The biggest thing that I disliked about *AYITL*? I hated Rory. She was one of my favorite characters in the original series, but she was nothing like the Rory of the original series in *AYITL*. She was selfish, entitled, and had fallen so far below her potential. I can't imagine what the writers were thinking with the Logan/Paul situation. She was terrible to Paul, and he did nothing to deserve it, aside from being boring? . . . The last four words were honestly tragic for her character. *Gilmore Girls* was never something that was supposed to come "full circle." Lorelai broke out of her parents' control and worked hard so that Rory could have a better life than she had. She worked her butt off, she found a way to pay for Chilton, she was constantly supportive and did anything she could to help Rory get where she was supposed to go—and that was right where Lorelai started? It makes no sense. It destroys the point of the entire show.

Many viewers thought of Rory as a more capable character and couldn't stomach seeing her rendered less capable or as having learned little from life. One wrote, "I think they pretty much destroyed Rory's character for no reason. She was pretty selfish in the later seasons of the original series, but OH MY GOD. She's the other woman AGAIN??? It's like she learnt nothing." Another opined, "I expected to catch up to my favorite characters and see some conflict but not the terrible story line for Rory. That was a major miscalculation. I've spent years believing she was good and capable and had integrity. This revival ignored all of that for her character." Another wrote simply, "I disliked how Rory was an idiot," while yet another elaborated, "I obviously did not like Rory's storyline.

She became this flighty character who forgets about her boyfriend of 2 years and is cheating on him with her ex. . . . She is unprepared for interviews and is clearly not a great journalist, which is not what the original series made us to believe. We can all relate to being lost, but I think they could have done that a lot better." In these and in another's comment, "I didn't like how much of a mess Rory was though. She just didn't seem like The Rory we knew and loved," a shared belief among many viewers became clear, that Rory was capable, smart, plucky, and self-sufficient but lost all these qualities in the intervening years.

An oft-repeated criticism was that Rory's development seemed stunted. To one respondent, "a lot of Rory's plot line would've made more sense if it happened 2 years after season 7 not 8 years later." Others said, "I expected more for Rory and was a bit disappointed with where she was in her life after all those years," "I hated how they made Rory. I didn't need her to be a successful journalist per se, but to have her so aimless and not seem to be trying or have learned anything in the past 10 years felt unrealistic to the character they introduced in the original series," and "Rory had no growth after the original series. If anything, she backtracked. . . . I just felt like it was all very wrong." At more length, another parsed,

> While I understand Rory feeling lost, her storyline seemed more accurate to a mid-20s than an early 30s woman. We're about the same age and education level, and I feel like the issues that are common to me and my friends have evolved beyond the "what am I doing with my life?!" and much more into balancing two-career families (with or without children), what compromises to make in life and career, etc. I feel like in real life, Rory would have had this crisis around 27, done the masters, and be working at Chilton by now (or similar path). She'd have some regrets, but there would be an upside, too. That's life, and there are some genuinely interesting and realistic stories in topics that resemble real life. . . . Overall, I just wished it was more true to 30-something problems since that's what she was supposed to be.

Many of these respondents listed Rory as their favorite part of the show originally, I note, so these were not cases of, say, Lorelai fans becoming distracted by Rory. Rather, as one stated, "[Rory] didn't seem consistent with the Rory I so dearly loved and identified with." This high regard for Rory clearly compounded their concerns and dissatisfaction. As one respondent, who set in boldface a response that "even now, months later, it still makes me furious," tellingly wrote, "I did not want to waste the precious minutes we had left with Rory Gilmore watching her be entitled, oblivious, and lacking in ambition or honor." This wording paints a pained scene, of a viewer who loved Rory deeply, mourned her absence from television and her life, and now therefore cherished the rare chance to have a few more "precious minutes" with her before she was once more taken. But instead, the writers stole those minutes. Many respondents used the language of what "they" (the producers/writers) did "to" Rory. Mobilizing a rhetoric often employed by fans, of weak writers "deviating" from characters' true selves,[12] the respondents posited Rory not only as existing independently of the writers but as victimized now by those writers. Some even employed more violent metaphors to describe what had happened to their beloved character, as when one wrote that Rory "was butchered into sensationalized nonsense. She was going to change of course but according to the revival, she grew into a completely new and entirely different person. She simply was not Rory at all." Or another "hated Rory becoming a monster," again employing words that suggested a violation and transfiguration of their beloved character.

Some detected or sensed a broader attack perpetrated by the writers, against Millennials in general. "I really didn't like Rory's storyline," one wrote. "It felt like a real let down after seeing Rory toil through Chilton and Yale, only for her to seem only alright at her job and like she hadn't come very far in the many years since graduation. It also seemed slightly demeaning to Millennials." Or another complained of the writers, "They could have stressed more why Rory was such a failure nowadays. It's not enough to just do a judgmental parallel to millennials, they needed to go deeper with her, maybe related it to her sheltered life with her mom and townies, or her fear of taking chances and going the conventional route, and i think that's why people found her character so unredeemable and annoying this time around. like we get it Amy [Sherman-Palladino, the head writer], you hate millennials, but to write about something you gotta know more than just the dislike you feel towards it." Such comments are themselves telling about how representative the character of

Rory had become for many viewers of themselves and their own generation, such that an "attack" on Rory would be read by some of them as by nature an attack on that generation. Admittedly, these are just two respondents, but many more framed their concerns by noting close identification with Rory in part on the basis of being the same age. Certainly, elsewhere in the survey, when respondents discussed why they loved the original, a great many noted identification with her as a smart woman of their same age. As Adrienne Shaw's audience-based work on "identification" shows, identification with a character is overpresumed to exist with many fandoms, and in fact many viewing (or, in Shaw's case, gaming) experiences are based on other, different appeals.[13] But Rory was overwhelmingly discussed as someone a lot of viewers saw as like themselves. When her *AYITL* iteration seemed stalled in terms of maturity, made bad decisions, and seemed significantly less confident in her abilities than before, this created a notable rupture that felt to some respondents like an attack on their generation, as if the writers were now casting aspersion on the notion that someone like themselves could (continue to) succeed.

In this case, then, asking after former fans' feelings of betrayal and dislike with *AYITL* allowed us to hear what was at stake, why *Gilmore Girls* truly mattered to many of them. If we recall from chapter 2, audiences regularly see all sorts of potential deal-breakers yet tolerate them. Thus, at the moments when fans instead ceased to become fans or felt the need to surgically remove and distance *AYITL* from their beloved object, we see what was truly special to them and hence what was lost. To many, that was Rory Gilmore as a particular image of capable, witty, affable, caring, involved woman "their" age.

What is more, the much-echoed concern with what Rory became as an adult suggests that *Gilmore Girls* and Rory in particular were perhaps especially endearing and important to audiences because Rory represented possibility and potential. The original show is embedded in something of an odd time warp, filmed on the Warner Brothers lot in ways that made its town of Stars Hollow feel familiar, since it was indeed the place in which numerous iconic American small towns were filmed too. Lorelai and Rory encounter problems of the real world but always have this space as a nostalgic, warm, encompassing home that's removed from the worst that the world has to offer. And so much of the show's directionality points to Rory's future—everyone in the town seems similarly invested in Rory making it and similarly confident that she will. This alone provides another layer of nostalgic warmth. But it's a layer that is therefore ripped away from those viewers when Rory's fated success never comes to be, when her worst decisions as a young person seem now to be the manifestations of deep character flaws, not just bad moments, when the town isn't enough to heal or restore her, when the promise and potential is at best on hold, at worst no more. This amounts to a marked tonal shift, and we should not be surprised that it left many viewers feeling violated—they went "home" and found no home there. Matt Hills has written of "sperosemic" readings of texts, those based in hopefulness and in an openness to the future,[14] yet Rory's characterization killed those hopes and threatened their earlier reading.

At the level of the text, we could of course find all sorts of elements that contributed to the show's original success. But whereas traditional adaptation studies have turned precisely to the text to parse differences between the original and the adaptation, here we see how helpful audience studies can be to direct us to appeals that mattered. Admittedly, these mattered to a specific audience. Our survey returned a lot of responses from people who were Rory's age, but we might expect that a survey of fans of Lorelai's age may have unearthed a different set of qualities that mattered. And this survey itself revealed a range of reactions to *AYITL*, not simply dislike. But for those who disliked and who centered an "attack" on Rory, the survey told us a great deal about what *Gilmore Girls* represented and meant to them at its core.

Unexpected Journeys from Frodo to Gollum: Disenchantment with *The Hobbit*

An audience-based approach to adaptation studies could and should go beyond just directly asking audiences to reflect on what is important to them. We can also take a more observational approach, seeing how fans discuss new iterations of a beloved text or franchise and how these discussions tell us about other sacred elements of the original text. Here I shift, then, from my interviews to reviews, blog posts, think-pieces, and fan-forum discussions about prominent franchises that have recently been revised, rebooted, or simply added to.

I start with published reviews of *The Hobbit: An Unexpected Journey*. I do so in part to offer a sequel of my own, following up on research I previously published about the paratextual framing of Peter Jackson's *Lord of the Rings* trilogy. There, I noted how the bonus materials included on the landmark DVDs for the trilogy frequently worked to elide the cast, crew, and characters, analogizing the story of a then relatively unknown Kiwi director who assembled an international cast and crew in New Zealand, somehow convinced New Line and Time Warner to extend them a massive budget, and went on to produce three of the most successful films in Hollywood history, the story of a small group of hobbits and an eclectic mix of a ranger, a dwarf, an elf, and a wizard who united to defeat the preeminent force of evil in their world. I noted that commentary tracks and making-of documentary shorts on the DVDs regularly talk of Jackson as if he were himself the simple, noble-hearted little hobbit Frodo, of Ian McKellen as the wise wizard Gandalf, of Dominic Monaghan and Billy Boyd as the playful Merry and Pippin, and so forth. New Zealand, meanwhile, is elided not simply with Middle Earth but with The Shire in particular as a bucolic, out-of-the-way, simple place minding its own business, and the unlikely success of its barefooted hobbit-like Peter Jackson in the looming industrial fortress of Hollywood has the air of a hobbit's mission to Mordor.[15] This determined effort to paratextually overdetermine the meaning of *The Lord of the Rings* struck me at the time as notable, which is why I was fascinated to see the reading that it proffered revived years later in disappointed reviews of Jackson's follow-up *Hobbit* trilogy. Reviewer after reviewer didn't see the first outing of *The Hobbit: An Unexpected Journey* as just "a bad film" but were clearly bothered by the transformation it represented of Jackson and his fellowship, suggesting that these meanings I had earlier found so clearly on offer in the *Lord of the Rings* DVDs had found their echo and resonance in some viewers' understandings of and relationships with those films. Here, then, I explore some of the published reviews to note exactly which elements and qualities of *Lord of the Rings* their reviewers thought, in Galadriel's terms, "should not have been forgotten [yet] were lost."

To find reviews of *The Hobbit*, I consulted the online review aggregator Metacritic.com and read all forty of the reviews linked to from the site. In exploring published reviews, I do not mean to suggest that reviewers are indicative or representative of "the audience" at large. Audiences are always varied, making the pursuit of representative responses a fool's errand at the best of times, but we should particularly not expect to find such representativeness in what a few elite reviewers note. Reviewers, too, are a particular class of disliker given that they are paid to pass judgment, and hence (as we'll see) their dislikes lean toward being more extravagant and performative than those of "average" viewers. For a more expansive consideration of *Hobbit* viewers, I highly recommend the reports from Martin Barker and Ernest Mathijs's World Hobbit Project.[16] However, on the one hand, I will note that the reviewers' criticisms were widely echoed in fan pages of the time, while on the other hand, I underline that my interests here lie not in locating the mystical one reading that unites them all but rather in noting one locus of power in a particular, shared meaning among many reviewers. Reviews are, in addition, interesting entities inasmuch as they not only document audience responses but, as paratexts, act to proffer and recommend particular responses to others. What, in this case, was that response on offer?

James Berardinelli opens his *Reel Reviews* commentary by situating the achievement of *Lord of the Rings*. "In 2001, only a few months after the fall of the World Trade Center," he writes, "Peter Jackson swept us away to Middle Earth with *The Fellowship of the Ring*." The film, then, is situated as a balm to the ills of modernity, a welcome escape from terrorism, violence, and despair. Or, strictly speaking, Berardinelli nominates Jackson as the active agent here, an auteur-healer. Only a sentence later, he notes, "It succeeded beyond anyone's wildest imagination," an extravagant comment given that the books had long topped Best Books lists but one that situates them as underdogs. Then Berardinelli argues that the trilogy "convinced Hollywood that there was unexplored ore in the fantasy mine," a clear act of suturing production to characters, given the importance of mining dwarves in each trilogy under discussion. However, Berardinelli thereafter notes that what was once "wondrous" is no more, since "the magic is gone" and though "Jackson is attempting to recapture something elusive," he is largely unsuccessful. Woven through Berardinelli's language, in short, are numerous instances of the original being magical, its production staff as unlikely heroes as the fellowship of humans, hobbits, dwarves, and elves, its provenance decisively "not of this world." By contrast, Berardinelli regularly criticizes

An Unexpected Journey in terms that make it more conspicuously industrial, Hollywood, produced: its stone-giant battle, for instance, feels to Berardinelli "more like an outtake from a Transformers film," and the film is criticized throughout the review for its "longwindedness" and its presumptuousness at taking up our time.[17] The Little Engine That Could has become a huge electric train.

Other reviews regularly criticize its length, too. To Andrew O'Hehir of *Salon*, for example, the film is "self-indulgent," and his title alludes to a more famed fall from cinematic grace, suggesting that "Middle-earth faces a phantom menace." It is an "overinflated blimp of a movie" that "gets off to a sour, soggy, bumbling start." Particular scorn is cast on its production process, and thus whereas the myth of *Lord of the Rings*' perfect production is upheld, it's quickly contrasted to a tale of fired directors and production woes. Even O'Hehir's seeming allowances for its being "a holiday film" and "definitely OK for most children down to about 10 or so" are both patronizing and designed to code the film as industrialized, formulaic, and inorganic. If the original was charming art, this is excessive capitalism at its worst: while writing with anger of a particular scene involving a character called The Necromancer, O'Hehir emotes, "Seriously? They spent the gross national product of Moldova on special effects and that's what we get for the freakin' Necromancer?" And the Rivendell set is likened to "the food court at a fancy architect-designed mall in Abu Dhabi." Jackson himself, meanwhile, is said to have "inflated both 'The Hobbit' and his own head to monstrous proportions," the comment proposing that the hobbit auteur has become the balrog producer who alongside his cowriters, O'Hehir reassures readers, "have to keep their paws off everything in 'The Silmarillion,' Tolkien's compendium of deeper Middle-earth history and legend, because they don't own the rights." Jackson, he writes, "hasn't just jumped the shark, but has dressed it up in dolly clothes and walked it around the block in a fancy English pram," an interesting critique that questions Jackson's masculinity at the same time, perhaps alluding tellingly to a deeper, less-noted critique of the film's being insufficiently "manly" for O'Hehir but also therefore emasculating the grand male auteur figure.[18]

Writing for *Slant*, Ed Gonzalez notes a similar arc from the wonder of Hollywood to shoddy industrial fare. In setting up *Lord of the Rings*, Gonzalez insists that "even disbelievers will attest to the movie franchise's breathless wonder," acknowledging the trilogy as "pinnacles" of filmmaking that used and advanced CGI in ways that "still feel state of the art, never employed by Jackson at the expense of his unmistakably classicist style." Compliments of Jackson as "classicist" and of his films as art thereafter go out the window, as instead we're left with a comparison of *An Unexpected Journey* to *The Adventures of the Gummi Bears*. The cinematic beauty of Middle Earth now, Gonzalez notes pejoratively, has "an unmistakably televisual quality," "undistinguishable from the land Tinky Winky calls home, or the bucolic set used for the part of the opening ceremony at this year's Olympic Games." To Gonzalez, then, this no longer even counts as film. His review settles down, and he admits to having enjoyed the ride; but in writing of its fall from grace and of Jackson as now working with a "toy camera," Gonzalez makes his disappointment palpable, a disappointment based on his sense that the film is no longer art, just a technical, industrial product playing on screens worldwide.[19]

Across multiple disappointed reviews, one encounters a veritable catalogue of metaphors that seek to reposition the film as no longer a film, no longer art, just plastic industrialized junk. To O'Hehir, it was a food court in Abu Dhabi, and to Gonzalez, it's a set at the Olympic Games, "televisual," and a world for Teletubbies. *Slate*'s Dana Stevens concurs on the latter note, saying it "looks like Teletubbies," while also offering criticism of how its forty-eight-frames-per-second presentation made everything look cheap, including Gandalf's staff, "an elegant Art Nouveau-esque creation that, in the earlier Lord of the Rings films, would have blended in as another part of the richly ambient whimsy" yet in *An Unexpected Journey* "looked like a cast-resin prop you might order online from a Wiccan supply house."[20] *Time Out*'s Keith Uhlich, for his part, dismissively calls it a "P.J. & Co. superproduction" that is a "mesmerizing study in excess."[21] And Ann Hornaday for *Washington Post* writes of the "Barnum-esque hype and rumors" that surrounded the production and complains of an "episodic series of walk-talk-fight sequences that often looks less like genuine cinema than a large-scale video game, its high-def aesthetic and mushy close-ups perfectly suited to its presumed end-use on a living room wall or iPhone."[22]

Most starkly rewriting Jackson as no longer the hobbit hero Frodo is *Time*'s Richard Corliss, who pivots from a discussion of Jackson wresting control of the film from Guillermo del Toro, the original director of *An Unexpected Journey*, to suggest a general transformation: "Jackson originally assigned Guillermo del Toro, the Mexican master of *Pan's Labyrinth* and the *Hellboy* films, to direct the *Hobbit* films (then planned as just two feature-length parts). Then Jackson took over; he wanted *The Hobbit* for himself, just as he had possessed the *Rings* movies. In this backstage story, there's a touch of the sad, covetous Gollum, who kept the Ring for ages and was corrupted by its possession before losing it to Bilbo and then Frodo."[23] Corliss backs away slightly from this uncharitable comparison, and from the suggestion that the movie should be called *The Hoard of the Rings*, to rather halfheartedly note that Jackson may still have an element of Gandalf to him, but this observed transformation, and accompanying concern, disappointment, and sense of betrayal, pervades many of the reviews of *An Unexpected Journey*. As Scott Foundas proposes in clear terms what many others allude to through metaphor, Peter Jackson "might have been stunted by his own mega-success."[24]

My point in assembling these critiques is neither to agree nor disagree with their critique of the film. Rather, it is their shared subtext that fascinates me, as they tell a story of a magical-mystical auteur-director who conquered Hollywood with his fellowship but tumbled headlong into darkness. Clearly part of the original films' charm and appeal to these viewers, in short, was precisely the "other" story it told, of its production. They loved not just the tale of Middle Earth but who was telling it and the myth of triumph in Hollywood that it enacted. In my earlier analysis of *The Lord of the Rings*' bonus materials' mythologization of both Jackson and the trilogy, I noted that it offered a drum roll to *Return of the King*'s success at the Oscars and the trilogy's general financial success, recoding that not as yet another big-budget Time Warner blockbuster success but as a tale of the little, barefooted, pudgy, Kiwi director who could. I noted the savvy in turning a massive industrial product into something that audiences were now allowed to like, as not American-centric, not paint-by-numbers franchise storytelling, not covered in Hollywood's smudgy fingerprints. And these reviews suggest the triumph of that tale (whether through the DVDs' telling of it or not), such that it set up an expectation for the sequel, one that perhaps would always be doomed to be violated. As the hobbits in Tolkien's *Re-

turn of the King discover at the tale's end, one can never truly go home again. Disappointment from many reviewers in *The Hobbit* suggests that a great part of the appeal of *Lord of the Rings* was that one could indeed go back again, to before Hollywood's industrialized takeover of art. But Jackson couldn't do this again—after having helmed such a series, he couldn't credibly be the Little Kiwi That Could any more (even sporting—perhaps disappointingly to some people—a new, more svelte figure), and his *Hobbit* trilogy couldn't deliver what may ultimately have been to some viewers its predecessor's most beloved offering.

Star Wars' First Order of White Masculinity

As with the preceding example of reviews, one need not go looking for disappointment in adaptations, sequels, and reboots, as it pervades popular culture. Sadly, a key site for this pervasion, especially in recent years, lies in the toxic white masculine policing of seemingly all franchises as belonging to white men and as supposedly existing first and foremost to sing the praises of white masculinity across the planet. Such instances therefore provide us yet more examples of how a refractive audience analysis of adaptations, sequels, and reboots can tell us a great deal about the values that matter to the audiences of their originals. And while, as noted in the introduction to this book, this is determinedly not a book "about" hate, since this chapter has endeavored to show transitions in audience reactions, focusing so far on shifts from like or love to dislike, these toxic posters' hate is illustrative both in showing how the tool of refractive audience analysis exploring disappointments can be used in some situations to reveal underpinnings to hate—not just engaged dislike—and in offering a case of like and love spiraling into dislike *and* hate. Functionally, too, they provide a sobering reminder that whereas I have generally focused on dislikers' more progressive demands, hopes, and disappointments, progressives hold no special control over engaged dislike, as it is felt and practiced across the political spectrum. My interviews offered very little of such hate, but as I worked on this book, the internet provided case after case of enraged "fanboys" decrying the diversified casting of their beloved objects. Thus, I supplement those interviews with a brief foray into that commentary here and into the realm of what Mel Stanfill dubs "reactionary fandom,"[25] both to acknowledge the "dark side" of dislike and also to suggest, even if my interviews didn't allow a deeper dive, how refractive audience analysis focused on disappointments can be applied to more toxic statements of dislike and of hatred.

A conspicuous example lies in the anger directed toward the 2015 and 2017 episodes of Star Wars, *Episode VII: The Force Awakens* and *Episode VIII: The Last Jedi*. Amid the many varied responses to each film were those that expressed anger at the supposed "tokenism" and "political correctness" in casting Daisy Ridley and John Boyega as lead characters in this new trilogy, then later with *The Last Jedi*'s addition of Kelly Marie Tran. I find this strain of criticism especially interesting, though, since it betrays the degree to which clearly many fans found it vitally important that Star Wars was and should remain a franchise for white boys or men. Admittedly, we should expect a franchise as large as Star Wars to attract many reasons for dislike from its former fans and longtime foes alike; indeed, in describing the concept of *neutrosemy*—whereby fans can render a text open to any and all meanings—Cornel Sandvoss gestures to fan research on Star Wars as a key example.[26] Thus, I do not mean to imply that all or even a majority of Star Wars fans share these feelings: as a Star Wars fan since I was a toddler, I certainly do not, and I hope that in this respect I'm not in the minority. But the fervid commentary and anger directed toward Ridley, Boyega, and Tran reveals a festering, rancid underbelly to the fandom that quite tellingly has the effect of insisting on the whiteness and masculinity of the franchise for those in the underbelly.

The Star Wars wiki Wookieepedia, for instance, was repeatedly edited to add racist attacks on Kelly Marie Tran and her character, Rose Tico. *Newsweek*'s Anna Menta reports of Tico's page being edited to change the character's name to Ching Chong Wing Tong and her home world to Ching Chong China.[27] The page was then edited further to describe the character as "a dumbass fucking character Disney made [who] is a stupid, autistic, and retarded love interest for Finn. She better die in a coma because she is a dumbass bitch."[28] Harassment of Tran persisted to the point that she left Instagram. In posting about her decision in a *New York Times* editorial, she noted of the trolls,

> Their words seemed to confirm what growing up as a woman and a person of color already taught me: that I belonged in margins and spaces, valid only as a minor character in their lives and stories.... Their words reinforced a narrative I had heard my whole life: that I was "other," that I didn't belong, that I wasn't good enough, simply because I wasn't like them.... Because the same society that taught some people they were heroes, saviors, inheritors of the Manifest Destiny ideal, taught me I existed only in the background of their stories, doing their nails, diagnosing their illnesses, supporting their love interests—and perhaps the most damaging—waiting for them to rescue me.[29]

This is quite clearly the message the trolls were trying to send Tran, and she astutely notes that the message became one about stories—whom they belong to, whom they should speak to, who and what doesn't belong in them. In being triggered to act by Tran's mere presence in *The Last Jedi*, the fan trolls showed how the story of Star Wars served for them as a monument to whiteness, one that required protection at all trolling costs.

Years prior, when John Boyega first appeared in a trailer for *The Force Awakens*, the Twitter hashtag #blackstormtrooper soon appeared, at first serving as a conductor and meeting spot for fans outraged at the casting. This twinned with a #BoycottStarWarsVII hashtag, with some people complaining that the film would be "ghetto garbage" or "obvious liberal pandering by casting the First Lady [Michelle Obama] as Han Solo's copilot." Others complained in clear terms about their supposed ownership of the text and story being challenged, arguing, "you can't market to 13% of the US population and ignore your primary demographic," dubbing the film "antiwhite propaganda" and worrying that "white children deserve wholesome movies, not more PC anti-white diversity crap." "Save your money white people," one concluded. "Everyone knows the best days of the franchise are behind them." Others using the hashtag complained, too, about director J. J. Abrams's involvement in anti-Semitic terms, griping that "Abrams ruins everything he touches, predictable jewish behavior."[30] Again, then, the defensiveness and anger of these fan trolls advanced an argument that Star Wars is and must remain a white (and/or non-Jewish) franchise for white children, its "wholesomeness" challenged by any incursion of people of color into the narrative.

Yet other (and at times overlapping) fan trolls were concentrating their anger on the increased centrality of women in *The Force Awakens* and *The Last Jedi*, liberally applying what Suzanne Scott calls "spreadable misogyny."[31] With the casting of Daisy Ridley as the new Jedi-in-training and primary hero, *The Force Awakens* inflamed many self-avowed "men's rights activists" who saw her addition and the specifics of her characterization as amounting to "feminist propaganda" and "man-hating" interventions.[32] Following the release of *The Last Jedi*, one fan even posted an edit of the film on Pirate Bay called *The Last Jedi: A De-Feminised Fanedit*. The edit removes Laura Dern's Admiral Holdo entirely, along with most scenes involving other actresses in the film. The alt-right group Down With Disney's Treatment of Franchises and its fanboys also boldly took responsibility for filling the online review site Rotten Tomatoes with critical reviews of the film via bots, leading in turn to numerous press pieces about the backlash against an "unpopular" film. A moderator for the group told Huffington Post that they couldn't stand the inclusion of so many women in the films.[33] And so again we see that failed expectations are key, where the expectations—here, that Star Wars be a franchise by, about, for, and upholding men—tell us the importance of the original story to the fans-become-dislikers in question.

These posters' dislike is wrapped up in hate, quite nakedly, but since at the very least it adopts the guise of dislike or perhaps more accurately mixes hate (for groups of people) with dislike (for certain texts featuring such groups), we can still ask the question of what led to the fans' transition to dislike and/or hate. Combined, they make a strong case that their Star Wars was in its best, most appropriate form when it was more clearly white and male. Indeed, they strongly counter the common disavowal of Star Wars as particularly white or male. Surely anyone reading this book who has taken or taught undergraduate classes on representation has watched as some students furrow their brows, roll their eyes, and otherwise reject outright the notion that white supremacy and patriarchy are buried deep, hegemonically, in many of the everyday media around them: some viewers will only admit they're in the presence of white-male-supremacist media when watching *Birth of a Nation* or *Triumph of the Will* but otherwise rankle at the suggestion that anything that is "just entertainment" might have a strong vein of white-male supremacy at work too. Star Wars, they might insist, is just a story "for everyone" set in a universalist universe. And yet here we have numerous white men loudly, angrily proclaiming the opposite, that to them Star Wars is precisely a white-male journey, that its white masculinity is absolutely vital to its value to them, and that deviation from that white masculinity is tantamount to a Death Star–like destruction of the story and its value altogether.[34] These racists claimed and were given significant power to proffer a particular vision of what the far-far-away galaxy's value was and should be to the contemporary viewing subject.

I have focused on Star Wars, but the lines of attack on *The Force Awakens* and *The Last Jedi* repeat themselves in many other instances when any text with white and/or male characters is remade with people of color and/or women. *Ghostbusters* antifandom is especially notorious here, focusing its rage tellingly not just on the three white women Ghostbusters in the 2016 reboot but in particular on its lone Black Ghostbuster, played by Leslie Jones.[35] Comic-book fans' anger whenever Spider-Man, Captain America, or other iconic heroes are rendered as Black similarly announces the degree to which those heroes exist in the minds of some fans as quintessentially white and male. News that the live-action remake of *The Little Mermaid* would star Halle Bailey, an African American, not a white redhead as in the animated film, led to especially bizarre arguments from white supremacists insisting that mermaids could only be white, with some even offering contorted, pseudoscientific explanations based on what a life in the depths of the ocean would in theory do to skin color. And Derek Johnson observes "neomasculine" mobilization around the franchise reboots of Star Wars, *Ghostbusters*, and *Mad Max*, noting both the potential for such reboots to recalibrate the franchises to allow more space for women characters and audiences and the "men's rights" activists' awareness and fear of precisely this. He writes, "By reproducing the media and market appeals of the past, the industrial practice of franchising bears the potential to retransmit preferred masculine identities and privileges, making them inheritable down the line. Yet because franchises reproduce in dynamic, iterative ways that carry cultural change, the equally built-in industrial possibility of reorientation also threatens this inheritance and legacy."[36] Suzanne Scott and Rukmini Pande have shown, between them, how very sexist and racist some fandoms can be.[37] In these and many other examples presented in recent years, though, one also sees not just angry fans but posters who seem to have no relationship whatsoever with the original version and who are posting to troll, in the process revealing that the text operates for them solely—at this moment in time—as an icon of whiteness and/or masculinity, important only inasmuch as it can be added to a list of popular and prominent texts about white men.

Emma Jane registers an objection to studying such bigots too closely and to risking a sugarcoating of their bigotry by considering them as "antifans," not bigots first and foremost. She notes, "If we observe hateful speech and we select anti-fandom as our lens, then we are situating this speech within a paradigm that has historically positioned such discourse as a response associated with audiences. These audiences, in turn, have historically been understood as having an agency that is subtle, idiosyncratic, and possibly even an admirable form of 'punching up' to hegemons."[38] On the one hand, though, here I study them (albeit in passing) not to hide or sanitize their bigotry but to reveal how it was being fed by prior texts, whether interpreted "correctly" or not. On the other hand, and in spite of my choice in this book to focus largely on dislikes that do tend to "punch up," Jane offers a clear reminder that dislike is never necessarily progressive or necessarily free from becoming interwoven with hate. The expressions of dislike based on thoughtful commentary on Rory Gilmore's wavering feminism that I have examined earlier in this chapter thus find their regressive counterparts in Star Wars fans editing female characters out of the film, just as the feminist deal-breakers that led some fans to stop watching *Game of Thrones* due to its sexual violence find their regressive counterparts in, for instance, as described by Holly Willson Holladay and Melissa Click, angry white men whose intense dislike of the character of Skyler White in *Breaking Bad* serves as an obstacle to their enjoyment of the text while also clearly communicating to audience researchers the seething misogyny that led to their hateful dislike and that undergirds all their media interactions.[39]

Conclusion

I have suggested that these various refractive audience analyses tell us about (some of) the elements and perceived contents of the originals that truly mattered to their audiences. Some readers, though, may be a little more suspicious that the "light" we see refracted through response to the adaptations may in fact emanate from audience members' responses to intervening time and from perceived trends in popular culture. Thus, while I have read responses to *Gilmore Girls: A Year in the Life*, *The Hobbit*, and the recent Star Wars films as saying a great deal about their audiences' sense of the value and values of *Gilmore Girls*, *Lord of the Rings*, and older Star Wars films, respectively, one might also or instead read them for responses to broader cultural concerns about how time and culture have changed since those originals, that opportunistically engage the sequels or prequels in question, but that have little "true" relation to the original stories.

In the responses to *AYITL*, for instance, one hears considerable anxiety about the place and treatment of women more generally. Rory, many responders worried, was never allowed to live up to her potential, but this might pain these respondents particularly if they saw society around them as similarly quashing young women's potential. Here, intertextual cues from Alexis Bledel's career in the intervening years may amplify that message: Bledel's career atrophied somewhat following *Gilmore Girls*' run, until she then appeared five years later in *Mad Men*, playing an unhappy character who is undergoing electroshock therapy. Then, a year after *AYITL* (and yet the same year as our survey), Bledel featured more prominently in *The Handmaid's Tale* as a woman who is brutally abused and victimized by the series's misogynist fascist government. Our survey also ran in the year of the large-scale Women's Protests around the world. The fate of Rory Gilmore, as such, could easily be seen as reflecting not just on what the writers did to the character but on what was happening to women—and to Bledel's characters in other shows—in general. Meanwhile, *Hobbit* reviewers may be responding out of concern as much or more with blockbuster culture in general as with any perceived damage done to *Lord of the Rings* or Tolkien; and Star Wars' racist, sexist detractors could be reacting to a perception of "too much" diversity or gender parity in society writ large, and Star Wars may be somewhat immaterial. As Jane notes of antifans such as the Star Wars bigots, their discourse can at times read as "a sort of metaphorical fig leaf for preexisting prejudice and bigotry."[40]

Christopher Bollas's notion of the disillusionment of "generational consciousness" might also be mobilized here. Bollas suggests that "a new generation (in a person's twenties) is allowed an illusion that it will single-handedly form and define contemporary culture," only to realize later in life that they no longer form culture.⁴¹ As Matt Hills glosses, "we thus move from being 'simple' selves who feel perfectly immersed in the events and media of our era, to becoming 'complex' selves who understand 'the self inside historical time' as we are culturally destabilised by rival generations."⁴² Bollas and Hills offer ways to consider generation as key to some of the foregoing discussions, albeit intersecting with race and gender, as the disillusionment of being pushed from the cultural center—of watching another generation and other sensibilities, values, and priorities matter more—could understandably lead to dislike. Hills poses that a "generational-transitional object, or a *life-transitional object*," might develop that comes to represent and embody this transition and disillusionment,⁴³ so perhaps Rory Gilmore, *The Hobbit*, new episodes of Star Wars, and other adaptations serve this role par excellence.

I have insufficient data to back up such readings, but I nonetheless mention them as possibilities. Even if they are in play, though, it would still be highly relevant if audiences' generalized concerns about contemporary society and culture were routinely being projected onto adaptations, reboots, and sequels and, thus, if adaptations, reboots, and sequels proved to be key sites for the communication of such values. As was explored in chapter 2, we would still be seeing audiences using scripts and statements about dislike to enunciate broader needs, expectations, and hopes for society. Dislike is once again deeply relational. And thus, whether or not audiences' reactions are "authentically" to the adapted original is beside the point if practically the adaptation, reboot, or sequel becomes a valuable cultural resource for enunciating concerns about the screened and real worlds around them, especially when that adaptation, reboot, or sequel marks a transition from love or like to dislike and/or hate for an audience member, as we have seen in this chapter.

To open the door to the possibility of "inauthentic" responses, though, and to the maelstrom of what is or isn't truly felt is to require a discussion of dislike's performative elements and of the ways in which identity is performed and announced through dislike, which leads us to chapter 4. I end this chapter on the note that adaptation studies, long "owned" by English or film studies, could be a rich realm in which audience studies could continue to explore not just dislike but changing tides of response and the textual and audience catalysts that lead to changing allegiances.

4

Performing Identity through Dislike

Throughout the early days of this project, I regularly asked people whom I'd just met what television shows they adamantly disliked. Many were uncomfortable with the question: we had just met, after all, and in asking them to share an engaged dislike, I was assuming more familiarity and intimacy. Another sizable contingent dodged the seeming familiarity of the question by offering a nebulous bad object—"I don't like reality television," they'd say, for instance, "since it's not real, is it?" And a third contingent would embrace the challenge, as though we were several rounds into a game of truth or dare, telling me first what they disliked and then their specific reason for doing so. In all instances, they were proving the degree to which dislikes perform identity: the latter group took the chance to offer personalized, deliberative performances; the middle group performed conformity; while the former group refused the exercise precisely because they did not wish to perform. The experiment also gave me a quick sense of how forceful a person was, with many from the latter group boldly asserting the supreme stupidity of such-and-such program, some from the former groups quite clearly not wanting to step on toes, both realizing how dislikes wag a finger not just at the disliked objects but at the "type of person" who watches such a show. Dislikes, in short, are regularly performative, laying claim to communities of belonging and distancing us from communities of approbation. This chapter focuses on such performances.

As discussed in the introduction, no single scholar looms over the study of media dislike as much as does Pierre Bourdieu. This book argues that we must escape from that shadow and explore the broader terrain of media dislike that is not guarded by it. So far, I've done so largely by placing Bourdieu to the side, but to consider dislike as a performance of identity, I must now turn back to him. I do so first to note how helpful and how generative his theory of distinction is. To Bourdieu, dislike is a performance of cultural capital and a classed act of claiming superiority.[1] However, over time, many liberties have also been taken with Bourdieu's theory of distinction, as some commenters play down the central place of class in the theory, instead seeing it as a theory of performative superiority in general and hence one that can explain distinctions based on gender, race, nationality, or other markers of identity. This chapter draws from my data to support this broader thesis. But in doing so, I want to acknowledge that as soon as we find other markers of identity being performed instead of or alongside class, we have moved beyond *Distinction*. Media and cultural studies, in other words, has been uncomfortable with the totalizing force of Bourdieu's macro theory of dislike and distinction all along, even if we haven't realized it yet. Accepting that Bourdieu's theory has strictly limited explanatory capacity if we wish to understand what dislike truly is and how it works, I wish both to explore the wealth and breadth of other identities that are performed through dislike and ultimately therefore to position Bourdieu not so much as "wrong" but rather as opening interesting doors that we should feel free to move through and well beyond.

Bourdieu's *Distinction*

As noted in the introduction, few academic works have been as important to media and cultural studies as Pierre Bourdieu's *Distinction: A Social Critique of the Judgment of Taste*, published in French as *La distinction* in 1979 and translated into English in 1984. Bourdieu set out to explain tasted preferences and drew on empirical work conducted in France in the 1960s to offer his thesis that they are performances of classed superiority. In his introduction, he writes, "The denial of lower, coarse, vulgar, venal, servile—in a word, natural—enjoyment, which constitutes the sacred sphere of culture, implies an affirmation of the superiority of those who can be satisfied with the sublimated, refined, disinterested, gratuitous, distinguished pleasures forever closed to the profane. That is why art and cultural consumption are predisposed, consciously and deliberately or not, to fulfil a social function of legitimating social differences."[2] This is a sweeping thesis, for it offers a master lens for understanding how class is perpetuated and rationalized, how social structure is reproduced through expressions of taste. Bourdieu explains that class—while premised on actual, monetary capital—begets social, linguistic, and cultural capital, too (respectively, whom you know, how you speak, what you like and dislike). These latter forms of capital are taught early, through immersion, such that one's cultural preferences feel "as natural as the air one breathes."[3] Then their insidious power is born, for they can do the work of classed distinction: one need not state anything about one's personal or family finances to justify one's higher position in society, as one can resort instead to a rhetoric of "cultural pedigree," thereby producing an "entitlement effect."[4] Cultural superiority, as such, can be performed and claimed through the displaced realm of what kind of music one listens to, which authors one reads, what art moves one's soul.

In particular, Bourdieu notes how cultural capital and the distinction between supposedly "pure" or "legitimate" taste and "barbarous" or popular taste follow a logic of class. Bourdieu quite carefully points out numerous ways in which bourgeois culture became bourgeois, arguing, for instance, that it is often characterized by a "distance from necessity" and is expected to be consumed with a cold, distanced "aesthetic disposition,"[5] whereas the working and lower classes will seek more direct and immediate relevance that might require less work to decode and enjoy and that may have a more participatory element (encouraging raucous cheering in the case of live performance, for instance, rather than a subdued, repressed clapping). Some of these points risk being patronizing in their suggestion that working-class culture is simpler and bourgeois culture more complex, but the specifics of the distinction clearly matter less to Bourdieu than does his general theory that this is a rigged game: the bourgeois could change what counts as "true art" or "culture" at any point.[6] Bourdieu also suggests that the devious brilliance of the system is that working and lower classes will regularly reify the system and its distinctions by claiming that "their" culture (or that which has been assigned to them) is the true, real culture. "At stake," he writes, "in every struggle over art there is also the imposition of an art of living, that is, the transmutation of an arbitrary way of living into arbitrariness,"[7] but over time, the working, middle, and upper classes all come to reify those arbitrary distinctions by accepting them as meaningful distinctions within the realm of taste.

Distinction hit media and cultural studies at an opportune time, for as the likes of Raymond Williams, Richard Hoggart, and E. P. Thompson were making the case for the importance of studying popular, mainstream, and often working-class culture, not just the cultural products of the bourgeois,[8] Bourdieu's *Distinction* provided a rich arsenal for attacking the elitism that aimed to rebuff their attempts. Williams even needed to argue that working-class culture *was* culture and that culture could not be a synonym for the products of the bourgeois, for "culture is ordinary." But Bourdieu offered a way to argue not simply that scholars should also study working-class and mass cultures, regardless of their disapproval of them, but that their disapproval, and their sense that high culture was in any way "better," was itself a deeply problematic formulation premised on an unquestioned elitism and privilege. In short, Bourdieu provided covering fire for anyone to engage with the cultural studies project of taking mass culture seriously, and his influence is palpable in early canonical work in media and cultural studies, including Paul Willis's *Common Culture*, Stuart Hall's "encoding/decoding model" and its "testing out" in David Morley and Charlotte Brunsdon's *Nationwide* studies, Brunsdon's work on taste and quality, and John Fiske's *Reading the Popular* and *Understanding Popular Culture*.[9] It also required continual engagement, for as Henry Jenkins notes, "taste is always in crisis; taste can never remain stable, because it is challenged by the existence of other tastes that often seem just as 'natural' to their proponents,"[10] thereby requiring both constant policing and continuing study.

Bourdieu in Action

Distinction has a lot of intuitive purchase, and one need not struggle to apply Bourdieu's analysis of 1960s France to parts of other contemporary societies. Within the realm of television, soap operas, reality TV, and quiz shows pale in the comparison of countless critics to HBO or FX dramas, while all of television can still be castigated as the dung heap of media by some ardent cinephiles or literature fans who see in film or the novel a far nobler form. The language used in such denunciations regularly reeks of snobbery, often tellingly losing focus from the media or texts in question to spew outward at the supposed unthinking, unwashed masses whose distinctive capacities are imagined to be so utterly broken if they choose to spend time with *The Price Is Right* over

Terrence Malick. Or, to move from hypotheticals to actuals, Diane Alters has research showing how parents, and mothers in particular, can often police what their children watch or don't watch in part on the basis of a strongly felt need to perform their class to others. Alters found several instances of lower-middle-class mothers banning *The Simpsons* since they thought it was "lower" than their class rank and they were keen for their children to perform that they were "above" that.[11]

Anne Gilbert's study of *Girls* and *Smash* hatewatchers also develops a Bourdieuian critique. Many of the hatewatchers' comments perform clear superiority, often in explicitly classed terms, as when one notes that "*Smash* was only made bearable with glasses of white wine."[12] Through such comments shared with others, Gilbert writes, the hatewatchers embrace a "mode of viewing behavior in which the personal use-value of the television text itself is of secondary importance to the exchange-value of performing a stance—critical and derisive—toward that text for others."[13] The performance is constitutive and constructive, though, for the hatewatchers "are effectively organizing themselves, other viewers, and fans into a hierarchical construct of the viewing audience."[14] Here, Gilbert echoes an earlier defense of fandom by Joli Jensen, who saw in the dismissals of fans an elitist performance of superiority, of being above the media fray, wherein the performance exists to announce that "we" cultured few are not like "them," the addicted masses.[15] Similarly, Roberta Pearson documents the complaints of longtime BBC Radio 3 listeners who "resent the fact that Radio 3's quest for new listeners [to the channel that specializes in classical music] entails catering to the less knowledgeable listeners' mainstream tastes rather than to their own supracultural tastes."[16] Radio 3, in short, aimed to collapse distinctions based on cultural capital, yet the keepers of that capital immediately found such a move threatening and felt the need to pen letters to magazines and newspapers to perform and announce their continued superiority.

Michael Newman and Elana Levine's *Legitimating Television: Media Convergence and Cultural Status* takes a discursive-based, not audience-based, approach but similarly offers a strong updating and application of Bourdieu. Newman and Levine criticize recent popular, industrial, and academic attempts to legitimate television directed predominantly at upper-middle-class white men that simultaneously deride legitimated television's Other. Each chapter attends to a different site of the "emergent set of discourses propos[ing] that television has achieved the status of great art, or at least of respectable culture, disturbing long-standing hierarchies that placed the medium far below literature, theater, and cinema in social, cultural, and technological worth."[17] In doing so, they argue that this legitimation "is premised upon a rejection of a denigration of 'television' as it has long existed" and hence upon discourses that "do not dismantle prevailing structures of status" but perpetuate them,[18] by allowing the likes of *The Sopranos* and *Mad Men* into the pantheon of high culture, while tossing "regular" television into the cultural trash can.

Our transcripts, too, are peppered with criticisms of the usual suspects of a lower-classed television. Reality TV, in particular, featured heavily when respondents were asked what they disliked. Candice, for instance, was a wealthy white woman who began the interview suggesting that she watched little more than documentaries and educational programming on television and only opened up about other viewing much later in her interview. Reality TV received particular scorn from her, as when she labeled the *Real Housewives* series "brainless" and "superficial," openly reflecting that she did so from on her "high horse." Linh, too, avoided reality TV because, in her words, "it kills brain cells." Thuy spoke ill of the entire medium: "I read an article a long time ago. It says when you watch TV, your brain becomes super passive and totally doesn't work—even more passive than when you sleeping. And people actually get dumber—dumber when you watch TV." Blake's disdain for reality TV viewers had even played a key factor in his deciding to break up with women when he'd found out they watched the genre.

Erin contrasted her disdain for reality TV with her own superiority as reader:

> I consider myself to be very nerdy and booky, and I read too much. I'm a bit of a book snob, and by a little bit, I mean by a lot. And I look down on people who don't read also. And I really do believe that . . . if you can read and if you're not reading all the time, that you're not doing anything for yourself. I love reading so much, I turn on the subtitles on TV just so I can read. Like, I read *everything*. I read every book recommendation that's ever given to me. So I'm very much a book snob. So I look down on people all the time.

Penny, too, proudly explained of reality TV shows, "I can't even tell you the names of them. I don't waste any time watching them. I can't even, like—I don't care about their lives. It means nothing to me. I feel like a lot of times the people they get on those shows are fairly trashy, in my opinion. They aren't living the lifestyle that I would live." She also referred to the genre as "worthless, a waste of time," and later repeated, now with specificity, "I can't even name a Kardashian," and then guessed, "To me it's probably just a bunch of trashy people living their lives out or putting on some kind of, I don't know—it just seems stupid." This response is interesting inasmuch as it's premised not on watching but instead on knowing from a friend community what she shouldn't watch, what is "below" her. Alongside Penny, numerous others clearly valued and appreciated the ability to claim an entire friend group that didn't watch "crap," as with Katherine, who said, "I can very proudly say that I don't know anyone who watched the Kardashians."

Other respondents didn't mention friends who agreed with them but discussed with candor how they loved being the elite who "got" how bad something was when those around them didn't. Ellen admitted, "I kind of like it when people don't love the things that I love because then it starts to seem like it's more unique to me, like it's more, like, a part of, 'Well, I like this, and if you don't, that just means we're different.' It's like I'm not just going with the crowd. I have my own interests." She claimed not to judge others too harshly for their tastes and yet also later noted, "I think that if someone were to say to me that they like *The Bachelor* and they meant it nonironically, I'd think that we probably wouldn't be great friends."

Snobbery, as such, was definitely present in these interviews. Perhaps, of course, some respondents felt a need to perform snobbery and disdain to us as a professor and graduate students, but either way, we have a confirmation of Bourdieu's basic thesis, as they either look down their noses at reality TV (or TV in general) and announce their distinction to us or felt that these would be the answers they should share with academic researchers. We also heard pushback against upper-middle-class media and characters by more working- or lower-middle-class respondents, performing a classed identity by, for instance, noting dislike for "any show that's framed around white-collar problems," as Vincent said. Or Simone couldn't stomach *Girls* because its characters represented the class barriers and its guardians, who had held her back throughout life. "I know all those girls, and I don't like them in my real life," she explained. "And the amount of privilege in just all those broads" was nauseating to her. Liz hated *The Bachelor* because all the characters are "just so rich and white and unaware of it." Jenna struggled to engage with any show in which characters enjoyed easy lives, given how much of a struggle she felt her own life to be. Jim, meanwhile, attributed his hatred of sports to its "classism," elaborating, "Like, I was very poor. Couldn't play sports, often because the equipment cost too much money. . . . It favored people who had money and favored people who were—and so I always say, whenever people are like, 'Why don't you like sports?' I'm like, 'Because I didn't like the jocks who I had to fight with in high school.'" Annie even balked at some shows' explicit performances of distinction, noting, "I think *Sherlock* is the best example of that, because it's, like, you're supposed to feel so good because 'Sherlock is so smart.' But he's mean. 'But he's smart, so it makes it okay. And it's, like, such a sophisticated show. It's not like that trash you can watch on *any* network. It's a BBC show! And isn't it so delightful that *Sherlock* is doing all these things?!' And it's like, no!"

One hears echoes, in Annie's sarcastic attack on *Sherlock* reverence, of John Fiske's discussion of wrestling fans gleefully rejecting bourgeois values and virtues or of Kevin Glynn's defense of alien-abduction videos, supposedly tawdry daytime talk-show debates about who slept with whose spouse, and so forth.[19] Their combined work serves as a strong reminder that Bourdieu's theories of class performance were never just about bourgeois tastes and performances but also intended to explain how much pleasure existed in working-class performances of class that rejected elite criteria for value.

Applying and Critiquing Bourdieu

Within media and cultural studies, though, Bourdieu has been repurposed, so that class is neither the only frame for analysis nor the only identity marker being performed. Fiske, for instance, coined the concept of "popular cultural capital" in an essay about fans jockeying for relative status within a fan community, while Sarah Thornton proposed "subcultural capital," "a subspecies of capital operating within other less privileged domains," using the concept to analyze hipness in club cultures.[20] Both concepts have been applied many times since, without necessarily invoking classed distinctions, simply to note how cultural hierarchies of relatively good or bad media are employed to characterize their consumers (or nonconsumers) as relatively more or less entitled to cultural status within fan or other subcultural communities. Almost two decades later, therefore, we see Sarah Harman and Bethan Jones write of *Fifty Shades of Grey* haters as positioning themselves as "gatekeepers," variously to the BDSM community or to general fan communities, "thus reinforcing their subcultural capital which in turn enforces specific taste cultures."[21]

Many who have used Bourdieu have shifted focus from *classed* status expressed via the classification of texts and readers to *gendered* or *raced* status expressed via the classification of texts and readers. Following Andreas Huyssen's and others' discussion of the degree to which popular culture is feminized, many argued convincingly that "women's genres" are inherently derided and seen as lesser.[22] Soap operas most notoriously occupy a low rung on cultural hierarchies, for instance, in large part because they are seen as belonging to women. African and African American art forms and practice across media have often similarly been derided and coded as lower and lesser,[23] evident in Theodor Adorno's notoriously racist critique of jazz or anything with a beat but also in everyday derision of hip-hop sampling culture as "unoriginal" and, as Olufunmilayo Arewa notes, in the institutionalization of that derision in copyright law that diminishes the artistry of African styles of music.[24] We could apply Bourdieu to any identity marker, to see dislike as snobbery, whether at the level of nationality (e.g., disparaging remarks by Brits of American football or by Americans of what the rest of the world calls football),[25] region (e.g., mutual mockery of the Northeast and the South by each other), generation (e.g., ridicule of anything a Boomer or a Millennial has touched), sexuality and gendered identity (e.g., the vociferousness of attacks on divas with significant gay fandoms), and so forth. Easy proof of dislike frequently being a form of snobbery can be found, moreover, in the plethora of synonyms for "bad" in English that reference an Othered identity, as when something is called "gay" or "chick"-something.

In this regard, it's worth noting what Bourdieu helped media and cultural studies do, say, and argue and hence how this theory shaped the field in its early days while also pointing it away from asking deeper questions of dislike. Media and cultural studies took *Distinction* as part of its premise and backdrop, implying various classed, raced, gendered, nationalized, and other prior acts of snobbery and elitism that forced its questions off the academic table and hence promising a response to them. Much early work in media and cultural studies, for instance, explicitly opposed sexist and gendered dismissals of women's media, instead defending the pleasures and depths of, variously, soap operas, romance fiction, Madonna, and fan fiction.[26] Such work made the case for why media and cultural studies was necessary, namely, to back up and ask deeper questions about all the media and culture that previously had been written off as lower, female, Black or Brown, foreign, or unworthy in other ways.

However, when not about class, this work had already ceased to be truly Bourdieuian and was already—even if never explicitly—finding *Distinction* to be highly problematic at worst, radically incomplete at best. In contrast to the generalized theory of various performed superiorities worldwide that the field developed in Bourdieu's wake, Bourdieu himself did not discuss gendered, nationalized, raced, sexualized, or other performances of superiority in *Distinction*. Generation factors into *Distinction* tangentially, given Bourdieu's concern with how successive generations learn class and are taught cultural capital, and Bourdieu certainly analyzes generation and gender more closely elsewhere in his collected work;[27] but *Distinction* announces class to be the solitary heart pumping life into taste judgments. To pose, though, that gender, nationality, race, generation, or sexuality identity don't (or didn't) matter in France would be outrageous, so their absence in Bourdieu's data for *Distinction* invites us to ask whether they were unreported, whether he didn't see them, or whether he underplayed their role. This criticism may implicate Bourdieu as being clumsy in his analysis and in neglecting to realize how intersectional dislikes can be. Or perhaps it points to an ebb and flow of identity factors that matter—perhaps at the exact point in time when Bourdieu conducted his study (the mid-1960s), class mattered most to the French (or at least his respondents claimed it mattered most and performed it the most), but perhaps with time, other currents would matter more, class less? Either way, missing from Bourdieu is an acknowledgment of the multiplicity of identity: his *Distinction* subjects are only classed subjects, not raced, gendered, or otherwise marked. But what if we were to revisit them and ask explicitly about other aspects of their identity?

Another key limitation and hence simplification of Bourdieu's *Distinction* is that while it helps us to understand taste *between* class ranks, it doesn't always help *within* class ranks. This failing exists in part because it is intended to be a macro theory about cultural patterns, not necessarily a tool for explaining taste at a more personal or communal level. Thus, Bourdieu helps us to explain why HBO dramas as a whole might be culturally adored and celebrated more than reality shows as a whole but may not help us to understand why, for instance, one person loves HBO's *Game of Thrones* more than HBO's *Westworld* or why another loves *Real Housewives of New Jersey* more than *Real Housewives of Beverly Hills*. In the former instance, both are big-budget "quality drama" shows, both draw from genres that are sometimes derided (the fantasy and the western, respectively), and both have complex, interlaced narratives. A classed analysis, in short, might help paint a broad picture but does little to help with nuances and detail.

As the media industries have produced exponentially more content, these flaws in Bourdieu's argument have become more corrosive to its overall utility, for while we might invoke Bourdieu to question the moniker of "quality drama," when the American television industry alone produces well over a hundred "quality dramas" yearly, the explanatory power of Bourdieu may do little to parse differences between them. Indeed, if the multiplication of content since Bourdieu's *Distinction* offers it less explanatory traction, this is because the last five decades have seen the ascendance of a commercialized media system that produces a large amount of content for the same class group, more or less. A great deal of media in the United States, at least, is aimed at the middle classes, and at the upper middle class specifically, due to their greater disposable income and hence desirability to advertisers and merchandisers. And thus, if much US media has been produced for the same class group, Bourdieu's theory would seem to be less operable in explaining differences in taste expressed between them. Why does one upper-middle-class person love *this* "quality drama" yet dislike *that* one?

Within this current media environment, adherence to Bourdieu has at times led to some scholars drawing odd and arbitrary distinctions within the upper middle classes. Thus, for instance, scholars' and critics' plaudits for HBO or FX dramas are seen by some as clear attempts to "legitimate" "our" media over that of the supposed working classes who watch CBS procedurals like *NCIS*, even when the available data offer no support to the implication that CBS procedurals are watched by viewers who are below academics and television critics on the class ladder.

Let me offer an example here, not to call out its writers in particular but rather to indicate a general if problematic use of Bourdieu. As noted, Michael Newman and Elana Levine's *Legitimating Television* helpfully questions logics of "quality TV," updates Bourdieu, and at times clearly shows how gendered these logics of distinction can often be. But the Bourdieuian frame through which Newman and Levine work proves constricting, inasmuch as it requires them to regard all preferences for "quality TV" as elitist, all defenses of more culturally derided television as of-the-people. "The work of analyzing patterns of taste judgment and classification," they write, "is thus to unmask misrecognitions of authentic and autonomous value, bringing to light their political and social functions. Such is the project of this book,"[28] and thus they announce their Bourdieuian unwillingness to regard any taste judgment and classification as something other than a "misrecognition" and denigration of "authentic and autonomous value." At one point, for instance, they quote a criticism of *Two and a Half Men* from the *Party Down* cast member Lizzy Caplan, who after complimenting her own show for having fans who were "exactly the type of people" the show was "hoping to impress: smart and vocal and funny and almost snobby about their comedy preferences," attacks *Two and a Half Men* by stating, "I think if a girl who liked *Party Down* found out that her boyfriend liked *Two and a Half Men*, she would break up with him." Newman and Levine regard this as an "emblem" of how *Two and a Half Men* has come to be "despised by elites, whose distaste for it—however authentically felt—effectively marks their social and cultural positionings."[29]

First, though, I question Newman and Levine's choice to read the comment through the lens of class alone and to see little more than an elitist looking snidely down her bourgeois nose at media intended for the working classes. Caplan's tale, after all, is preeminently one about gendered taste—about a "*girl*" and "*her boy*friend." Where Newman and Levine see Caplan and her hypothetical woman as elitists, we could also see both women expressing dismay, anger, and annoyance at the frequently misogynist *Two and a Half Men* and, by extension, at ("dumpworthy") men who find its humor unproblematic. The story could instead be more about gender than about class, in other words. Or we need not see these two interpretations of Caplan's comments as mutually exclusive, since likes and dislikes will often be multilayered, as I will consider more in chapter 5. Caplan and her hypothetical character may be snobs. But why attack *Two and a Half Men* in particular? US television provides no shortage of options for a snob to deride. If a snob chooses to mock *Two and a Half Men* rather than something else, therefore, this choice is relevant, as is the choice to elaborate on this dislike by offering a tale of a woman dumping her boyfriend because he watches it.

Newman and Levine generalize outward from Caplan, though, to "elites" in general, but here we could again ask why this show in particular drew the ire of critics, more so than *Big Bang Theory* or *Modern Family*, equally successful prime-time sitcoms. We should also question the assumption—born out of no data—that *Two and a Half Men* is watched by (or even intended for) the working classes and not by an audience equal to or above the bourgeois academic in class standing. And I note the rather loaded choice of dislikers here: Lizzy Caplan can stand in comfortably for "the elite," given her success as a Hollywood actress, as perhaps can the alluded-to professorial elite pontificating in our ivory towers. But what of working-class women who are disgusted by seeing Charlie Sheen's character grooming his nephew to become a misogynist, in his multimillion-dollar Malibu beach house no less? Or what of queer viewers who are alienated and excluded by its regular homophobic and transphobic humor? Or, for that matter, what of feminist social-justice-minded bourgeois professors who look down their snobbish noses at working-class culture at times but whose dislike of this show is deeper and more involved? A quick look online for expressions of dislike for *Two and a Half Men*, not just from Lizzy Caplan's imaginary friends, yields snobbery, yes, but also the comedian Gil Ozeri's report on a weekend spent watching the show, during which he counted thirty-five homophobic jokes,[30] while Joanna Schroeder targets its rampant sexism, observing, "Every single man on that show is an asshole! We have the womanizing, alcoholic Charlie Harper who exists in a morality-free zone where women are objects and everyone lives to serve him. He's a jerk to almost everyone he meets . . .

[and yet] is rewarded with a giant waterfront Malibu home and a plethora of young, beautiful women just begging to felate him."[31] In adhering too closely to Bourdieu, Newman and Levine present a fine theory of legitimation at a broad level, and often offer strong analysis at a fine-grained level, but offer little explanatory texture to understanding why individuals such as those just quoted or why entire communities might dislike *Two and a Half Men* or any other show.

In short, Bourdieu only gets us so far. In previous chapters, we have already seen many other reasons to dislike. Mike Savage and colleagues have also noted that Bourdieu's class rankings themselves may need updating for contemporary contexts and realities, as they use survey data to rethink Britain's class ranks.[32] But Bourdieu's basic suggestion that dislike performs identity and distinction between identity categories, creating an I and a we versus you, they, and the Other, is a proverbial baby I do not wish to throw out with the bath water of necessary class specificity. As Carl Wilson summates following his own skeptical treatment of Bourdieu, "even if Bourdieu was only fifty percent right—if taste is only *half* a subconscious mechanism by which we fight for power and status, mainly by condemning people we see as 'beneath' us—that would be twice as complicit as most of us would like to think our aesthetics are."[33] I will now turn to my data to analyze a range of other fights for power and status and other performances, articulations, and constructions of identity that used dislike as resource.

Malawi and the Nation

I turn first to my research conducted in Malawi to consider performances of national and cultural identity.[34] Whereas most of the data offered in this book come either from interviews designed to elicit discussion of dislike or from sections of interviews with that design, when I went to Malawi, it wasn't to ask about dislike at all. Instead, clear pronouncements of dislike kept erupting through my discussions about engagement with foreign media. I was asking about national and cultural identity and regularly found that respondents were clearest and most passionate in claiming and performing national and cultural identities precisely in the act of discussing media from elsewhere that they worried about, resented, or otherwise disliked.

In shifting focus from the predominantly American respondents discussed throughout the rest of this book to Malawi, I am of course shifting cultural contexts. Malawi is regularly listed as one of the poorest countries in the world. As should be expected, therefore, the country is responsible for little television or film production. Malawi has only one terrestrial broadcaster based in Malawi, the national public broadcasting station TV Malawi (TVM). When I was there in 2008 and 2010, there was no film production, at least none that anyone had heard of or seen. Satellite television was prohibitively expensive for most Malawians, but many neighborhoods had well-established communal watching practices, whereby those who could afford satellite would allow others to come over and watch, sometimes charging a nominal fee. Most towns also boasted one or more "video shows," in which patrons could pay the equivalent of three or four US cents to sit down on planks of wood placed over plastic cartons for however long they wanted to watch a parade of movies on DVD. DVD players were relatively common among the general population, moreover, contributing to a thriving economy of pirated DVDs that ensured every village or trading outpost had at least one stall or store selling DVDs, while towns and cities boasted many.

It was this media ecosystem that fascinated me and that led me to Malawi following reports from my wife, who conducted research there. Global media studies has spilled no shortage of ink in discussing "cultural imperialism" and US media's competition with local media around the world.[35] However, such examinations have more usually focused on cultural contexts in which competition is more legitimately possible, when a local production industry must deal with the shadow cast over it by imports. Malawi presented a different situation, one in which next to no local production was occurring, such that *all* film and the vast majority of television were imported. How, I wondered, would the tale of cultural imperialism and its active audiences play out in this cultural context? In 2008 and 2010, I spent my summers in Malawi trying to find out both how Malawians interacted with and thought about media and, quite practically, how media moved around the country. I split my time largely between Liwonde in the South and Rumphi in the North.[36] English is ubiquitous in Malawi, a former British colony in which English is taught in its universal education system, thereby allowing me to conduct many interviews myself: I regularly encountered people who wanted to "practice" their (usually very good) English and who would therefore happily let me walk with them for an hour asking questions. In Rumphi, though, I also hired a research assistant, Stanslous Ngwire, so that he could conduct interviews in outlying villages with some older Malawians who didn't speak much English and simply so that not all of the interviews were colored by the dynamic of being conducted by me.[37] Placing these interviews alongside those conducted mostly in the United States may seem at first blush rather odd, but these are still people talking about media and dislike. Malawians are also people who watch films and like them or don't and whose cultural lives have as much depth and as much banality in them as those of their counterparts in the United States.[38]

Film and television in Malawi were dominated by US, Nigerian, and Chinese options. Most video shows I saw played a steady, unbroken stream of action movies, predominantly from the United States but some from Hong Kong or China, except in a few instances in which Nollywood dominated. The DVD stalls and stores, meanwhile, were regularly stocked with 50 percent to 80 percent US films and television, with Chinese martial-arts films and Nigerian film and television splitting much of the remainder and occasional Indian, Korean, or British content available too. In larger towns or shopping districts, some stalls or stores would specialize solely in Nigerian and other African film and television. Satellite television took the form of the South African–owned DStv, a service with many channels, most of which were predominantly US or British.

I was soon struck by the division I heard between preference for US film and television or Nigerian film and television, such that enjoying one—whether passionately or mildly—quite often entailed strong dislike of the other. This cultural duel never included China, but the ascription of value changed radically, nearly always centering on opinions about what Malawi was and what were Malawian values. To some, US media brought worrying values. The United States was universally spoken of as a rich land of opportunity and access to wealth, yet many respondents also saw it as an extremely violent country led by corruption and characterized by little sense of togetherness. Americans were seen by many as foul-mouthed, as prone to sexual recklessness, and as not caring about family. "I feel like a lot of people are very careless with their lives in America," Zubeda told me. Such concerns were often generational, voiced by the older Malawians to whom I talked, and the voicing of these concerns inevitably led to fears of cultural imperialism taking hold of younger Malawians, who, it was said, no longer cared for their parents and extended families, would sleep around, would kill each other or become hooked on drugs because they followed in US media's footsteps, and who did not understand traditional Malawian ways of dealing with problems. Chimwemwe told me that "American films teach people to be violent, teach people how to steal, how to kill, and apart from that, they also teach a lot about drug abusing. A lot of youngsters these days are taking after the celebrities which are found in America, with ill morals."

To these viewers, Nigerian film and television represented a refreshing alternative. Nigerian media has plenty of sexual infidelity and violence, but most respondents felt that sex and violence were dealt with in ways that they regarded as more authentically "African" and that honored family. Nigerian film also *showed* less, said Masida, who complained about US films allowing "people to show their private parts in the air." Several of these viewers also valued the Nigerian media's interest in magic, spirits, and curses, as I was frequently told by such viewers that this is "how life is." Some viewers in this group did not actively object to US media as much as they saw its characters and plots existing in a different world devoid of ghosts, magic, and witchcraft and thereby as less useful or representative of everyday life. For instance, the video-show owner Mabvuto noted that he rarely played US movies because his customers saw them as too fanciful, whereas "the Nigerian film is real life. Most of the people from this area have experienced witchcraft problems in their villages. So when they are watching such movies, they just feel like real things happening."

Most women we talked to favored Nigerian drama, too, not necessarily or not just because of the witchcraft but because many Nigerian dramas tell tales of love, marriage, deceit, and friendship, whereas the bulk of US films in Malawi are male-centered action films. The comparative verisimilitude of Nigerian drama to these women resulted from stories that focused on women's everyday issues: "Most Nigerian dramas," Sinya said, "really base their stories on real-life experiences and on what people really go through, such as love affairs, families, marriages, communities, schools, etc." She explained that she used to enjoy US films but then had an affair with a married man that ended in her being badly beaten by his wife; soon after, Sinya saw a Nigerian drama with a similar story line, which gave her courage to continue. She explained what that meant to her: "It's not only me who has ever faced such kind of hardship in life. American films never showed me people like me. Their culture is different. So I stopped watching them, and now I enjoy very much Nigerian drama." Dofasi saw US life as so completely foreign but Nigerian drama as dealing with monetary struggles, love, and what she called "village life" in a way that made it more recognizable and of more utility to her. Wonanji wryly told us, "Nigerian films tell how to end problems that we have. American films are about war, drug abuse, and being rich: I do not have these problems."

To these viewers who favored Nigerian over US media, an interesting slippage regularly occurred, whereby Nigerian media soon became, in discussion, "African" media, "our" media, and "village life" and was talked of in other ways as local and familiar. The video-show owner Lusungu, for instance, noted, "A lot of older people say that Nigerian films are the best films which are supposed to be watched by Malawians, because they teach about how an African should be behaving as per demands of his culture. They also try to educate the people from Africa about their own dressing styles and culture, telling them to be happy and proud of their tribe. But they also try to safeguard our own traditions, such as eating the food using hands, kneeling down when greeting the old people, and many other traditions." Ntchindi explained, "I like watching Nigerian films because I see African culture and identity and dignity." As in these passages, "African," "Nigerian," and "Malawian" often blended into one when respondents justified their preference for Nigerian media. At times, moreover, respondents would outright declare, as did Goli, that "all Africans are one, and they are well-known as Bantu people, so they have one thing in common and most of their culture." And Vayireti said, "people feel at home when they are watching their fellow Africans." And thus, while US media was seen as an invading force that could harm Malawian culture, Nigerian media was regarded as the local (pan-African) antidote.

Opposed to this group, though, was an admittedly smaller group of respondents, who objected instead to Nigerian media and clung to US media as better. To these viewers, Nigerian media was silly and/or insulting in its use of witchcraft, and they often elaborated at length on how damaging these "backward" beliefs were to Malawi. For instance, one day Ngwire encountered three men who had come to a video show but who refused to pay to see the Nigerian drama on offer. Stoniard explained, "American films are better than Nigerian dramas. It's better to go and sleep than to watch stupid drama. What do people enjoy when they are watching Nigerian films?" Chiguliro responded, "Those films talk about witchcraft. What does that mean? That they want to believe in witchcraft? They promote the witchcraft business. They are stupid." Zakhi, similarly invoking third-person effects, worried that "these kinds of films are making a lot of people in Malawi believe in witchcraft and that these situations actually happen. Malawians are visiting witch doctors to get rich because these films tell them it will happen." Stoniard then interjected that this is why Nigerian films weren't successful in the United States or Europe, because "Americans and Europeans are modern," and he speculated that Nigerian films were popular largely because they were cheaper than US films, because they were easier to copy. All three bemoaned the impediment to modernization that they saw in what one called the "flood" of Nigerian drama.

To these viewers, US media was valued more because of what it wasn't, modeling how they wished Malawian life would be conducted, without any belief in curses, spirits, or charms. Abdallah told me, "African films are only just developing and still use too much witchcraft. Some Nigerian films have moved past this, but most have not," thereby positing a line of development, wherein an industry's modernization could be read off its adherence to witchcraft. Interestingly, these viewers, as with their counterparts who preferred Nigerian media, still often referred to it as "African" and as local, but they saw it as a weight tied to the country's (and continent's) foot, disabling Malawi from developing and modernizing. Hamza insisted that "the world is becoming a global village where cultures are mixing, and so whoever thinks American films are hurting Malawian culture has got problems, because our culture is changing, and it should change." Given that Hamza had just criticized Nigerian film for being "backward," again there is a telling elision between Malawian and Nigerian culture when he notes that "it" should change.

Clear throughout was the battle over cultural identity into which many respondents enlisted US and Nigerian film and television. US media was regarded by both groups as containing the capacity to change Malawian culture, and regardless of whether respondents worried about or welcomed such change, statements of dislike became powerful testaments of distinction. Some of this distinction rings of classed differences, for sure, as "modernization" and "backward" become heavily loaded terms, but the distinction is also quintessentially about national and cultural identity. We can see parallels of this debate in Marie Gillespie's study of Punjabi Brits in Southhall coming to terms with who they are, with teens distancing themselves from traditional Indian devotional texts and gravitating toward British soaps and ads to embrace a more decisively British subjectivity and identity, and their parents urging or outright ordering them to eschew soaps and watch more texts from the "home" that their parents nominate as such (the Punjab).[39] In that study, too, what one dislikes proves as important to a declaration and performance of national identity—if not more so—as what one likes.

When I originally published the foregoing material, I was especially intrigued by how respondents moved back and forth between characterizing film or television from Nigeria—approximately five thousand kilometers away from Malawi—as "ours," in opposition to US or Chinese film. The article aimed to nuance discussions of cultural imperialism that are too often based on simplistic models that envision one imperialist and one essentialized locality. But for my purposes here, I want to underline that this work also challenges us to move beyond global media studies' more binaristic view of global media as variously ubiquitous, welcomed, and hence culturally destructive or gloriously and deviously resisted by active audiences. Both ends of this binary have presumed and focused on fandom and/or positive engagement, without paying much attention to instances of imported media that are vehemently disliked. As I've aimed to show here, disliked media can be a powerful cultural resource and tool with which people can reflect on processes of cultural imperialism and power imbalances and hence with which people can create, articulate, and perform a sense of cultural identity. And precisely because imported media often arrive from more than one would-be imperialist, in ways that can naturally lead to the construction of various "rivalries," not just of the local to the foreign but of one type or kind of foreignness to another, this invites forms of competitive, mutually sustaining fandoms and dislikes to develop. For many of my respondents, though, one would be misunderstanding and mishearing them if one were to focus only on the fannish part of these sustaining duos: yes, some respondents preferred Nigerian film to US film, some vice versa, but their reasons for disliking one of the two were often as or more central to their enjoyment of the other.

Often, in short, fandoms appeared more accurately to be outgrowths of a dislike, and the reasons and utility for disliking and for sharing and articulating that dislike were considerably higher than for engaging closely with the supposed "fannish" element of the partnership. Thus, although, as noted in this book's introduction, "dislike" carries with it the lexical appearance of something that is constructed entirely as a negative—the lack or absence of like—some "fandoms" and likes may more accurately exist as the lack or absence of dislike. When film aficionados scoffed at the witchcraft of Nollywood or the debased morality of Hollywood, their accompanying statements of approval of their opposite were regularly offered with more relief than passion. We may not be able to escape the lexical challenges of "dislike" sounding forever as if it's the shadow of "like," but as Bourdieu noted of classed distinctions, here we see how much more discursive utility disliked objects had, with their liked "opposites" or alternatives posited definitively in their shadows. Reading this back against earlier work on cultural imperialism and its active audience rebels therefore makes me wonder how often the embrace of an imported object (whether unproblematized or playfully complex) by many other scholars' consulted audiences may have been hinged to a stronger dislike. If millions globally watched and loved *Dallas*, *Baywatch*, or *Friends*, what *weren't* they in the eyes of their viewers? What was being said or worked out about cultural identity by watching them instead of something else or by watching that something else, *whatever it was*, instead of watching *Dallas*, *Baywatch*, and *Friends*, given all that they represented worryingly, odiously to viewers?

Gendered Performances

If Bourdieu tells us that class performances occur through dislike, and if the preceding case study shows that performances and constructions of national identity occur through dislike,[40] now I turn to other performances, articulations, and enunciations from my data. First, and most prominently, audiences regularly situated themselves as gendered subjects, and made clear what that subjectivity meant to them, by talking through dislikes. Several such instances are evident in already-quoted material. Deanna's hatred of *Basketball Wives*, for instance (cited in chapters 1 and 2), tells us about her as a classed, raced, and gendered subject. Sophie objects so vehemently to *Two and a Half Men* with a "deep and intense hatred" (discussed more in chapters 1 and 2) because of its construction of women as things to be stared at and used and because its women are allowed no personality, only hotness or the lack thereof. Simone (discussed in chapter 2) disliked *The Newsroom* because it has "the worst female characters" that are as anathema to her own image of what being a woman should mean as are *Mad Men*'s Betty Draper and *The Way We Were*'s Katie Morosky to Laura (also discussed in chapter 2). Samantha (in chapter 2) said that Taylor Swift "represents weakness" to her, leading to her strong dislike for the singer, and parents Andrew and Rose (quoted in chapter 1) and Rachel (quoted in chapter 2) wanted to steer their kids clear of, respectively, Disney princesses and Barbie and Bratz dolls, given their sense of what kind of femininity was represented by those figures. All of the deal-breaker discussions and many of the *Gilmore Girls: A Year in the Life* dislikers from chapter 3 performed versions of what a woman should (according to those quoted) be. And of course many of the toxic fanboys discussed at the end of chapter 3 are performing a virulent masculinity through their professed dislike of any woman in any franchise they love.

As with the respondents from Malawi, in each of these cases in which dislike is declared, one hears both an explanation for the dislike and a further performance of identity. As earlier, I use performance in the sense not of deception or of acting as something that one is not but of reiterating one's role to an audience. Performances are to the self, on the one hand, as the act of "saying it out loud" can play an important role in insisting on, checking back in with, and renewing membership in a particular type of identity. On the other hand, performances are to others, sometimes testing our constructions out, sometimes presenting them proudly. And those presentations can in turn be reiterative, welcoming, defiant, or intentionally alienating, in ways that aim to pay homage to an already-existing group identity, to propose a new or changed group identity, or to draw distinctions between the group "we" and an Other. Joke Hermes writes that "popular culture is a domain in which we may practice the reinvention of who we are,"[41] a phrasing that makes clear this multipartite focus of performance, of creating for the self, for groups of "we" (whether that we exists already or is brought into being by our performance), and for groups of others. In Henry Jenkins's championing of the term "participatory culture" is a similar reflection that it is not just with individual items or texts of culture that audiences wish to participate: we wish to participate in the construction of culture writ large.[42] And audience research has shown how we can participate (albeit to different levels and degrees) through the performative acts of being an audience, whether they be fan productivity as Jenkins defines it,[43] semiotic participation as defined by Fiske,[44] or "TV talk."[45] To Nicholas Abercrombie and Brian Longhurst, "in an aestheticized and commodified society, consuming is like being a member of a diffused audience because both involve *performance*."[46] And picking up on the constructions and creations involved by such performances, Cornel Sandvoss insists of fandom (though we may apply his comments to dislike too) that it "is constitutive of the self . . . [and] reflects *and* constructs the self," while also creating scripts of home, Heimat, and belonging.[47]

I am indebted here to Judith Butler's writings on performativity, for she writes of identity not as something that simply or ever just "is" but as something that is created in acts of performance that presume exterior pressure and scripts. She writes of gender performance, for instance, as a form of self-fulfilling prophecy, operating "as an interior essence that might be disclosed, an expectation that ends up producing the very phenomenon that it anticipates," such that "the anticipation of a gendered essence produces that which it posits as outside itself."[48] The interplay that Butler posits here among interiority, essence, and external forces is key, for it both allows the feeling of having an inner, "true" being and acknowledges how that being can still be fashioned from outside. Butler refuses to see "the internal world of the psyche" as entirely a myth, and allows room for agency and individuality, but nevertheless regards identity as always at least in part scripted. She also posits acts of performance as key, wherein the internal and external truly impact each other. Performativity, she writes, "is not a singular act, but a repetition and a ritual, which achieves its effects through its naturalization in the context of a body understood, in part, as a culturally sustained temporal duration"; "what we take to be an internal essence of gender is manufactured through a sustained set of acts, posited through the gendered stylization of the body."[49] Butler writes of theoretical possibilities, but her work has motivated considerable work in media and cultural studies that examines media consumption and discussions of media consumption as key sites of gender performance, as is especially evident in Robyn Warhol's work, for example, on "having a good cry."[50] Admittedly, my own use of this concept operates at a simpler level, for I do not pretend to illustrate how external scripts and internal senses of being ignite each other here. Instead, I am motivated by an interest in how identity is spoken, articulated, enunciated, and hence *performed* through acts of disavowal and expressions of dislike, situating these acts and expressions not just as descriptions of who one is but as acts and expressions that invoke and solidify identity through their utterance.

Matt Hills, himself working with a Butlerian notion of performativity, writes that "pleasure-as-performative is always a cultural act, an articulation of identity."[51] Hills observes the benefits of working with such a notion:

> Performativity becomes useful as a way of thinking about the pleasures of popular culture ... precisely because it allows us to treat accounts of pleasure not only as descriptions, and because it also allows us to challenge, from the outset, any notion that consumers of pop culture are simply voluntaristic agents going about their interiorized, individualized business of leisure. As a methodological and heuristic device, it opens the door to addressing "the question of agency not as a ... definite property that fans [and nonfans] do or do not 'possess' ... but rather as a claim that can be made at certain points in time but not at others."[52]

And while Hills talks of pleasure as performative given his own titular goal to explain "the pleasures of horror," in the book's conclusion, he notes that the same lens could profitably be used to make sense of the *displeasures* of horror, for such performances will be as articulative and constitutive of identity as performances of pleasure are. While here not focusing on horror, I similarly find it helpful to consider statements about dislike as "claims" to identity that simultaneously instantiate, conjure, and articulate both individual and communal identity when "performed."

Practically, meanwhile, in an immediate sense, these performances were to my research assistants and me. As much as we all tried to keep good "poker faces" at other times, I'm sure our own feminist leanings played out and were performed through body language, choice of wording, and so forth, to the point that our respondents may have felt some need to perform especially feminist versions of themselves to us. Sometimes, these performances came out through declarations of fandom and elaborations on favored texts and characters, but on the whole (and even when, I remind the reader, none of the interviews were framed as "about dislike," and all contained sections inviting respondents to discuss fandoms too) collectively we witnessed far more performances of gendered identity through the nomination of, and elaboration on, dislikes.

Elsewhere in our interview with Rachel, for instance, she noted that she loved it when her kids "sing 'Let It Go' and they're so dramatic and powerful." But she quickly pivoted to offering *Frozen* and Elsa's counterparts in other Disney tales, asking, "Can I swear in this interview? It's not like fucking Snow White, who's, like, out singing to birds in the woods, or [*Sleeping Beauty*'s] Aurora, who is, like, learning how to bake cookies in a cottage in the woods." Rachel is trying to talk herself around to not disliking *Frozen* so much because of its merchandising and hence notes that at least Elsa offers an image of femininity for her children that is far superior to that of other Disney films, where *Snow White and the Seven Dwarfs* and *Sleeping Beauty* serve as handy resources to enunciate the docile, domesticated image of being a girl or woman that she's keen for her children to avoid.

Joining Deanna, Sophie, Simone, Laura, Samantha, Andrew and Rose, those with deals broken, *Gilmore Girls: A Year in the Life* dislikers, toxic fanboys, and Rachel were many other respondents to whom a key utility of discussing dislikes was to make clear the versions of being a woman they sought to avoid. To Angela, it was Hallmark movies, which her mother loved but she "can't stand" because she saw the women as too passive and domesticated. To Melanie, it was endless movies "like *American Pie*": "if the most important part of those films, like to convey plot or make people laugh, is to see some girls naked, that's so stupid to me." Olivia shared Laura's concern with *Mad Men*, explaining, "I never really saw the women, like, stand up and be something I would want to be," but she also really disliked *Gilmore Girls* and Lorelai Gilmore in particular, stating,

> I just think she's annoying. She doesn't come off as that smart. Comparing her to, like, Kerri Washington [in *Scandal*] or Viola Davis [in *How to Get Away with Murder*], it's just, like, she doesn't come off as that, like—I mean, she's a single mom, so partly she is strong, but, like, I don't think she comes off as a strong, intelligent woman. And I think I don't like that. Just annoying. And I think that's something a lot of guys—I feel like that's a word that's used to describe women a lot—as just "annoying" or "talking a lot" or something like that. And I felt like she really embodied that. And I just didn't like it. I felt like it was kind of perpetuating the stereotype of just being, like, annoying and kind of an airhead—not someone with a lot of drive or direction. She just bothered me.

Elle reached back to *The Mary Tyler Moore Show*, saying that Mary Richards (Mary Tyler Moore) "was supposed to be setting this feminist thing, you know, working and being a single woman in the seventies when nobody did that, or very few people did that, and blah, blah, blah, blah, blah. But, I mean, she completely lacked self-confidence, she cried all the time about dumb stuff, and she was completely beholden to Lou Grant; I mean, what kind of feminist . . . ?"

Or, as noted in chapter 2, several of our respondents needed their feminist shows to be intersectional, too, leading to critiques of the lack of intersectionality elsewhere, as when Ellen criticized *Girls* for being "problematic": "It happens in New York City, and that's a very diverse place; but it's just not true to that. Like, it's a liberal white perspective. It's, like—I consider myself to be a very feminist kind of person, but there was a type of feminism that I started falling into that I've had to sort of pull away from, which is very much the feminism of the rich white girl that is not—well, it kind of ignores the intersectionality of other cultures and other people that might be going through other things." Here, Ellen is quite reflective about a conscious process to avoid *Girls* because it spoke to a part of her she was trying to overcome and improve on. One hears her talking through the gears of performativity.

Several men similarly talked us through the obstacles that they found themselves lurching away from in constructing notions of what they should be as men. Wes explained why he strongly disliked action movies: "because a lot of them aspire to, like, toxic masculinity and, like, patriarchal norms of, like, the hero gets the girl at the end and blah, blah, blah, and I'm, like—none of this matters to me." Kyle stated a general preference for media directed at women but struggled to articulate what was especially excellent about such media, instead framing his preference as based on a dislike of media directed at men, which he characterized as "a dick-measuring contest," "invested in hitting you over the head with things that are supposed to impress you": "I just don't like feeling like producers and writers are tricking me into thinking something is so clever and great when it may not be." He saw much Emmy fare and "quality television" as pretentious and appreciated how media directed at women seemed less interested in announcing its brilliance and thereby offered a clear critique of masculine auteurism and need to declare itself, preferring a subtler, more understated mode.

While (as cited earlier in this chapter) Jim framed his hatred of sports primarily in class terms, as he talked further about it, its toxic masculinity was clearly operative in his dislike too. He detested what and who was valued by sport culture, noting particular disdain for the NFL player Michael Vick, infamous for training dogs to fight, "and other characters in our society that have really had these things that have been played out": "And I'm like, whoa, are we fricking dogfighting? Like, what the fuck is that about? Or, like, you punched your girlfriend in the face and knocked her the fuck out in an elevator, and somehow, like, you didn't get jail time for that? You're not ejected from the league?" Likewise, Green Bay Packer fandom and even just games bugged him, because "you get revved up by a bunch of extremely, like, hypermasculine men who are warring, essentially," and he extended his critique of violent, "warring" masculinity to the Olympics: "[It] is another catastrophic—I can't even—it doesn't work for me. I don't understand how, why we have the Olympics. We have wars. We don't need to have the Olympics. It's almost like the Olympics are supposed to replace war, and yet somehow, they, like, just embed it more." Jim regularly felt alienated by the objects of his dislike, acutely aware that they placed him outside the norms of men around him. But he also alluded to how performances of dislike could lead to community and to a gathering of like-minded others, as he told us with great pride and excitement of how a bar at which he worked had instituted, on his suggestion, a weekly "Fuck Sports Day." And just as Andrew and Rose and Rachel aimed to steer their kids away from texts with problematic women, Andrea spoke of how she tried to pass on her intense dislike of *Family Guy*—which she saw as reinforcing "a lot of toxic masculinity" and peddling "a combination of fart jokes and really low-grade dick jokes, then combined with really sexist things"—to the thirteen-year-old boy whom she regularly babysat, trying to use her dislike of the show as a resource not just for her own performance of gender but ideally for his too.

Mark, meanwhile, showed how a performance of gender may stand in direct opposition to prevalent scripts of dislike. "I love romantic dramas, romantic comedies," he told us. "I love a good romcom. You can't watch a romcom and not love it. Get your toxic masculinity shit out of here. That stuff is great. *50 First Dates* is a great movie. It's cute, it's funny, it's wonderful. A lot of guys are, like, 'I don't like romcoms.' I'm, like, 'Get the fuck out of here with that. You take your toxic masculinity elsewhere. I'm going to enjoy it.'" Here, he's offering a fandom, not a dislike, but his enjoyment of and identification with the genre is articulated in relation to an assumed dislike by "a lot of guys." These guys become the presumed audience for his performance of fandom (even when his interviewer is a woman): "*You* take *your* toxic masculinity elsewhere," he notes. He employed a direct address that we heard in numerous interviews when subjects engaged the performances that they liked or despised. Tess, for instance, similarly found herself "performing" to her (absent) granddaughters when explaining why she disliked Kiefer Sutherland and *24* and shows of that ilk:

> Like, what the hell can be the message in a program like *24*? . . . "I can do whatever the hell I want to you, because I'm the big guy and I'm carrying a gun?" Maybe it's that their message is so demoralizing and it glorifies violence. Almost all of them have a white male character as their hero. You know, whoever he is comes in and saves the day. It's like, I have four and, now with this new marriage, five granddaughters. That is not the message they need to get. No boy needs to rescue you from anything. Sorry. Don't give him that kind of power. You have your own power. Use it.

Overall, we should not be surprised to find feminists opting for the language of dislike, given how relatively little avowedly feminist media exists. It is depressingly rare for even strong female characters to explicitly claim to be feminists. Fan studies have shown the capacities for fandom to offer prospects for forcibly taking promising characters from their writers' and actors' hands and delivering them into a realm of purer feminism through fan fiction, vids, and other fan productivity. But feminist and other marginalized positions will by nature be ones that appear less often and less flatteringly, thereby inspiring—as our data show—many feminists and other marginalized positions to find many media texts and figures more useful as opposites and obstacles.

Nevertheless, as Mark's comment about widespread hate for romantic comedies suggests, identity performance through dislike is by no means limited to those who have more progressive identities. On the contrary, our data also offered numerous instances of men and women voicing and performing more conservative and hegemonic gender roles through announcing other dislikes. Courtney, for instance, voiced strong approbation of MTV's *Teen Mom*, nominating it as one of her greatest dislikes and explaining, "I just think you need time to get your own priorities in time and make sure you have a career that you can provide for yourself, so if you're bringing a child into this world, you're totally altering your abilities to be able to do that. Not saying it's impossible, and people do it. But just saying it's not something that is easy to do, and I don't think that you need to be promoting people doing that and thinking that's okay." Fiona, meanwhile, replied to a question about what she doesn't like in the media by noting, "I personally do not care to watch shows that are sexually explicit, so many along that line." She then continued to voice displeasure with shows with "unusual family situations," which she later explained to mean LGBTQ or unmarried families. "I do not care to watch those," she said, explaining, "I'm just not into that lifestyle or what's happening with them." Candice's intense dislike of the Kardashians was pegged in large part to their "getting a little too caught up" in "obsessing over glamour," intoning, "I certainly don't like that we idolize, that that female, that that role is something we hold dear and that we put on magazine covers and we aspire to. I think that is worrisome."

Kenneth, for his part, offered a lengthy attack on *Madden*, EA Sports' popular series of football video games, that broadened into an attack on any video game based on a sport. Why? "I refuse to go out and spend $60 every year for the same game," he argued, "when I can go outside and play myself. I won't play any game I can do myself. I won't even play UFC games. I can go to my gym and do that. I'm not gonna pay money for it. Why bother if I can actually do it in reality? To me, that's just sad." By contrast, he noted, "I can't go shoot down a helicopter, so I'll go do it in a game. But on the same hand, I refuse to play a football game, when I could be outside playing football. To me, at that point it just gets kinda sad. Just don't do it. Like, if the game is there, go do something you can't do. Go play football outside. Go play basketball. There are basketball courts everywhere. Don't do something you can do in real life. It's just weak." This disdain for something being "weak" was clearly a gendered attack, and he contrasted his own willingness to go to the gym to the "loser" men (as he later called them) who are incapable of doing so. Even the hypothetical game he will deign to play oozes a performance of rugged masculinity—shooting down helicopters—and his dislike is articulated in a clear manner to advertise his own perceived superior masculinity.

Comments such as the preceding ones find echoes in work by others. Leila Green, for instance, heard broadside attacks on soap operas from Australian men performing their masculinity by calling them "sickening" and "bullshit."[53] Catherine Strong frames much dislike of *Twilight* as enacting "a form of symbolic violence, in that the underlying point of the discussion is not about *Twilight* at all, but about constructing teenage girls as a group not worth taking seriously."[54] And Holly Willson Holladay and Melissa Click document haters' palpably sexist commentary on Anna Gunn's Skyler White from *Breaking Bad*. White is called a "shrieking harpy" and a "fuckin' histrionic bitch," while other criticisms regularly focus on her looks, such that "fan criticism is deeply influenced by gendered expectations of female characters and of women more broadly,"[55] while performing a rugged, aggressive masculinity, even through continual threats of physical and sexual violence against Gunn. Our respondents were not being encouraged to share their hates, and my interviewers' feminist convictions probably asserted themselves in enough ways to warn away the more sexist respondents from spouting too much misogyny; but these other scholars' work makes the existence of regressive performances clear.

However, lest we construct an easy binary between wholly progressive performances on the one hand and wholly regressive ones on the other hand, I also note the high prevalence with which our respondents nominated bad women as objects of dislike. This was to be expected in the feminist deal-breaker interviews, given a general frame of performances of gender, but holds firm throughout many more interviews. A notable pattern announced itself, whereby a clear majority of the bad objects, characters, and celebrities that respondents nominated to us were women, real or fictional. Think back to Mark's comments quoted in chapter 2, for example, in which Ariana Grande stood out as the absolute worst celebrity to him. Or see Rachel's previously quoted comments about "fucking Snow White, who's, like, out singing to birds in the woods," or the many other echoes in previously quoted material from earlier chapters. Even when the disliked, unhappy objects were being used to perform more progressive versions of gender, race, national identity, parenthood, or more, the hegemonic power of judging excessive, egregious women all too often exerted itself.[56] In true Butlerian form, therefore, even when respondents aimed to perform progressive feminism, the specters of a hegemonic patriarchal culture regularly haunted those performances, reminding us that perhaps no performance is ever truly agential and individual, instead always performing other scripts at the same time.

Performing Race

Another key type of performance we heard was of race and racial identity. Some of these have already been discussed. Most prominently, the toxic white fanboy screeds against people of color appearing in "their" texts, examined in chapter 3, are especially loud performances of whiteness. Deanna was quoted as performing and proffering a version of Blackness through sharing her dislike of another version on show in *Basketball Wives*. And Alfred Martin's previously cited study of Tyler Perry antifans similarly shows his subjects discussing competing images of Blackness and of Black cultural identity through their dislike. For example, Martin writes of one of the women that she "describes the images Tyler Perry writes for his films as 'coonery,' suggesting that the images are closely associated with the coon stereotype, in which black characters are presented as objects of amusement and as black buffoons."[57] Or another sees Perry as constructing "positive" imagery "in a monolithic way: educated black people, who enter into intraracial, heterosexual marriage and produce children. To be granted membership within this group of 'positive' black media images, then, one has to, without deviance, subscribe to such fashioning,"[58] which the antifan in question does not, and thus her dislike of Perry aims to perform a different version of what Blackness is.

Ralina Joseph also writes of a screening group that she and some students created for watching and talking about *America's Next Top Model*, and her account of this group details the women offering strong articulations of their own identities as women of color, not as fans but instead in opposition to host Tyra Banks and her preferred contestants. Prior to describing this group's responses, Joseph offers careful readings of Michelle Obama's, Oprah Winfrey's, and Shonda Rhimes's performance and use of "strategic ambiguity," wherein "a privileged minoritized person . . . gauges microaggressions in a room and uses the failure to *name* racism—one of the primary tools of postrace—in order to . . . claim a seat at the table," a technique that she sees as "a necessarily subtle form of resistance and risk that balances on an escape hatch of deniability," one that admittedly "the powerful can use to shore up hegemony but also that the powerless can use to chip away at that hegemony."[59] As Joseph notes, though, such a performance is steeped in respectability politics and by nature requires a restriction of articulation—"the failure to *name* racism."[60] In turning to these women hatewatching *America's Next Top Model*, then, she finds them appreciating and capitalizing on the opportunity to name that racism and to articulate more freely a sense of who they are as women of color, who they want and don't want as role models, and what behaviors they valorize and villainize, together in a safe communal space. Hatewatching together, in short, "provided the women with a tool to, quite simply, be neither strategic nor ambiguous,"[61] to perform a different version of racial identity from the one that they felt society and Tyra Banks demanded of them.

Similarly, Michelle Rivera's previously cited study of Latinx antifans of reggaetón also quotes unmitigated critiques and attacks on the artists, music, and fans of reggaetón, often on the basis of, and feeding into, rival performances of what it means to be Latinx. For instance, one poster objects online, "You guys realize that reggaetón contributes to the formation of the stereotype of the stupid Latino? Haven't you guys thought about that? Are our countries just sexual games and 24 hour parties?"[62] Another writes, "I respect a person who is fair, honorable, hard working and decent, things that reggaetón imbeciles are not, and who have the balls to do nothing other [than] dishonor and bring the culture of South American down to the ground, because it is a music of delinquents, drug traffickers, gangbangers, bitches, and a million other things, and I am from Asturias, and here there are many decent immigrants that are against this b%$#ass garbage and all that it entails, they work, they make a dignified living."[63] Certainly, there is a distance between the more academic critiques of Martin's and Joseph's respondents and the sprawling screeds quoted by Rivera, but all have in common an articulation of dislike that is intended to create distinctions between an us of the good or proper people-of-color subjects and the bad ones.

My research assistant who interviewed Vietnamese Canadians found many instances in which respondents negotiated and performed their nationality and racial identity through discussing dislikes. Linh, for instance, offered a particularly clear breakdown of two stages of her identification as first not Vietnamese and then as more proudly Vietnamese:

> I didn't really like watching Vietnamese stuff when I was little because I thought it would make me a FOB,[64] make me different from the white kids who were cool at school and I was just the boring Asian kid. And I didn't fit in, so I was like, maybe if I watch like Western stuff, you know, start speaking English to my parents, they wouldn't think I was a FOB anymore. Now that I'm older, I'm just, like, "Why did I ever think that? I'm so stupid." ... [Now] I want to watch Vietnamese stuff to make up for all those years I tried to be a white kid.

Steven disliked Korean dramas and talked about this dislike to underline how he wasn't "that type" of Asian, while also trying therefore to delineate difference from Vietnamese and—just as viewers from Malawi worried about imported media—to voice concern with Korean "invasion" of Vietnam and Vietnamese Canadian communities. "Personally," he stated of Korean drama,

I feel it is invasive. It's sort of, like, skews other cultures in ways. Like, take a look at Vietnam and how, you know, how Korean culture is such a big thing and people are, you know, trying to look ever so more Korean— Vietnamese people trying to look Korean. You know, that happens when there is a pop culture that's really popular and everyone is doing it, it's trending. Why not? Of course. So that I don't, you know, accept. But why I don't want to do that is because it's not my culture. It's not particularly what I want to be, but it's just very popular. . . . It's become so ingrained into Vietnamese pop culture that, you know, I just don't like it.

For both Linh and Steven, dislikes once again allow them to make moves in declaring who they are, who they aren't, and who they want their communities to be and not be.

This research assistant, Tony Tran, pulls from his wider data elsewhere to discuss diasporic Vietnamese online discussions of the YouTube star Michelle Phan's beauty videos and richly mines what he playfully calls "anti-Phandom" to find discussion (and hence performance) of what diasporic Vietnamese beauty could or should be. Tran notes that comments such as "Way to go at shunning your own culture and monetising on another" (when Phan wishes viewers Happy New Year in Mandarin) or "Maybe Vietnam is not interesting or sellable for her. Maybe deep down she's always wanted to be seen as Chinese or Korean" charge Phan with being ashamed of being Vietnamese, while performing counternarratives of Vietnamese diasporic pride and femininity.[65]

Meanwhile, Marina, who is Malay, framed most of her nominated dislikes in terms of their commentary on race. Of *The Mindy Project*, she said, "To see stuff like that was a little uncomfortable, even though it's nice that they have an Indian character on the show and she's kind of ditsy and she's not meant to be the typical smart Indian or smart Asian nerd or whatever. But there's still instances where the way her ethnicity is portrayed that's still very stereotypical and very eeeeehhhh, no it's not really like that in the community." After noting slight improvement in the state of Disney princess films, she gestured to a great deal of media in noting,

There's also a part of Hollywood and stuff that is just doing a lot of whitewashing. And I guess that we are targeting a certain population, and they think more profit is going to come from having a white lead character, I don't know, whatever their reasons are. So it's kind of like, is it getting better? Hopefully it's getting better. But then there's, like, these chunks of movies where you have some Tibetan guy character from Marvel or something being played—this actress, I forget who she is [Tilda Swinton in *Doctor Strange*]—but you could get a Tibetan woman to play her. Scarlet Johansson playing an Asian character [in *Ghost in the Shell*]. It's just really frustrating, and it's really shocking, because you have advancements being made, but the way that they're casting characters in a big-budget film isn't really going with that.

Vincent, meanwhile, is a Black man who spoke at length of his dissatisfaction with numerous filmic and televisual accounts of Blackness. Of *Being Mary Jane*, for instance, he opined,

Okay, many people would disagree with me about *Being Mary Jane*, because it positively and accurately represents a Black woman in power. So, yeah, I feel that. And there are other reasons people like it, and I can recognize that. But I personally don't like the moments of weakness that aren't represented in the main character, Mary Jane. I think perhaps it's something that I'm not totally understanding of why the representation might be important. She has moments where she—so she feels lonely, she feels lonely that she doesn't have a partner, a male partner. And sometimes that loneliness leads to her just having sex with this guy, and then she thinks this guy really loves her, and he says he really loves her, and then he breaks her heart because he says that he's married. So at first, you know, I started to like the show. It's cool, she's in power, she really just wants someone she can share herself and her life with. So like, that's really just what she wants. But it turned into her just making certain decisions to go back and continue to have sex with someone while recognizing that he's just using her for sex. So it's hard. It's a very weak moment that I thought was harmful to her and harmful to images of Black women because Black women have been historically hypersexualized and represented as not making strong decisions and stuff like that.

Vincent's critique here is based on a viewing of a lot of the television show, as compared to Marina's critique of *Doctor Strange* and *Ghost in the Shell*, two films she admitted that she did not watch. But both not only told us about these dislikes but shared that these were critiques they'd discussed with others, and though both of them framed their acts of sharing as careful and not forceful, Marina in particular saw it as imperative that she share these opinions with the people around her. Marina even talked of herself as an audience for her concerns, noting that she regularly talked out loud while watching television alone. The dislike didn't just exist: it begged performance and enunciation.

Samantha, an African American woman, couldn't stand Amy Schumer, stating, "She's always talking about sleeping with Black men, and she's like, 'Oh yeah, I love to sleep with Black men.' But she does it in the sense where she's like objectifying the person, rather than just, like, talking about the person. . . . I think she tries to stereotype relationships and put people in boxes." Samantha was joined in this assessment, as noted in chapter 2, by numerous white feminists, who also took issue with Lena Dunham and with *Girls*. Numerous white feminists also took issue with *The Bachelor*, which Zoey amusingly glossed as "just like a bunch of white people standing in a row" and which Liz glossed as "just like white people, just so much white people, just so much affluent white people." Indeed, these white feminists' insistence that feminism needed to be intersectional and to include the voices of women of color was its own performance of race, namely, of a more progressive whiteness, as were some of their discussions of white privilege. Here, the disliked objects proved key to articulations of disavowal, wherein white supremacy and its long, hegemonic reach could be called out and criticized in ways that lay claim to belonging not to white-supremacist culture but to a progressive, intersectional ally culture.

My interviews were structured in ways to hear performances, not to hear from those performances' audiences per se, but an interview with Violet offered a rare glimpse into a moment when a performance worked not only to dictate identity but to compel a reappraisal of a text. As described in chapter 3, Violet discussed a former fandom for *Unbreakable Kimmy Schmidt* and for (cocreator) Tina Fey in general that ended when a woman of color in one of her college classes "did a whole presentation about how Tina Fey is kind of racist by breaking down the movie *Mean Girls*, and then they also started talking about *Unbreakable Kimmy Schmidt* since that's a show that she produces": "I never, like, really realized that before, and I used to really like *Unbreakable Kimmy Schmidt*. But as I continued watching it and noticed more things, it kind of turned me off of it." Violet then rehearsed her classmate's critique to the interviewer, in significant detail, admitting that she continued watching at first; but the damage was done, and eventually she stopped watching. Such moments underline the stakes of performances that are personal and personally constitutive but that in being enunciated to others may attempt to "win over" converts to the "we" that is opposed to the disliked text and that which it represents. Or we might more cynically read some such moments of performance as performing virtue, but even then, the performance is designed to create an "us" and a "them" and to invite others into the "us."

Silent Performances and Dark Stages

To talk of performances, though, is to imply volume and is to envision a voice projected from the metaphorical stage that is loud enough for even the worst seats in the house. Thus, I close this chapter with a reminder that performances of identity are often directed to smaller audiences. Our interviews actively, repeatedly, asked respondents about their dislikes, so what we received was in many cases a command performance, not the equivalent of hearing someone offer up an impromptu monologue. Granted, some respondents enjoyed discussing their dislikes (as will be discussed further in chapter 5), and some articulated them with a precision that suggested they were speaking from scripts used in other conversations. But as chapter 1 nevertheless reminded us, many interviewees felt that their dislikes were more generally and universally liked, and while some rebelled against the presumed expectation to perform approval and acquiescence, many told us of instead feeling that they needed to carry their dislikes privately. In short, many were expending far more energy in offering a markedly different performance by pretending either to approve or to tolerate.

Here, we might think back to all those who noted being in social situations or jobs that required they grin and bear their dislikes. That includes Alex, Ilana, and Melanie being forced to watch and silently dislike because their family and/or friends love; Blanche, Tom, and Winona watching shows their partners enjoy and keeping quiet about their dislike; Portland, Sophie, and Jim suffering through *The O'Reilly Factor*, *Two and a Half Men*, and sports at their workplaces; Amy, Charlie, and TJ all dutifully watching disliked shows at home so they can fit in with friends or coworkers later; Jacob and Aida, Marta, and Chelsea tolerating disliked media for their kids' sake; and many more. In these cases, two performances are occurring, the first as they pretend to like or tolerate in order to be part of a community. This is why Sara Ahmed refers to the feminist killjoy as an "affect alien," for one becomes alienated when one is "out of line with an affective community—when you do not experience happiness in the right things." Killjoys must decide whether to feign acceptance at the cost of silence or to disrupt at the cost of alienation.[66] The second performance, meanwhile, is private and personal to the self, a performance that may still perform identity in Butlerian terms and superiority in Bourdieuian terms.

But some others weren't performing dislike at all. As much as my interviewers and I collectively succeeded in eliciting discussion about dislikes from our interview subjects, we sometimes failed too. Sometimes, as noted at the conclusion of chapter 2, we instead heard some respondents perform positivity and a refusal to dislike, another position not mentioned by Bourdieu wherein we perform superiority not only through our judgments but through our judgments about judging and through our (professed) refusal to judge. This may seem to make them "cultural omnivores," a position discussed by Richard Peterson wherein someone "commands status by displaying any one of a range of tastes as the situation may require," claiming to like everything (or at least a little bit of everything) and performing high cultural status not through snobbery but through omnivorous appropriation.[67] But these respondents didn't perform omnivorousness, just a disdain for dislike; I don't doubt the omnivore's existence, but none of our respondents presented themselves as such.

Meanwhile, at yet other times, some respondents simply struggled to articulate their dislikes. I have turned to dislike in this book to try and hear some of the unspoken dislikes, annoyances, and alienations that are as characteristic of our encounters with media as are like and enthusiasm and that are well documented by many other researchers trying to make sense of why and how silences enshroud our understanding of audiences,[68] as well as descend on the body politic.[69] My interviewers and I found no shortage of such scripts. But we also heard those silences and sometimes heard only those silences. As much as I have filled this book with some of the more articulate and engaging discussion from our interviews, our transcripts also include stuttered responses when respondents struggled to express themselves. The writing up of audience research perhaps inevitably requires a privileging of what was said, but palpable in some interviews was a sense of the unsayable; and though my interviewers did noble work in getting people to open up, the preference of some to remain closed should not be written out of the record. One might even expect those who volunteered or agreed to be interviewed to be more willing to share than most, yet some respondents tripped over their words, hesitated, and/or fell silent when the interviews turned to dislikes. Such moments suggest that what I earlier called the "vocabularies of engagement" may be differentially developed and that—as documented in chapter 1—we often do not feel at liberty to speak dislike. Scripts and performances of dislike, in other words, may at times be hard to construct, perhaps even harder than scripts of like.

Conclusion

Bourdieu oversimplifies the wide range of dislikes and reasons for dislike that exist. He is not wrong to note that classed performances regularly undergird judgments of taste, but in this chapter—as in the rest of the book—I have argued that many other reasons for dislike exist. Some of these reasons are themselves performative of other identity markers, whether nation, gender, race, sexuality, generation, or beyond. In the preceding section, I offer a reminder that they are not only performative, as some audiences variously struggle to articulate their dislikes or refuse to articulate them for fear of the social prices of doing so. But audiences also regularly use their dislikes to draw lines between an us and a them, an I and a you. Bourdieu only scratched the surface of the performative capacities, intricacies, and utility of dislike, as such, and a great deal more work exists to be done to explore how disliked texts are engaged to create scripts of identity, self, and other. One of media and cultural studies' most important activities has been to chart the complex roles that media play in situating us within or outside communities, within or outside power, within or outside agency, and this chapter has aimed to show some of the complex ways in which our dislikes, and both our talk and our silences about them, do this work, thereby demanding further study.

And yet to note the complexity of such processes and the complexity of dislike bridges us to chapter 5. Bourdieu's key error in trying to make sense of dislike was to offer one overarching explanation and reason, instead of allowing for greater complexity. To this point, I have argued for numerous other explanations and reasons, but in chapter 5, I turn to moments when these reasons overlap and multiply, whether because a performance is intersectional by nature or because a dislike contains multitudes and layers.

5

The Multiplicities of Dislike

Dislike is complicated, and though each chapter so far has focused on particular forms and articulations of dislike, in practice many of these forms overlap. Let us return briefly, for instance, to several of the already-quoted dislikers in this book. Deanna disliked *Basketball Wives* because she resented its messages about Black femininity, but her dislike was framed in ways that clearly showed classed stakes too. Mark disliked Ariana Grande because of how thoroughly apolitical and hence, in his eyes, meaningless her music was; in telling us of this dislike, he used terms that rang of misogyny, even though elsewhere in his interview he spoke out against toxic masculinity and proudly declared his love of romcoms in resistance to gendered expectations. Rachel and several of the other parents discussed would quickly nominate children's media that had become their own bêtes noires, and yet in doing so, they could easily wax poetic, seeming to take pleasure in their dislike, actively enjoying the discussion and the challenges of articulating why and how they disliked. Each of these cases serves as an example of the multiplicities of dislike. So far, I have presented several reasons why one might dislike, each reason with its own stakes. But Deanna, Mark, Rachel, and many of our interviewees made it clear that reasons and reactions could have multiple layers. Deanna and Mark each nominated specific reasons for their dislike, but we could easily hear other reasons in operation too. Rachel, meanwhile, professed dislike but offered evidence of a dislike that was intermixed with degrees of like. This chapter turns to the complexities and multidimensionality of dislikes such as these, arguing that the various reasons offered so far regularly operate alongside one another.

First, I will discuss the joys of dislike and instances when one feels both pleasure and displeasure in consuming or even just considering the item of media in question and when one's dislike and like are inextricably linked. To best chart the landscape of dislike, we cannot simply examine moments of alienation, annoyance, and anger, as practices such as hatewatching, professions that one "loves to hate," and the voluminous pleasures that are often experienced variously in describing one's dislikes and in reading or hearing others' dislikes demand inclusion in any map of dislike. The first half of this chapter will thus probe further the joys of dislike. The second half then turns to instances when one has multiple reasons to dislike, whether stated honestly or not. Bourdieu presents his theory of performed superiority in relation to class alone, but if we allow for performances of gendered, raced, sexualized, nationalized, generational, or other superiorities of identity, we must allow for intersectional performances, wherein one text provokes response across numerous dimensions of identity. I will also consider instances of deception, self-deception, and fauxtrage, when one reason for dislike is claimed, in spite of evidence to the contrary. Finally, I will consider how communities of dislike can pressure their members into consensus reasons for dislike even when a greater range of reactions is present.

The Poetry of Putrescence

Statements of dislike regularly communicate disappointment, displeasure, annoyance, and a sense of pain. But some statements of dislike also or instead communicate joy and pleasure, or at least contain a poetry to them that may allow the hearer to enjoy the statement. Indeed, as a starting point for an exploration of the joys of dislike, I note that these joys are widely available in most media markets. Many utterances of dislike are marginalized by, as was noted in this book's introduction, a system of reporting on and consulting "audiences" that privileges fans, and I have argued that both the media industry and academia have not learned how best to listen to dislikers' experiences of alienation, annoyance, and pain. By contrast, though, when dislike can be turned into entertainment, it enjoys a healthy presence in popular culture, such that I begin my exploration of the joys of dislike with its professionalized outpost of negative criticism.

As much as the craft of being a professional critic may be envisioned to be one of passing judgment in thoughtful, expansive terms, it can regularly involve the skill of eviscerating beautifully. I have already quoted several critics' playful attacks on *The Hobbit* in chapter 3, likening the film to a food court, for instance, or to a children's film about anthropomorphized candy. And I have quoted Carl Wilson's *Let's Talk about Love*, because his meta-analysis of why he and others dislike Céline Dion is thoughtful and expansive, but he also has a great deal of *fun* in expounding on how he dislikes Dion. Dion's music, he shares, struck him as "bland monotony raised to a pitch of obnoxious bombast—R&B with the sex and slyness surgically removed, French *chanson* severed from its wit and soul—and her repertoire as Oprah Winfrey–approved chicken soup for the consumerist soul, a neverending crescendo of personal affirmation deaf to social conflict and context," and he later asks, "Is Céline Dion's music a dishwasher-sized blue landscape?"[1] The metaphorical play in these attacks cues a process of aestheticizing statements of dislike that is common through many critics' work.

Some critics are as famed for their takedowns as for anything else they write. On opposite sides of the Atlantic, Roger Ebert and Mark Kermode stand out here. Ebert even published collections of his more eviscerating reviews, their titles a clear indicator of the pleasures of critique on offer: *Your Movie Sucks*, *A Horrible Experience of Unbearable Length: More Movies That Suck*, and *I Hated, Hated, Hated This Movie*.[2] Many of these offer memorable comparisons: *Half Past Dead*, for instance, is said to be "like an alarm that goes off while nobody is in the room. It does its job and stops, and nobody cares," while *Battlefield Earth* "is like taking a bus trip with someone who has needed a bath for a long time. It's not merely bad; it's unpleasant in a hostile way."[3] Statements of excess abound, as when Ebert closes his review of *The Hot Chick* by noting, "The MPAA rates this PG-13. It is too vulgar for anyone under thirteen, and too dumb for anyone over thirteen."[4] His reviews even tend to insist on the inability of the language and genre of the review to encompass such bad filmmaking, as when he writes near the end of his review of *Dirty Love*, "I would like to say more, but—no, I wouldn't. I would not like to say more. I would like to say less."[5]

Mark Kermode, for his part, is similarly renowned for his diatribes against numerous films, especially for those offered in his BBC Radio 5 show *Kermode and Mayo*. A particularly notorious review of the *Entourage* movie—freely available on YouTube—begins, "Well, I mean, it's no surprise: I do hate it, I absolutely hate it. I hate it. I loathe it. I despise it. I detest it. I feel contempt for it. I just—everything about it rattles every one of my cages." Calling it "a comedy with no jokes, a satire with no satire," he evokes two other disliked films to suggests that, "compared to this, *Sex and the City 2* is a call to arms for, you know, the dispossessed masses of the world to rise up. In terms of its gender politics, *Human Centipede* is more sensitive."[6] Elsewhere, a *Buzzfeed* article offers "11 film posters improved by Mark Kermode's scathing reviews," superimposing onto the posters comments such as, of *Revolver*, "I feel bad for Guy Ritchie. I can wake up tomorrow and think 'I didn't make that film.' He has to wake up and think 'I made *Revolver*,'" and of *Keith Lemon: The Film*, "At one point I lost this 5p piece down the side of the chair. I put my hand down the side of the chair, and there's all manner of filth and scrounge and putrescence.... I thought 'that's disgusting.' But I realized it was less horrible than watching the screen. I spent 25 minutes getting foul filth under my fingernails because it was less revolting than watching the screen."[7]

Not only professional critics get to play this game, though, as numerous interview subjects in my study aestheticized their displeasures. Chelsea, for instance, said *Mickey Mouse Clubhouse* is "like white bread with salt on it," while opining that the titular character of *Caillou* was "a whiny little piece of crap. Like, if he were your kid, you would hate him." Ralph suggested that "if *The Bachelorette* or *The Bachelor* was on, I'd go outside and dig a ditch: at least I'd be getting exercise." Or Kenneth in particular offered lengthy denunciations of numerous films and filmmakers. Of *Signs*, he noted,

> At the very end, the aliens are allergic to water. So . . . you're an advanced race whose flown halfway across the galaxy in giant mile-wide ships that can turn invisible, so obviously you know something. You've been on this planet for like two weeks already, and you just now find out you're allergic to water? You remember the scene with the birthday film, where they're watching the alien walk across the alley? So that was in Brazil. It rains in Brazil like every two days! Nobody figured out, like, "Steve, it burns my skin when it rains." So how is this a surprise?

Or of Michael Bay films, he shared,

> Don't get me wrong, I love action sequences. I love—I'm a guy—I love stuff exploding. Like, I've blown stuff up in my backyard just for gig-

gles. . . . But there's a way to do it. If just done for the sake of blowing stuff up, then it's insulting. Like, Michael Bay is the king of everything bl—did you ever realize the average person believes if you flip a car over, it'll explode, because of Michael Bay? . . . Like, no, Michael Bay blows stuff up for the fun of it. A car does not explode like that. If you wreck a car, it does not burst into flames. You'd be the worst car company ever. Think about it. What would happen if a car hit you, and you just blew into flames? Oh my God. The freakin' car fatality rate would be like quadrupled. . . . Any Michael Bay film, you drop like a glass, it will explode, shrapnel will hit people.

All of these comments offer excess, whether at the level of extravagant metaphors and comparisons, overstatements, or even discursive piling on. Granted, the *Hobbit* reviewers, Wilson, Ebert, and Kermode are paid for their protestations of dislike, meaning that the stakes, motivations, and rewards for our respondents vary significantly from the professional critics, but all still clearly *enjoy* their dislike.

Of course, these comments are performative, and especially from the paid critics, they can sound very Bourdieuian. Stoner comedies such as *The Hot Chick* or reality shows like *The Bachelor* rank so far down a hierarchy of acceptable taste that we should expect not just denunciations of them but effusive, heavily performative takedowns. Both the speakers and the laughing audience of such criticisms can take comfort in their supposed mutual superiority to such fare. Or, though not quoted here, we might expect—again in Bourdieuian fashion—that others might enjoy lambasting the products of high culture, using elaborate, poetic language to eviscerate them in a way that still insists on cultural superiority, albeit based on an inversion of usual cultural hierarchies. But context is important and insists that more is going on, since Ebert and Kermode also regularly share their gleeful appreciation of other "low" fare. Ebert sounds like a snob when deriding *The Hot Chick*, but his review of the tonally similar *American Pie* is glowing; and in general, he deserves credit, alongside his *At the Movies* cohost, Gene Siskel, for dedicating a large part of his career to making it acceptable for film critics to engage with and utterly enjoy films up and down established cultural hierarchies. They're not *just* performing superiority, in short. What else is going on here textually?

First, we might see the aestheticization of dislikes as a process of making one's statements more of a text, or a fully realized paratext. Each metaphor, instance of excess, overstatement, and wild analogy aims to elevate these comments from being "mere" reactions to being texts in their own right, ones that will be remembered, shared, and referenced. *BuzzFeed*'s act of plastering Kermode quotes on the films' posters literalizes the rhetorical pitch made by the critic's statements, attaching them to the films, as textual/paratextual elements in and of their own right. Excess and the aestheticization of dislikes are thus techniques for endurance, for ensuring that the criticism stays attached to its text, haunting it, dangling from it conspicuously. Or, in the terms of Henry Jenkins, Sam Ford, and Joshua Green, they make the criticisms, and the dislike they enunciate, "spreadable" in ways that beg for circulation and sharing.[8]

Certainly, some of Ebert's critical reviews invert classical marketing techniques, offering themselves up as counterhype. Whereas film marketing regularly mythologizes the creators of the film, his negative reviews regularly resituate them as supremely untalented. Of *Death to Smoochy*, for instance, he writes, "Only enormously talented people could have made *Death to Smoochy*. Those with lesser gifts would have lacked the nerve to make a film so bad, so miscalculated, so lacking any connection with any possible audience. To make a film this awful, you have to have enormous ambition and confidence, and dream big dreams."[9] Or of *Dirty Love*, he opines that it "wasn't written and directed. It was committed."[10] Moreover, whereas film marketing often highlights particular scenes as representative, so too does Ebert, often offering long deconstructions of especially awful scenes and regularly of scenes featured in official advertising. Take, for instance, his review of *Slackers*, which offers its own edited montage of scenes: "Consider a scene where the heroine's roommate, interrupted while masturbating, continues even while a man she has never met is in the room. Consider a scene where the hero's roommate sings a duet with a sock puppet on his penis. Consider a scene where we cut away from the hero and the heroine to join two roommates just long enough for a loud fart, and then cut back to the main story again."[11] The poetry of putrescence is strategically and rhetorically helpful, as a way to encourage the spreading of one's opinions of dislike.

Second, though, the poetry of putrescence can also work as a bold retort, as a disliker's refusal to play the role of victim at the hand of the disliked object. As chapter 1 details, most media objects that we intensely dislike are those we (believe we) cannot escape, whether because they're so popular that they're "everywhere" or because our social communities, workmates, and/or loved ones enjoy or demand them. This ubiquity and inescapability create a power differential, and a perpetual *reminder* of that power differential, potentially salting the wound of the disliker with every subsequent exposure. One small way to fight back is to limit their power both by finding joy in one's dislike and by communicating their ills in extravagant, poetic fashion. Parents' frequent resort to vulgarity in describing, for instance, Caillou as a "bald little fuck" or "a whiny little piece of crap" or Bratz as "little bitches" palpably release built-up tension, as Lesley, Chelsea, or Rachel, respectively, feel compelled to allow Caillou and Bratz into their homes but, when interviewed by an adult, capitalize on the chance to "talk back" to their dislikes. What we hear in such responses is an affective escape from entrapment, pleasure as the last resort of bitterness. Or in other cases, as with Kenneth, the defensive position offered by the aestheticization of dislike allows one to find peace by evading affective attachment and concentrating on formalist or "realist" readings, strategically refusing to engage the disliked item of media on its preferred terms and instead approaching it with critical distance, reframing it as something to be analyzed, not enjoyed.

But even if a retort of forms is being lodged, a rhetorical game initiated, it is still striking that many of these denunciations are expressed as joyful by their speakers. Kenneth was not ranting angrily when he decried *Signs* or Michael Bay—he was smiling, laughing, and having a good time. Ebert and Kermode play the part of the angry film critic at times, and have been paid handsomely for doing so, but the sheer glee with which they roll around in their dislike, and their insistence on returning to movies that we and they both surely know they will dislike, betrays both their own significant pleasure and the expected pleasure of their readers. And even if they're drawing deep from their respective wells of literary techniques to hurt a film, both critics are often more interesting and well written when they're in attack mode, suggesting in turn that they might truly enjoy the act of dislike. To see strategy, then, is important, and throughout this book, I hope to have pointed out how dislikes can certainly be useful if they provide moments for enunciation and articulation of other hopes, expectations, wants, and needs. But we must also acknowledge the inherent pleasures of some displeasure, especially if we also consider why someone might buy a collection called *Your Movie Sucks!* Why might we *like* to dislike for reasons other than Bourdieuian snobbery alone?

Spectacles of Failure

At times, a poetics of putrescence will lift up a *declaration* of dislike, as some critics can deftly and even beautifully render an intense displeasure in terms that will be pleasurable to others and that will be sought out, circulated, and appreciated. But what of the dislikes themselves? Enough audiences take enough pleasure in seeing media fail, in discovering new dislikes, and in cultivating existing dislikes that we must also conclude that, paradoxically, displeasure can be a major source of pleasure. Spectacles of failure are commonplace throughout media consumption.

We see the relishing of such spectacles in the healthy audience for "bad" media. We see them in camp, as media are lauded for their flagrant disregard of normative guidelines of quality.[12] Related, we see them in the deliberate production of "bad" film, from B movies of yore to Syfy specials such as *Sharknado, Dinocroc,* or *Mega Shark v. Giant Octopus.* We see them in many of the pleasures of reality television and daytime talk shows, when people's outrageous and bad behavior is often a key offering of each genre. We hear them in music-appreciation cultures for songs and performers branded as cheesy, whom listeners claim to listen to ironically, as with yacht rock, for instance. We see and hear them in the growing popularity of texts in which comedians read "bad" writing: for instance, the podcast *My Dad Wrote a Porno* consists of Jamie Morton, James Cooper, and Alice Levine reading from and pausing to mockingly unpack an erotic novel written by the former's father. We see them in video-game culture's embrace at times of low-grade graphics and painfully bad acting.

Indeed, video games are an interesting port of entry to spectacles of failure, precisely because, as Jesper Juul has argued, failure is so central to playing games, in ways that should demand that we take failure and frustration more seriously as pleasures—or at least required features—of media consumption. Although Juul says that he is "a sore loser," he reflects, "I play video games though I know I will fail, at least part of the time. On a higher level, I think I *enjoy* playing video games, but why does this enjoyment contain at its core something that I most certainly do not enjoy?"[13] And yet Juul is quick to note that games require failure, as games that one can "beat" with minimal labor are judged as too easy and poorly designed, such that, Juul says, "I dislike failing in games, but I dislike *not* failing even more." This leads to what he calls the paradox of failure or "the paradox of painful art":[14]

1. We generally avoid failure.
2. We experience failure when playing games.
3. We seek out games, although we will experience something that we normally avoid.[15]

Juul is discussing video games specifically and sees them as "the singular art form that sets us up for failure,"[16] but we might easily apply his comments to other types of games—tabletop, school yard, gambling, and sports, for instance—since these other realms seemingly require failure at some level. Witness, for example, the intense dislike generated for sporting teams that regularly win and that spend seemingly endless money to ensure even more wins: as with the video game that one can't lose, these teams have their fans, but many others see them as threats to the sport, such that most of us could accurately be said to actively want and need "our" teams to lose at times.

Reworded in the terms of this chapter, Juul suggests that games actively produce moments and experiences of dislike, frustration, and annoyance, but these are all central to the production of enjoyment. How? Failure, he is careful to note, comes in different magnitudes,[17] and the art of designing a good game requires working out what lower-level failures can set up higher-level successes. When playing *The Last of Us*, therefore, I have been caught and eaten by zombies hundreds of times—a failure—but all the while I am learning better how to move, attack, flee, and strategize to avoid future death. Juul notes that game players regularly even add obstacles or playing strategies that make it harder to succeed yet that aren't self-defeating: they might handicap themselves, for instance (refusing to use a powerful weapon, to see if one can get by with lesser ones), or otherwise play badly to the keep the game interesting (what happens if I lose this fight?), to avoid social consequences (letting one's child beat one so that they don't throw a tantrum), or to explore other aspects of the game (*will* I fall off this cliff as I suspect, or is there a hidden area over there?).[18] In short, we play games with all sorts of goals and desires, meaning that some failures and displeasures promise or guarantee other successes and pleasures.

While accepting Juul's premise that games are an especially rich medium for considering competing goals and learning curves, I wish to export from game studies this notion that some media pleasures may need to be set up with or otherwise involve displeasure. Failures and displeasures may teach us something that allows yet more pleasure. Chapter 1 details numerous instances of viewers subjecting themselves to unpleasurable media to avoid social consequences, thereby allowing other social pleasures (of watching together, of belonging, etc.). But we might also seek out failure and displeasure precisely to reflect on and appreciate success and pleasure. Seeing bad performances, bad lighting choices, bad representation, or bad anything in film and television (where "bad" is personally adjudicated, not necessarily what one is "supposed" to consider bad) can help one see a greater range of possibilities, such that one's appreciations and pleasures of seeing their superiors is heightened. Simon Frith notes that "'bad music' is a necessary concept for musical pleasure, for musical aesthetics," and "a necessary part of fandom,"[19] precisely because it serves as the contrast for, and hence the frame around, concepts and appreciation of "good" music. As in gaming, then, we may need to fail either to learn how to succeed or to enjoy success. As in gaming, too, although some of those failures will simply be frustrating, annoying, and laced with nothing but displeasure, some of those failures and dislikes may be pleasurable in their displeasure precisely because of the role they are playing in setting us up for future pleasures and likes.

Notably, J. Halberstam has written of the "queer art of failure" and of queer appreciation of failure in ways that may seem to challenge Juul's and my proposition.[20] However, failure to Halberstam is that which has failed by conventional, hegemonic norms, its appreciation and reclamation coming from those who reject the evaluative schema behind those norms. Thus, the (conventional) "failure" is in fact experienced (by Halberstam's queer subject) as an object of like, not dislike, whereas the (conventional) bar of success and expectation is experienced as an object of dislike. In short, then, Halberstam is still allowing that pleasure can come from the reflection on that which has failed and that which is personally or communally disliked (aka that which is conventionally framed as success) in ways that pose an opposing possibility of like and appreciation (even if that which is liked is conventionally framed as failure).

As was discussed briefly in chapter 2, competitive antifandoms might also produce situations in which pleasures and displeasures are inseparable from each other. When one loves a sports team, one is by nature invested in its rivals doing poorly and may easily find oneself enjoying the spectacle of one of its rivals failing. For instance, Annette Hill describes professional wrestling (anti)fandom as an arena in which the pleasures of supporting one wrestler are interchangeable with the pleasures of rooting against another. She offers the telling example of a wrestling fan congratulating a wrestler after a match by saying "good match, love to hate you."[21] But since competitions are rife within media, anywhere a competition is invoked or constructed, the grounds for enjoying spectacles of failure have been created. Talk-show hosts, news anchors or pundits, time-slot rivals, box-office peers, or any rivals for an award or record can all quickly be pitted against each other in competition, thereby creating vibrant possibilities for some audiences to enjoy watching failure. Celebrity also provides rich terrain for actual or perceived rivalries, sometimes when celebrities feud with one another but sometimes simply when they become symbols for various competing beliefs or logics. Thus, celebrities with clearly spoken political or social beliefs offer themselves up as objects of delicious derision when they or their ventures fail, and video of them looking crestfallen can circulate quickly among those who actively enjoy the spectacle of failure. Whenever, in short, one person's, text's, or organization's failure might mean or simply imply the success of another person, text, organization, or belief, that failure will probably be enjoyed by someone else parlaying their dislike into pleasure.

A form of this competitive antifandom is seen in contrarian pleasures of disliking that which is popular or commonly framed as "good." Quite a few of our respondents reported actively disliking something and yet, upon being asked why, offered simply that they didn't like that it was popular. As chapter 1 details, almost everything nominated by our respondents as especially irksome was regarded as occupying too much space in popular culture and as ubiquitous and inescapable. Thus, such items' "rivals" were relative silence or the hope of something better. As chapter 2 details, moreover, most of these objects of engaged dislike were regarded as representative of a greater ill, crime, or indignity. Consequently, any spectacle of failure involving these objects would at least potentially offer itself up as a spectacle of pleasure, given what that failure could suggest about the conquest of rival senses of logic, aesthetics, and/or decency.

Singing in the Shit, Alone or Together

Spectacles of failure may take the form of a team losing a game, of a film performing horribly at the box office, or of a celebrity brought down or otherwise shamed, but the spectacle may be the item of media itself, wherein the enjoyment comes from seeing just how bad it is. Jeffrey Sconce's work is illustrative here, as Sconce has both explicated and performed the joys of disliking "bad" media. In "Movies: A Century of Failure," he turns to the enjoyment of bad films by a cadre of critics. "United in the principle that the cinema has become an unimaginative and perhaps irredeemable sewer of cliché and stupidity," he writes, "these critics collectively articulate a voice that ranges from the bitterly comic to the comically bitter," and that takes the form of a "mock and mocking despair" that is popularly dubbed as "snark."[22] Sconce argues that such critics see so little to legitimately enjoy in cinema, and so much cynical production of garbage, that all that is left to do is to celebrate the end point of cinema and "a world where the cinema's unending compromises have finally produced a complete and irreversible artistic collapse, leaving only derisive irony and disengaged contempt as viable modes for enjoying the vast majority of contemporary cinematic product." This produces "an audience today that appears to go to the movies, not out of an expectation of actually being moved, engaged, or even remotely entertained in any conventional sense, but rather to wallow in the cinema as a faltering medium in a failure culture. Often the goal is less to watch an individual title than bear witness to an entire cultural institution in collapse."[23]

Sconce posits an audience that definitively has a sense of a better alternative, whether rooted in history, in the avant-garde, or only in ideal, but here the pleasure is less of actively rooting for failure by a rival and more one of bearing witness. Meanwhile, there is something here of the playwright Samuel Beckett's famous suggestion that "when you're in the shit up to your neck, there's nothing left to do but sing." Sconce invokes a poetry of putrescence to discuss the awfulness of much Hollywood fare and yet, in that awfulness, therefore finds a pleasure and documents a similar enjoyment of the awful from various other critics. In doing so, he offers a key pleasure and joy of dislike. Sianne Ngai dubs this affective position one of "stuplimity": "a concatenation of boredom and astonishment—a bringing together of what 'dulls' and what 'irritates' or agitates."[24] In contemporary usage, "awful" means horrible, but it stems etymologically from "awe-ful" or "awe-inspiring," and in "confront[ing] us with the limitations of our capacity for responding in general,"[25] Ngai's "stuplimity," and its seemingly paradoxical wedding of the stupid and the sublime, thus unites the root and the end of the word "awful," finding them working together in the mixed reaction of joyful disgust.

Though Sconce never says so explicitly, another obvious pleasure that he finds in reading and writing about putrescence is that of finding comrades and community. After all, if one utility of dislike is that it serves as a site for the articulation of desires, needs, hopes, expectations, and preferences about the media, while another key utility is in allowing a performance of identity, ideally those articulations and performances should be witnessed by others. Sara Ahmed notes that "even when the experience of pain is described as private, that privacy is linked to the experience of being with others. In other words, it is the apparent loneliness of pain that requires it to be disclosed to a witness."[26] When our pains and displeasures are witnessed, and more so when they are acknowledged and when others agree, another key utility of dislike presents itself as community creation. Though by contrast I maintain that some performances of dislike may either be intended for the performer alone or be frustrated and held secret, Anne Gilbert suggests that "hatewatching" is an "inherently communal" practice,[27] as she points to the significant and extensive joys and pleasures of community that arise from sharing an engaged dislike. The *Smash* and *Girls* hatewatchers she studies enjoyed each other's presence and were given both the confidence of their convictions and simply a lot of pleasure from watching and discussing mutual dislikes together.

As previously discussed in chapter 4, Ralina Joseph has also studied hatewatchers. The young, women-of-color *America's Next Top Model* viewing group was united in its dislike of the show and in its "unmitigated disgust" at host Tyra Banks, whom they found "to be fake, a misogynist, racially biased and unapologetically and disproportionately cruel to women of color. They did not see Banks as a woman of color role model they aspired to be like, but rather as a villainous figure against whom they identified."[28] But Joseph notes how fond they became of the time they spent watching it together, given the space it opened up for them to bond over their largely agreed-on criticisms: "The women formed community through their oppositional reading." And thus while none of them *liked* the show, they nevertheless "received another form of pleasure in creating critiques," a pleasure that was powerful precisely because it was communal, shared, and hence reinforced and acknowledged by each other.[29]

My own interviews weren't set up to discuss communal hatewatching per se, but they did offer many moments when respondents noted the pleasures of finding other dislike-minded souls; and whenever my interviewers betrayed their own agreement with certain dislikes, respondents regularly got excited. Parents in particular often recounted narratives of being subsumed under the weight of disliked media and their associated paratexts, and when the interviewer laughed at a statement about *Caillou*'s titular character being "a whiny brat," a "whiny little piece of crap," "terrible," "annoying," "atrocious," a "bald little fuck," or "the bane of all parents' existence," for instance, at the statement that *Mickey Mouse Clubhouse* is "like white bread with salt on it," or at the admission that *Dora the Explorer*'s song about her backpack "gets under my skin," the parents offering such condemnations all responded to the laughing acknowledgment. For a brief moment, the parents were with someone "like them," not with a child who loved Caillou. And thus one should expect that the pleasures of such moments of community, belonging, and agreement might lead to *Caillou*, *Mickey Mouse Clubhouse*, and *Dora the Explorer* paradoxically providing enjoyment and pleasure for parents, even if only in the acts and moments of denunciation.

Given the pleasures offered by such moments, we might understand the snowball effect that leads to Bad Objects being crowned, wherein general approbation is directed toward specific, seemingly commonly disliked texts or individuals. Caillou certainly appeared to have taken on the status of a Bad Object among parents, regularly invoked in a derogatory and often vulgar manner. Reality TV and the Kardashians in particular were also commonly complained about. *Two and a Half Men* featured prominently. Or we might think about how commonly *Twilight*, Nickelback, Justin Bieber, and Miley Cyrus have been criticized in recent years, each becoming a go-to Bad Object to be invoked and attributed with all manner of ills. Such Bad Objects allow not just a community but seemingly a society to come together in shared approbation, thereby allowing a pleasurable experience (though I'll discuss the hegemony of and behind Bad Objects later in this chapter).

Of course, some pleasures and likes will, conversely, be premised on others' dislikes. Camp as a viewing, reading, or listening strategy, for instance, relishes in mainstream and regularly heteronormative culture's dislikes and discomforts, to find pleasure and joy therein.[30] Many other subcultures, too, predicate their appreciation of some items of media on the mainstream, hegemonic culture's disdain. I do not consider such practices or communities of consumption here, since they seem not to *layer* dislike and like with the individual or community of consumers—the focus of this chapter—as much as they exhibit fandom and regard for media that eschews (other audiences') normative ideals of taste, quality, and value.

The Ridicule of Joyful Dislike, and Why Dislike Isn't Necessarily Trolling

Joyful dislike, as I have shown in the preceding section, takes many forms. Most of these forms, though, are looked down on. Dislike, it seems, is something we're more usually expected to do in pained silence, and one need only see the contempt that oozes from many critics toward ironic, snarky declarations of joyful dislike—redoubled when they include vulgarities and excess, both common markers of joyful dislike—to realize how nonnormative joyful dislike has been. Before moving on to consider other layerings of dislike, then, I find it important to challenge the value judgments that undergird this abnormalization of joyful dislike.

Much of the debate over the "appropriateness" of joyful dislike can be seen in another of its key artistic forms, namely, satire. Satire, as George Test notes, is marked by the copresence of aggression, judgment, play, and laughter,[31] and in mixing the first two with the latter two, it regularly offers joyful dislike. Satire is further marked by many of the qualities noted earlier of other forms of joyful dislike, as it peddles in excess, snark, and vulgarity, while at its best often proving to be remarkably witty and poetic. These qualities, alongside its refusal to be wholly sincere, working as a tool of irony, have regularly seen it criticized as apathetic, cynical, and nihilistic. In a broadside attack on irony, cynicism, and satire, for instance, Jeffrey Goldfarb charges that satirical irony and cynicism "is a form of legitimation through disbelief," with its philosophic base in relativism":

> When we no longer know that our way of life is the best way, we learn to respect others, but we also begin to doubt ourselves. Our positions on political, social, and even religious issues come to appear accidental, more the product of who we are—our class position, nationality, and limited interests—than a product of how well we think and act. Thus the quality of what we say and do and what others say and do come to be understood cynically. Words and actions are interpreted as manifestations of the limited positions of specific individuals and groups, not believed or judged on their own terms.[32]

Goldfarb paints a picture of a slippery slope: when we begin from the position that something is wrong and insufficient, and when we take pleasure in noting that error, he says, we lose all sight of values and soon find ourselves a society without values. Admittedly, many critics offer more measured versions of this criticism, but satire and cynical irony's apparent unwillingness to nominate a better way and the pleasure that the satirist or cynic take in undercutting and ridiculing are seen as deeply problematic by many.

One of satire's best critics and theorists, Mikhail Bakhtin, by contrast offers us a way to consider satire and the acts of relishing one's criticisms as bona fide modes of criticism, albeit different ways of speaking. Laughter and ridicule, he writes, have "the remarkable power of making an object come up close, of drawing it into a zone of crude contact where one can finger it familiarly on all sides, turn it upside down, inside out, peer at it from above and below, break open its external shell, look into its center, doubt it, take it apart, dismember it, lay it bare and expose it, examine it freely and experiment with it."[33] This is an admittedly romanticized declaration, but Bakhtin's point is that we must too often do battle with the ideas and objects we dislike on their own territory, or on neutral territory that allows us little power. Most dislikers, I have shown, feel that their objects of dislike are ubiquitous, inescapable, and hence hold power over them. But drawing an object into a realm of ridicule allows one some momentary power over it. Bakhtin thus sees a ridiculing laughter as "a vital factor in laying down that prerequisite for fearlessness without which it would be impossible to approach the world realistically."[34] Joyful dislike and laughing ridicule, in short, might allow us moments—however small and sparse—to develop traction in a more sustained critique.

As I hope to have shown, most statements of dislike *do* propose what the dislikers believe to be better alternatives, contra Goldfarb and his fellow critics' frustration with cynical, satiric approaches. They may not announce them explicitly, and hence may require us to listen further, but this is a mode of enunciation and articulation that the speaker has chosen to engage rather than surrender to the object of dislike. "To degrade," insists Bakhtin, "is to bury, to sow, and to kill simultaneously, in order to bring forth something more and better," and thus at its best, ridicule "does not deny seriousness but purifies and completes it."[35] In short, then, what I am calling the poetics of putrescence that accompany joyful dislike are a poetics with a long history: Bakhtin traces them back several centuries, while others trace them back to Diogenes.[36] They have endured and developed given their uncanny abilities to mix critique, fearlessness, hopefulness, and an unwillingness to be silent, all while providing joy and laughter. Singing in the shit is perhaps understandably an oft-misunderstood act, but it is an approach that allows its chorus a joyful, raucous camaraderie in frustration.

However, I want to distinguish between those who sing in the shit and those who play in it, namely, trolls. At first glance, trolls' purposive antagonism toward fans may seem to be yet another form of pleasurable dislike. In a book on trolling, Whitney Phillips writes of trollery as devoid of, and hence not articulating, deeper sentiment; on the contrary,

Phillips notes, for trolls, "No matter the circumstance, and whatever their source, emotions are seen as a trap, something to exploit in others and ignore or switch off in yourself. Abandon all feeling, ye who enter here."[37] Trolls, Phillips argues, "do not, and in many cases cannot, connect their object of ridicule . . . to the emotional context out of which it arises."[38] Suzanne Scott also writes of "the detachment that characterizes trolling."[39] However, that detachment is a guise, and Phillips's subsequent reflection on her work on trolling in light of her experience of abuse serves as a strong, sobering reminder that the troll's motto, to "do it for the lulz," is classic abuser crap, since it is still and always very much motivated by hate and malice.[40] Trolling has evolved (devolved?), such that Phillips's initial definition may have been rendered moot by everyday usage and understanding. But there is still something to that detachment; working within her original terms, I would distinguish the troll from the joyful disliker as someone who still speaks a pain received from the text. The joyful disliker may attempt to laugh it off or to return fire, but nothing they say or do attempts to suggest the pain was not felt. Pure trolling, by contrast, is detached from the supposedly disliked text and is aimed solely at upsetting, angering, or otherwise inflaming a fan. Trolling works within a mode of critique, ridicule, and negation but is directed at its own audience, and the claimed reaction to the text exists only as kindling for its fire.

In offering this distinction, I do not mean to "rescue" joyful dislike as in any way always good. Dislike rests on *perceived* ubiquity, inescapability, power, and harm, and the disliker may quite categorically be wrong in their perceptions. So, for instance, angry, white, male Star Wars fans of the ilk discussed at the end of chapter 3 may legitimately *feel* threatened by people of color and women, thinking their world to be collapsing, and may consider *The Last Jedi* and its casting of people of color and women to be an act of cultural erasure of them, of whiteness, and of masculinity. They are wrong, offensively and stupidly so, but their reaction is still perceived. Under Phillips's terms, though, a troll would be someone posting about women of color in *The Last Jedi* ruining the film, with no legitimate feeling of having been harmed yet using that language to garner a reaction from women, people of color, and anyone else with sense. Whether the common usage of "troll" still holds is up for debate, though. Bluntly and functionally, in any given situation, both the joyful disliker and the troll may potentially be abusive assholes,[41] but analytically we should avoid rolling *all* joyful dislike in with trollery and assholery, as the joyful disliker still has a grievance to be heard and interpreted, while the pure troll is working through hate and/or malice, their "grievance" a game and a façade.

Intersectional Performances

While like and dislike, pleasure and displeasure, can often overlap, so too can various *reasons* for disliking. These reasons will intersect, at times working in harmony with one another while at other times either seemingly or actually working against one another. Thus, for example, although chapter 4 examines dislike as a performance of identity, we should expect postmodern and intersectional identities to produce various intersectionalities of dislike that complicate one's performance.[42]

Following Bourdieu, one could easily set about the task of deciding which items of media are low-, middle-, or highbrow in classed, elitist terms. But one could repeat this exercise distinguishing now between items of media deemed superior due to their masculinity, ranking easy listening, daytime talk shows, and romantic comedies near the bottom and rock, HBO dramas, or indie films about men in crisis at the top. Then one could repeat the exercise with race and ethnicity serving as the distinguishing lens, placing media associated with people of color (such as rap or hip hop) near the bottom and whiter media (such as *Mad Men* or TED talks) near the top. Then one might consider sexuality, nationality, generation, and so on. Each of these metrics would offer one a fair degree of predictive power over who might be inclined to like or dislike anything on the list. If one read through our interview transcripts armed with these lists, one would at times be impressed with one's predictive powers, as our interview subjects quite often followed suit (even if, in some cases, flipping the evaluative poles, given their own identities as working class, women, or people of color, respectively). However, one is of course never just a classed subject or a gendered, raced, sexed, national, or aged subject. And thus, predictive powers can at times falter when a person's various identity components interact, forcing us to consult across our various lists. In such instances, we should not even expect one identity component to "win out," as instead we might expect audiences to feel conflicted.

Intersectionality may work harmoniously, admittedly, for in some cases, the lists will superimpose on each other, and one's performance of identity will be intersectional without creating tension. In Malawi, for instance, the women with whom we talked were more likely to profess appreciation for Nigerian film and television. As women, they regularly expressed appreciation of Nigerian media's greater perceived relevance and attention to the social lives of women, while bemoaning the endless parade of violence on display in the predominantly action-film fare that made it from the United States to Malawi. And as Malawians, some clearly took pride in watching *African* melodrama that addressed African issues and specificities, while disliking the cultural remoteness of US film and television. In such cases, then, their identities as Malawian and women worked in stereo to produce a dislike of US media. Or, in the United States, Imani framed her dislike of *Breaking Bad* as speaking to race, gender, and generation—to her, it was a middle-aged white man's show, and her discussion of it refused an analysis along one plane of identity alone. Carly's dislike of the *CSI* franchise and its "guys your dad might have a long, boring business meeting with" was situated comfortably at the intersections of generation and gender.

In other cases, though, audience members' identities will interact more dynamically in performative terms. For example, I refer the reader to my earlier invocation of Newman and Levine's criticism of Lizzy Caplan, the Hollywood actress who voiced her dislike of *Two and a Half Men*. Newman and Levine read that dislike as classed, and I posed that it may instead be gendered; but it could of course be both: Lizzy Caplan may be a snob who looks down her nose at three camera sitcoms that she sees as artistically inept *and* be a woman who resents aggressively misogynist shows. Deanna's dislike of *Basketball Wives* was explicitly tied to its representation of race and framed her quite clearly as a *middle-class* ("bourgeois," in her own terms) African American woman, who looked down on women who behaved as did those in *Basketball Wives*. Boyd struggled to articulate what he disliked about US television for half his interview, though during that time, he often zeroed in on the inanity of "chick flicks" in a way that seemed to perform traditional masculinity and portrayed US television as feminized and hence, to him, lesser. But he then turned to the news, and we gained a sense of his profound alienation as an Ethiopian American who despised how Africans were represented in the news. His general dislike for US television, then, was both nationalized and gendered. Or, while Malawian women could easily identify against Hollywood when seeing it locked in a battle with African melodrama, Malawian men were often more conflicted, at times appreciating the action of a Jean Claude Van Damme or Arnold Schwarzenegger film yet distancing themselves from the US values embedded in the film.

Or for another example of one's various identities and their performative expectations actively clashing in one's reaction to media, I turn to Candice, whose strong dislike for the Kardashians rang of some elitism mixed with a generational concern with "young people." "I do think," she said, "there are some people that get a little too caught up into it. They obsess over the glamour, or they think that that is something to aspire to be, and that's where I might have concerns, especially with women that are younger and more impressionable." And she continued to express concern about younger people's "obsession," while also complaining about the overall "quality" and "trashiness" of the shows. Earlier in the interview, no less, she professed only to watch documentaries and educational programming, and she spoke critically of sitcoms. However, after offering the foregoing criticism, she then stopped herself in her tracks and backed away somewhat from its sweeping judgment: "They're not hurting anybody," she conceded, before continuing,

> And you can also look at the side of they're making a crapload of money doing this. So whether it's them or the people they've chosen, they've certainly made very good business decisions, and they're laughing all the way to the bank. So in some ways, you almost have to respect them for getting somewhere out of nowhere. So when those comments start coming up, then I almost want to revert to defending because I really—I don't like when, especially toward women, people say, "Oh, well, you can't do that" because of, like, the sexist argument, whereas if it were men, that argument wouldn't be happening. So then all of a sudden, I see myself wanting to defend the Kardashians, who I really can't stand, and I would imagine that if I met them, I probably wouldn't like them. But I feel almost like wanting to protect them out of a sense of feminism or wanting equality of the sexes and seeing an unfair bias against them.

As wealthy and middle-aged, Candice is happy to look down upon the Kardashians as vacuous, trashy young people. But as a woman, and as one who elsewhere in her interview is quite thoughtful and concerned in discussing representations of women, she feels the need to pull back and to limit her critique lest she seem or *be* antifeminist and out of respect for women who have made "a crapload of money."

Similar to Candice, one of my Malawian interviewees, Auna, had drawn a stark contrast for me between US film and television as culturally irrelevant and invasive on the one hand and as overly masculinized in their zeal for destruction, war, and gang violence on the other hand, as compared to Nigerian film and television as culturally relevant and welcome on the one hand and attentive to what she saw as women's issues on the other hand. But near the end of our interview, when I asked if she watched anything else, she excitedly told me that she had recently been watching a lot of Korean dramas. When I asked if she found them as invasive as US media, she paused for a long time to consider the question and eventually smiled at me, saying, "So you have found me out. I want to support African media. But there is a beauty to the stories from Korea that I just cannot resist." She proceeded to describe how popular these stories were with a group of friends, all women studying at the university like herself. "We will quote the lines to each other, because they are beautiful lovers and they can say such beautiful things that my friends and we wish our Malawian men had such poetry." Thus, her identification as a highly educated woman, and the performative expectations of this role, seemed to clash with her identification and wish to perform identity as a Malawian.

Identity, in short, can be performed through dislike, but sometimes those performances are challenging and complex, needing to speak (across) various levels of identity. Indeed, my interviewers and I could learn comparatively little about our respondents in half an hour to an hour, meaning that although we were drawn to performances aligned with those more visible, obvious components of identity—gender, race, sexuality, class, and nationality—if we knew our subjects much better, we could undoubtedly see the ways in which other striations of identity played out in their performances. Even, then, when we think we saw clear performances and even when they marked their performances in explicit terms, I want to avoid the essentialist trap of assuming they liked or disliked what they did simply because they were women, African American, Malawian, or so forth. Each and every performance may well have had yet more intersectional depths and complexities that we could not see.

From Multiplicity to Duplicity: Deception, Self-Deception, and Fauxtrage

To invoke the language of "performance" in this and chapter 4, though, is to open the door to another multiplicity, namely, to the possibility of deception. I have largely used the term "performance" as synonymous with "enunciation" and "articulation," whereby one constitutes who one is through the acts of speaking, being, and doing. But some performances carry with them aspects of either deception or self-deception, wherein one or more reasons are offered as cover for one or more authentic reasons for dislike. That slippage between "the truth" and what is spoken is unavoidable to the qualitative researcher. Clifford Geertz reminds us that "what we call our data are really our own constructions of other people's constructions of what they and their compatriots are up to."[43] Sometimes other people's constructions are interested. John Thornton Caldwell has sounded the alarm that interviews with media professionals are not trustworthy, given the professionals' inherent desires to present themselves and their organizations in a favorable light,[44] and though one would hope that my own interviewees would see less need to offer PR, for all had been promised anonymity through pseudonymity and none represented organizations, they still may wish either to have impressed or simply not to have looked bad to my interviewers and me.

David Morley addresses this concern adeptly, by noting, "even if it could be demonstrated that my respondents had systematically mispresented their behavior to me . . . , it would remain as a social fact of considerable interest that these were the particular forms of misrepresentation that respondents felt constrained to offer of themselves."[45] Keeping with the language of performance, even if one's performance is fictional, it is relevant that they constructed this performance, that they felt that my interviewers and I should be treated to that performance. Such performances, "authentic" or not, therefore, still tell us about how dislike is presented and are probably crafted with a sense of what are normative performances. They still tell us something of the ideals and aspirations of the performance.

I do not mean entirely to explain away the problem of deceptive performance, although I would hope that across this many interviews, none of which has been treated as singularly important or indicative, the research design was set up to withstand the stress test provided by some respondents variously lying, withholding information, or stretching the truth. What interests me more than the prospect of some people performing to us, though, is the prospect of people performing to themselves. Contra Caldwell's media professionals, our respondents had little to gain *from us*, but a self-deceptive performance might help them keep in tact certain constructions of who they are. In saying this, too, I do not mean to allege necessary "delusion," as instead I believe that we all regularly deceive ourselves, constructing versions of who we would like to be, even if only to deal with some of the inherent tensions faced by a postmodern, fractured identity and with the challenges of fully knowing ourselves and being able to articulate precisely why we do and feel everything we do.[46] Matt Hills has noted that "the belief that fans can fully account for their fandoms [is] a 'fallacy of internality,'"[47] and it is extravagant to assume that dislikers would be any better endowed than fans with the ability to account entirely for their actions.

Rather than necessarily posit—in the absence of strong evidence—instances in which my respondents "lied" to themselves, instead I point to some moments when it was precisely the multiplicity of dislike that resulted in ambivalent reactions, when they offered more than one reason for dislike, thereby demanding that I as analyst wonder which if any of those reasons was primary, which secondary. Such moments were particularly evident when respondents offered both an aesthetic reason to dislike and a political reason. In such cases, the political reason was regularly presented as key, but I was left naggingly wondering which came first: Did the interviewee dislike the show for more personal, aesthetic reasons, then embrace a political reason to dislike, or did the political dislike initiate a search for structural, aesthetic reasons to dislike too?

Consider, for instance, Charlie's account of his dislike of *Game of Thrones*:

CHARLIE: *Game of Thrones* is not, in my opinion, a particularly good piece of television. And everybody treats it like it's literally the best television show that existed. . . . I think if something is filmed a certain way, like, if it's filmed in a cinematic style, I would say, everyone thinks, "Oh, this is quality television!"

INTERVIEWER: And that bugs you?

CHARLIE: It does! Because we all know . . . that there are many distinct styles, and I think videographer style is underrepresented—but that's not important. What's important is that I think a lot of people just like it because it's really violent and has a lot of sex in it, and they try to use the fact that it's filmed professionally to justify their [fandom], when the plot is nothing special.

Only later in his interview, conducted with his partner, Trent, did both Charlie and Trent note concerns with the show's sexual violence. When they did so, however, it's unclear to me whether the charge of sexual violence was a convenient weapon to wield against a popular show that they thought "everybody" liked, when they simply did not care for it, or if their aesthetic concerns overlaid their political concerns. Hills has written of fans' "discursive mantras,"[48] easy and commonly shared explanations for why one loves what one loves, and we might note that some dislikers will have their own mantras, forcing the listener to sort out whether the mantra is legitimately felt or a better attack. Charlie and Trent are not alone here, as most of the feminists who reported *Game of Thrones*' sexual violence as a "deal-breaker" surrounded their critiques of its sexual violence with commentary on not liking fantasy as a genre, on not appreciating its narrative style, or on other aesthetic-affective responses that similarly left me wondering how to allot blame for their dislike.

Melanie offered a similar doubled-up reason for disliking Taylor Swift. "My thing with Taylor Swift," she said, warning, "I'm going to get slightly political, but she preaches about being this feminist icon, but her feminism isn't intersectional. And she uses this as a cover for her poor song lyrics, and all of her songs are, like, four chords. So I'm just not a big fan of her music and her cultural relationship with sexism." Two reasons to dislike Swift are presented, one because "her feminism isn't intersectional," the other because "all of her songs are, like, four chords." Does

Melanie "weigh" these evenly, though: is one the greater crime, or is one simply a cover for the other? Patricia offers yet another example, noting a dislike for *Girls* and that most of her distaste for the show "just comes from Lena Dunham," in a way that would seem to center Dunham as prime offender. But when the interviewer asked about her history with *Girls*, she reflected about what happened when she started watching: "I don't know, it just didn't really hold my interest for very long. And then all—Lena Dunham started saying all this stuff that really rubbed me the wrong way, and so I just never [returned]." Here, Lena Dunham's comments are presented as arriving after the fact: Patricia already disliked the show, since "it just didn't really hold [her] interest," but she then found a political objection to the show, such that she leads with that objection to the interviewer.

I repeat that I am not charging my interviewees with lying. On the one hand, I imagine that many of them might struggle themselves to adjudicate precisely how much they react to a show on the basis of one reason, how much on the basis of another reason. That is because, on the other hand, their comments suggest to me the degree to which dislikes are cancerous, metastasizing into other realms. The show that one dislikes because it seems poorly told can draw critical attention, especially if it is popular, encouraging one to dig deeper for political objections. Or vice versa. And thus we should expect that many dislikers will present a range of reasons to dislike. For the analyst, it would be lovely to find some magical means of sorting them out, and sometimes their narratives of dislike seem to present a linearity to the types of and reasons for dislike, as with Patricia. But even narratives can be told differently later in time, such that ultimately no magical means exist. Instead, this should signal the need to listen to all of a disliker's stated reasons for disliking and to think multidimensionally about the disliked objects' many stated crimes.

A utility of being skeptical and thinking multidimensionally would be to help us better unpack, deconstruct, and challenge a specific type of clear deception, that of fauxtrage. Here I refer to publicly shared "outrage" that announces one line of exuberant critique, even while additional reasons for dislike seem more or as decisive. So, for example, Fox News' pundits regularly rail at athletes or Hollywood stars trying to insert themselves into politics or at films or television shows with obvious political views, in a way that stages a performance of their supposed belief that the field of entertainment should be distinct from the field of politics. Laura Ingraham, in particular, infamously instructed LeBron James to "shut up and dribble." Not only does this betray a radical misunderstanding of the inseparability of entertainment and politics, but the performance is usually staged only in response to left-wing athletes or stars trying to insert themselves into politics, whereas Tom Brady's or Jon Voight's conservative statements are regarded lovingly. Political reasons for dislike, in short, are buried, to proffer an ethic of entertainment-politics field separation that is unevenly applied.

One also sees fauxtrage most clearly in attacks on young women singers, who are freely accused of all manner of ills from commentators who seem quite obviously to also or instead dislike them intensely because of the young femininity and often young sexuality that the women represent and champion. Or similarly, a thriving, bubbling racism regularly undergirds the continual assault on the supposed moral ills of rap and hip hop. Kimberlé Crenshaw offers the specific example of 2 Live Crew's obscenity case, agreeing that the band's *As Nasty as We Wanna Be* contained misogynist lyrics but noting that the charges against the band members were filed because they were Black.[49] Rap and hip hop are regularly charged with sexism in such fauxtrage campaigns that awkwardly seek to place a feminist mask over a racist face.[50] When we hear or discern multiple reasons for dislike, we need not excuse one as entirely inauthentic per se, but a more careful analysis of the fauxtraged speaker's words and rhetoric may well be in order to unpack the fullness of what they are saying. Discursive mantras can circulate widely, and though they help some who invoke them to articulate the previously unarticulated, they are also available to be used as masks, producing a situation in which the landscape of dislike is fraught terrain.

The Sociality of Dislike

Another key form of multiplicity comes at the level of the group or community, as each individual's reasons for dislike interact with others'. My project design didn't allow us to see this process in action, given that I opted for individual, not group, interviews. Subjects' dislikes surely would have interacted with others' outside the interview, but unless they reflected on and recounted these experiences, I had less to work with. And yet still, the sociality of dislike erupted through some interviews and transcripts, reminding me how important it is. I heard it, as charted in chapter 1, in how audiences' dislikes were nearly always premised on the assumption of a text's general approval by others, of its social centrality, and in how audiences regularly turned casual, mundane dislike into principled, engaged dislike when their social surroundings subjected them to repeated exposure to the offending text. I heard it, as charted in chapters 2 and 3, in how audiences regularly discussed dislikes as doing harm not just to them but to their communities and in how some audiences therefore greatly appreciated being able to share their reasons for dislike with others. I heard it, as charted in chapter 4, in the performances of identity that were regularly directed outward, requiring an audience of their own. But to say that dislike is social means that it will at times be constructed socially, deliberated on, and thus for the remainder of this chapter, I will turn to some of the few moments when interviewees discussed the social construction of dislikes, wherein their own reasons for dislike were forced to interact with and overlay others' reasons for dislike and/or with others who actively liked the text. I work with less data here, though, and hence I submit a humble request for intrigued readers to do more work into the sociality of dislike, so that collectively we can better understand how dislike and like "face off" against each other, how communities of dislike and like interact, and what etiquette is foisted on the disliker by their social situations.

I start by echoing my comments in the conclusion to chapter 4 regarding the silences of dislike, noting that some interviewees expressed significant discomfort at the notion of sharing their dislikes with others, if those others were presumed even potentially to be fans or casual likers. For many, then, the "sociality" of their dislike, and its interaction with others' opinions, was a quiet one, personally negotiated. For instance, Barry noted, "A lot of times I'm sitting around after golf league socializing and someone will say something, and I'm just like, 'ignore.' I don't comment on it," since "the moment is inappropriate. If I would bring up what I object to, it would be more challenging. So the particular social setting I'm in, it wouldn't fit." He quickly revised this to allow that even outside this group setting, "there are other cases where I'm sitting down to dinner with another couple and he'll bring up something, and I'm just like, eh, I don't want to get into something. It's just not the appropriate setting." Later, too, he noted that when discussing things with his daughter-in-law, he absolutely must bite his tongue, or else they're "going to have a fight about it," so instead the two of them try their best to avoid any and all discussions about potentially divisive dislikes. Andrea similarly noted an overarching preference not to discuss her dislikes, except with a very few people, self-reflecting that her dislikes regularly produce "a shutdown moment" for her: "I leave the room in those situations if I can."

While Andrea's choice of terminology suggested self-criticism, and while others described their acquiescence and silence regretfully, clearly wanting and preferring that they could speak up, several respondents framed their own discomfort with conflict over dislikes in more positive terms. Greta, for instance, described her choice not to engage others in discussion about dislikes with a sense of a personal ethic of self-care: "I've found it's far more effective to not patronize something you don't like rather than try to fight it actively, which tends to suck you into the dynamic that you don't like in the first place." Candice, for her part, focused on strategy; although she will speak up occasionally, she insisted, "I do try to be very careful about who I say something to. It's gotta be somebody I'm very close with because . . . you can almost alienate people [more] than you can draw them in. I try to keep my sensitivities and my perspective to myself a good chunk of the time. I kind of believe in a less is more." Melanie, too, saw more likelihood for a profession of dislike to backfire, saying, "I feel like when people have a thing, like a program that is their baby, they kind of take it as a personal offense if you don't like it. So I'd rather just try to see why they enjoy it than making them feel bad about their taste, like, 'Oh, your taste is so horrible. Let's watch something I would watch instead.'" And Molly spoke forcefully of how "you can only fight so many battles in your life," so you need to "pick your battles."

Admittedly, some other respondents either used little restraint in debating their dislikes with others or actively relished combat. Ellen noted matter-of-factly, "I've been having a lot of fights recently about superhero movies. After I saw *Guardians of the Galaxy 2* with my friends, I thought it wasn't a great movie, like, it didn't have a strong plot, blah blah blah. They were all upset that I would have that type of opinion because they're like, 'Superhero movies are just fun. Just have fun and don't dissect the plot or go into anything,' which is sort of how I watch things. I'm a very critical, analytical person." She later confessed, "I kind of like it when people don't love the things that I love because then it starts to seem like it's more unique to me, like it's more, like, a part of—well, I like this, and if you don't, that just means we're different. It's like I'm not just going with the crowd. I have my own interests." Mark was more abrasive in noting, "I have no problem telling someone to their face if something sucks. . . . I get why you might, but I think it's trash." And just as those who were reticent to engage in disagreements with others could sometimes undergird that decision with a personal ethic, so too could those who engaged others more commonly. Thus, Patricia explained why she would regularly share her dislikes: "I almost think that it's, like, important—I think if I were to just stop watching it, that wouldn't really have much of an effect on anything, but I think . . . that's almost more important to have, like, a discussion about it rather than to just, like, stop watching it."

Outside my data, too, we need look only to the success of some censorship or activist campaigns to see how dislikers can, in the right circumstances, wield and weaponize their dislike to great effect. Martin Barker, Jane Arthurs, and Ramaswami Harindrinath document how arguably the strongest effect of a censorship campaign surrounding David Cronenberg's adaptation of J. G. Ballard's novel *Crash* came not from succeeding in banning the film, as the film was still released in many markets, but in surrounding the film with an air of its being a perverted film about perverted people. Based on their interviews with audiences, Barker et al. note that all the talk about the film often served "to so overload the film with expectations that *Crash* could not survive the demands made of it—perversely, especially where those demands were that it be thoroughly pornographic, gory, and awful."[51] Thus, the censorship campaign applied a filter of interpretation and expectation that even many who seemingly rejected the campaign accepted, namely, that this was a risqué, seedy film whose primary purpose was to foreground and lovingly study nonnormative sexual behavior. Even to these viewers, the film often couldn't be much else. Jason Mittell reminds us that precisely because genres are discursive categories, they are prone to definition from dislikers as much as from fans, and he backs up this contention in a chapter analyzing audience definitions of soap opera. "Even if they had never seen an episode of a soap opera," he writes, "they had effectively absorbed [critical, dismissive] central assumptions and generic conventions by being part of a culture that uses the generic category broadly to demean anything that is seen as narratively drawn-out or excessively sentimental."[52] And Lori Kido Lopez charts the growth and evolution of Asian American media activism that has, in Barker et al.'s terms, similarly "overloaded" some texts—or that seeks to overload them—with its criticism of offensive depictions.[53] In such instances, we see the possibilities of dislike, when it is martialed into campaigns or when it circulates throughout the discursive operating system of a society or community.

More simply and intimately, many of our respondents detailed instances when they were able to impact others with their dislike. Molly had a general policy of "picking her battles"; but one such battle was waged against *Caillou*, and she playfully recounted how her own dislike for the show "infected" her child: "She's heard me talk about people who don't like it, so she always says she doesn't want to watch it just because she's picked up on me talking about how other people talk about it.... We'll see *Caillou*, and she'll go, 'Nooooo! Not *Caillou*!'" Like Molly, many of the parents among our respondents spoke with pride of instances when they were able to curtail their children's viewing or to otherwise steer them clear of especially disliked entities. Ivy, meanwhile, talked from the perspective of someone whose dislikes had been heavily affected by what she read on Tumblr and by what she heard in her university classes. She said, "[Tumblr] definitely brought me towards feminism and being more like critical about things. And also in, like, my television and film classes, like, we dissect things all the time." And Zoey's interview offered multiple instances of her nominating shows that she "knew" were "bad" and antifeminist, because friends had warned her away from them. Of *Game of Thrones*, for instance, she claimed that she "really wanted" to watch it, but she said, "The last year or two, I have heard a lot about, like, the gratuitous rape scenes in *Game of Thrones*, so . . . I don't really, like, need to watch that." *Girls* and *The Bachelor* had similarly gone unwatched, though Zoey could detail reasons why the interviewer should also not watch them, based on recommendations and critiques from friends.

To note that a spectrum exists, ranging from intense discomfort with conflict to impassioned insistence on engaging those who have contrary viewpoints, and hence from affecting nobody with one's dislike to actively infecting many with it, is in and of itself unremarkable and wholly to be expected. However, I do so in part to note what should be a similarly unremarkable truism in audience studies, namely, that different audience members' opinions take on different social status and power, as some people try to foster interpretive communities while others stay away from the fray. Barry, Andrea, Greta, Candice, Melanie, and Molly all offered us pictures of themselves as playing little to no role in the spread and replication of their dislikes, whereas, by contrast, Ellen, Mark, and Patricia all embraced the challenge of spreading their dislikes. Or, to shift to the language of Horace Newcomb and Paul Hirsch's theory of media's "cultural forum,"[54] not everyone chooses to or can engage in the cultural forum equally. As several scholars have documented, in the realm of politics proper, many people choose to be quiet, to lie low, and not to contribute to the forum.[55] And similarly, when discussing the variously political or apolitical pleasures and displeasures, objections and agreements, with popular culture and media, again many audience members will lie low. I framed this book in my introduction, in Couldryian terms, as in part an attempt to hear these often silent voices, but many of them insisted that they more regularly keep their silence.

As such, further study of the sociality of dislike would need to consider who is more likely to be quiet, who is more likely to speak up. Dan Sperber poses this as a challenge for ethnography in general, noting that the world is full of meaning, full of cultural representations, but a key question for the anthropologist should be to ask, "Through which process of selection, as a function of what factors, does a tiny fraction of all the mental representations that humans build become shared cultural representations, and invade, either temporarily (rumors, fashions), or lastingly (traditions) the networks of social communication? A cultural anthropology must comprise—I am tempted to say, must be—an epidemiology of ideas."[56] Or within textual studies, Stanley Fish's notion of "interpretive communities" garnered significant attention, with its suggestion that interpretation is rarely wholly personal, instead enacted through groups with shared tools for analysis and meaning creation.[57] Applying this idea to audience studies, David Morley poses "a model of the audience, not as an atomized mass of individuals, but as a number of sub-cultural formations or groupings of 'members' who will, as members of those groups, share a cultural orientation towards decoding messages in particular ways."[58] However, while Fish postulates interpretive communities without much consideration of how such communities begin, end, gain or lose members, and interact with each other, the interest in people, communities, and audiences that the likes of Sperber and Morley propose demands attention to precisely those dynamics, asking who are the Marks or Patricias who actively engage others in an attempt to win them over to their interpretive communities and who are the Barrys or Andreas who don't. Who determines the discursive mantra of a community, who commands the cultural forum, and who doesn't?

Alas, I again note that I have no firm, heavily data-driven answer to this question, as much as I'd love to see others engage in such an "epidemiology of ideas." Rather, then, as I edge toward the end of the book, I edge toward the requests for future work that often accompany a project's closing. But I will note with concern that since functionally many dislikes will need to live through the social and hence through interpretive communities, we have a situation in which many progressive dislikes will variously be deflected or silenced by their normative, hegemonic counters, whether those counters take the form of fandom and approval or of alternate reasons to dislike.

Ilana offers us an image of the former process in action, when she noted how a group of her friends went to watch *Kid Cannabis*. She described the show as "the worst." But she "just quietly disliked it": "I sat on my phone. I think all the boys liked it and all the girls didn't because afterwards we were like, 'What the hell did we just watch?'" This comment echoes Melanie's earlier-quoted story (from chapter 1) of watching movies with friends and needing to take off her "feminist goggles." These two women's silence, in short, allowed the men and their approval of the media in question to command their respective social groups. Or we might compare them to the women profiled in Alfred Martin's examination of Tyler Perry antifandom and their own discomfort with speaking up about how much they disliked Perry, and especially his portrayal of Black women, for fear of angering friends and family.[59] In my own study, Vincent echoed these women, for while he at first noted an overarching willingness and even enthusiasm for engaging others in debate with regard to his dislikes, he then noted of his dislike for the "white-centricity" of *Grey's Anatomy* and *American Horror Story*,

> When I'm around someone who does like the show, that mind-set can be a problem, especially if someone who likes the show is Black. Because then it's almost like I'm making the claim that you like everything white and you don't like things that are Black. It's almost like I'm trying to box in the identities of Blackness and disregard the complexities of Black identity. So that could be an issue for reasons I don't have to expand too much into. So it can be a problem, and sometimes in order to avoid that problem, I will just resign myself to not expressing my thought on a show.... If I'm in a space with someone, I'll just bear that show, if I value being in a space with someone and just enjoying having a moment with that person more than enjoying the show.

In short, Vincent's ethic of not wanting to "box in the identities of Blackness" leads this African American man to self-censor his critique of shows he sees as white-centric and to back away from engaging others with opinions that may sway their own. In such cases, we see how the presumed social etiquette of (not) voicing dislike may regularly allow the status quo to go unchallenged, even when silently disliked.

Disagreements do not simply occur between fans and dislikers, though, and my data offered several windows into the awkward mechanics of negotiating reasons for dislike. Earlier in the chapter, I quoted Melanie's reasons for disliking Taylor Swift, but after discussing her own doubled-up reasons, she also discussed other people's reasons for disliking Swift: "I know other people who dislike her but because she's been with so many guys and, like, she's 'easy,' but then they're also contributing to the problem of sexism by saying that. And especially with big celebrities like that, it's easy to attach the label of not liking someone almost out of jealousy because they never have to confront them. They'll just be, like, 'Oh, Taylor Swift is so stupid.'" And thus Melanie was quite aware that any expression of her dislike for Swift may need to be explained and elaborated on, lest those other reasons be presumed.

Daniel, too, discussed at length his dislike of *The Force Awakens* but felt the need to defend his dislike and to distinguish it from other reasons for disliking the film up front. "I really hated *The Force Awakens*," he insisted but then quickly added, "but not in the same way as you're probably seeing online. It's awesome, really, that Star Wars isn't just about a whole bunch of white people and that the new Jedi is a woman. I want to defend it for that, 'cause there are so many trolls and racists and assholes on Twitter and pretty much everywhere actually that, like, that clearly hate it because it's not all white, all male. That's not me." Instead, he offered another well-traveled critique of the film, namely, that it's "just" a nostalgic remaking of *Star Wars Episode IV: A New Hope*, and he complained about what he saw as director J. J. Abrams's lack of artistic vision and unwillingness to take risks with the franchise. "*The Phantom Menace*," he said, "was shit, but at least [George] Lucas was rolling the dice. Not Abrams," he declared. However, Daniel explained:

> It's hard to say I don't like this crap movie, except to my good friends, since, like, people must totally think that I'm a racist, sexist jerk. I mean, that's what they hear and read, right? That the movie sucks 'cause, like, it has a Black stormtrooper or 'cause there's a strong woman who could kick Luke or Anakin's asses. I hate the jerks saying that crap. I mean, I hate them 'cause they're stupid racists. But I also hate them 'cause now I can't talk about the film and why I don't like it without people looking at me wrong.

The interviewer asked if he'd interacted with any such dislikers, and this set him off again:

> Oh, oh, yeah. I hate that too. Like, I met this guy, and we got to talking about the movie 'cause he had a Star Wars T-shirt on and I commented about it. He, like, asked if I saw this one [*The Force Awakens*] and what I thought of it, and for this minute we were bonding, 'cause we both hated the crap out of it. But then—this is bad—then he goes and says some crap about hating Finn and Rey, and all of a sudden I'm getting suspicious. I'm wanting to talk about artistic vision and taking chances and doing something, and he's now just, like, railing against "political correctness," and, uh, like, it was *ugly*. I really wanted to get out of that conversation quick, so I just looked at my watch and acted like it was time to go see my sister.

Both Melanie and Daniel, then, found themselves in uneasy coalitions of dislikers, where Melanie's more progressive, feminist reasons for disliking Taylor Swift encountered a more regressive, misogynist reason or simply "jealousy" of stars, while Daniel's more aesthetic concerns came up against the sort of misogynist, racist rationale for disliking *The Force Awakens* that is discussed in chapter 3. Of concern, though, both noted extraction and removing themselves from the discussion as their adaptive responses.

Melanie and Daniel contrast with Kyle, who strongly disliked *The Beguiled*, offering nominally aesthetic reasons that quickly betrayed an intense dislike of and disrespect for its director, Sofia Coppola. Kyle, though, was aware that popularly the film had been criticized heavily for removing Black characters and one character in particular from the original, a charge that Kyle found specious. To Kyle, Coppola probably had nothing to offer the character anyway—"you can't be mad that a fork's not a spoon," he said—but he discussed actively engaging people with that critique. Even though he too disliked the film, he felt the need to "set the record straight" about precisely *why* people should dislike it. He didn't recall ever having such a discussion with another disliker, but he nevertheless generalized from this experience, noting a desire to intervene in future such debates: "I think I would defend it, even a film I really didn't care for, from what I thought to be unfair critique. I think I would do that. In the case of *The Beguiled*, I don't think I did. I wasn't all that fired up about it, but I don't like when I think that a critique is unfair. That really bothers me even if I didn't care for the thing at all. So I probably would step in. I can't think of an example where I would step in, but I could definitely see myself doing that." It's thus a pity that in the three clearest examples presented to us of "coalitions of dislike," the two dislikers whose reasons for dislike challenged a regressive status quo were moved to silence, while the disliker most likely to challenge others' reasons was one who wanted to challenge concerns for diversity and equitable representation. Obviously, we cannot use three people alone to draw grand conclusions here, and I would love to see future research on the topic; but in concert, the three cases left me worried that progressive reasons for dislike, and the kind of enunciations I've attempted to focus on in this book, may face strong headwinds from within a community and coalition of dislike itself, before even being presented to fans or more neutral parties. Melanie and Daniel may, in short, have opened a window for us not simply into how dislikes interact with each other but also into how and why so many dislikers' voices remain relatively silent and unheard in the first place.

Conclusion

Any audience research requires a lot of interpretation, and this project has been no exception. However, if there is a key conclusion to this chapter, it is that singular interpretations will regularly be insufficient, requiring second, third, or subsequent additional levels of analysis and interpretation. Dislike can perform who one is or who one thinks one should be; dislike is a response to feeling forced to engage; dislike identifies texts that represent larger pains and grievances; dislike can be a yearning for something the text is not offering; dislike can be a letdown from something once loved; dislike can fight back against annoyances; dislike can be joyful and laughing even while pained; dislike can be aestheticized; or dislike can be a combination of any of these. Dislikes interact with each other, moreover, and with likes and pleasures, in a plenitude of ways that should deny us the comfort of applying just one interpretation to a dislike and that should always ask for more. Thus, while each chapter of this book has aimed to offer ways of "hitting media studies' dislike button" and of engaging with dislike further, this present chapter both offers yet more ways—centering the joys of dislike, intersectional performances of dislike, and the social negotiations of dislike—and makes a plea for interactive approaches that consider dislike as regularly working in many ways at the same time for the same person.

Conclusion

The Rhythms of Dislike

To conclude this book, I want to cast some lines out from its focus on dislike of media entertainment to consider what could be learned about the broader cultural context in which media dislike nestles. Kurt Vonnegut quipped that "any reviewer who expresses rage and loathing for a novel or play or a poem is preposterous. He or she is like a person who has put on full armor and attacked a hot fudge sundae or a banana split."[1] However, throughout this book, I've attempted to show that far more than tilting at hot fudge sundaes is going on when dislikers articulate their concerns, annoyances, and grievances with various texts. But what might this study of our armored ice cream antagonists tell us about citizenship and dislike outside "just" the media frame? Embedded in Nicholas Abercrombie and Brian Longhurst's deceptively simple statement that "in contemporary society, everyone becomes an audience all the time" or in S. Elizabeth Bird's somewhat similar proclamation that "the 'audience' is everywhere and nowhere" is the notion that audiences are representative and reflective of citizens.[2] Audiencing and audience behaviors are indicative of, and can tell us a great deal about, being a citizen in general. What, then, does this study of textual, media dislike indicate about how dislike, annoyance, intolerance, anger, and displeasure work in general?

In recent years, numerous scholars have shown us how meaningfully a better understanding of *fans* can inform a better understanding of citizenship. "In its proliferation, its growing importance in the construction of identity and its social and cultural classification," Cornel Sandvoss writes, "fandom has something to say about the very substance, premises, and consequences of everyday life,"[3] and Sandvoss is one of numerous scholars whose work has drawn direct lines between fan practices and citizenship.[4] However, if the study of fandom tells us a lot about engagement, passion, commitment, love, and enthusiasm, our "mattering maps," as Lawrence Grossberg calls them,[5] are incomplete without attending also to dislike, alienation, displeasure, annoyance, and anger. Grossberg writes, "How a specific text is used, how it is interpreted, how it functions for its audience—all of these are inseparably connected through the audience's constant struggle to make sense of itself and its world, even more, to make a slightly better place for itself in the world,"[6] and in so doing, he draws a direct line between the study and consideration of audiences—of any ilk, whether fan, nonfan, or disliker—and consideration of how we interact with the world around us. That line may be short and straight in some instances, as audiencing immediately and directly impacts acts of citizenship, or it may be long and winding in other cases. But acts of audiencing always carry with them the potential to be sites at which larger commitments variously begin, amplify, quieten, or end, such that audience behavior is often a rich site both for feeling the tremors and after effects of the political realm—the realm where groups make decisions and work toward turning thought, belief, and conviction into action—and in turn for feeling where various tremors that will in due course hit the political realm originate.

Jeffrey Jones notes that "daily citizen engagement with politics is more frequently textual than organizational or 'participatory' in any traditional sense. For better or worse, the most common and frequent form of political *activity*—its actual practice—comes, for most people, through their choosing, attending to, processing, and engaging a myriad of media texts about the formal political process of government and political institutions as they conduct their daily routines," for it is these that "constitute our mental maps of the political and social world outside our direct experience. They provide a reservoir of images and voices, heroes and villains, sayings and slogans, facts and ideas that we draw upon in making sense of politics."[7] Jones here privileges texts about "the formal political process of government and political institutions," but if we allow for politics to include identity politics and the politics of the personal, then an even wider range of texts—along with our reactions to them—network our inner lives to the political world around us.

At various points throughout this book, I have gestured to ways in which our interview subjects connected their targeted dislikes of specific texts to broader concerns about society and culture, to their place in or alienation from various communities, to their individual and communal attempts to create a sense of identity, and to their hopes and fears for the world around them. Granted, I have not followed these acts to A Political Outcome or to activism. Only a tiny few of my subjects spoke of activism or other organized political action based on or strongly connected to their dislike. And thus, on the one hand, if I now wish to insist that their actions and beliefs are connected to the political realm, I am doing so somewhat speculatively and must leave this as a hypothesis to be tested by others. I would love to see a flourishing of studies of dislike and politics to match the flourishing of studies of fandom and politics. As I have been writing the book, I have often heard echoes of its contents in the political world around me. Chapter 2, for instance, charts how unmet expectations and disappointments regularly fostered the more vociferous, deeply felt dislikes, and it was hard not to see a parallel in how many people talked about the Democratic primary process in the United States in early 2020, with more bile, more charges of racism and sexism, more concern about "selling out" and abandoning a more righteous cause regularly directed by self-identifying Democrats toward other Democratic candidates and their supporters than toward Donald Trump and his base. Or chapter 4 poses that our dislikes give us identity, and in the political realm, again one can regularly hear stronger articulations of identity posed through declarations of dislike, as subjects parse out what is wrong with various candidates and their platforms, than through noting what is virtuous, noble, or preferable about other candidates. And if chapter 5 calls for attention to the complexities and multiplicities of dislike, all of the aforementioned discourses often cry out for thoughtful unpacking in terms of their various contributing feeds, even in the face of political opposition that often woefully and deliberately "hears" expressions of dislike as more singular, less complex than is the case. In short, everything I've been examining and saying about dislike of texts could, at least in theory, have application to dislike of policies, candidates, and platforms and may help us distinguish between various vocabularies, modalities, and motivations behind an agora that is full of dislike.

On the other hand, though, we risk belittling people if we do not count their opinions as mattering until we see them acted on in ways we personally consider appropriate political action. In calling for more work into dislike and organized politics,[8] therefore, I don't wish to imply that dislike is worthy of attention only if and when the analyst can see it feeding *directly* into the realm of organized political action. This conclusion also argues, then, that we need to reappraise the role that expressions of dislike play in discussions about the cultural world writ large, such that we might connect them more *indirectly* to political action and to a general cultural citizenship, as well.

As scholars drawing lines between fandom and politics have themselves encountered, the headwinds into which any attempt to connect audiencing and citizenship must march consist of a long-standing suspicion of the presence of *any* emotions in the political realm. Buoyed by a wholly unscientific distinction between heart and mind, a great deal of political theory fetishizes rationality, believing it both possible and preferable for political thinking to be rational but never emotional. Jürgen Habermas was by no means the first to subscribe to this notion,[9] but his theorization of the public sphere enshrined for contemporary media and communication studies a particular idealization of rationality, given the degree to which he sees no room for emotions therein.

The Habermasian romanticization of rationality and suspicion of emotions, though, have come under heavy and justified critiques from some people. Nancy Fraser's infamous rejoinder to Habermas already noted that the public sphere's theorization excludes women, the poor, and many others, along with issues germane to them and their lives.[10] John Hartley builds on Fraser by castigating the "male nobility model of the public sphere" that separates "rationality" from "emotions" in large part by segregating "public" and "rational" concerns from "personal" and "emotional" ones in highly gendered, highly problematic ways.[11] In short, he shows that the division of the world into rational or emotional issues already enacts an insidious hiving off of women's issues. George E. Marcus, for his part, helpfully consults science on brains to show that far from allowing reason to work independently of emotions, our brains require the two to work together and don't even *allow* a Cartesian mind-body split. "Emotion systems enable reason," he notes, and he offers practically that "politics most often is at least initiated by emotion. Politics often begins with the pursuit of some local interest or grievance . . . which to become political demands specific emotional support, courage to confront those often more powerful whom one decides to oppose, or sympathy that attracts one to join someone else's fight."[12]

More recently, Karin Wahl-Jorgensen has similarly argued, "The insistence on the primacy of rationality, the undesirability of emotion and subjectivity reifies the liberal binary between rationality and emotion. In doing so, it obscures the messiness and conflict that inevitably characterize political discussion. . . . Such a position is not only at odds with lived realities, but also fails to reflect the ways in which we actually come to understand and appreciate the experiences of other people."[13] Wahl-Jorgensen thus turns to a variety of emotions and their place in journalism and political reporting in particular. Of particular relevance to my interests here, Wahl-Jorgensen veers away from some of her predecessors in examining not just love, like, and fandom but also dislike and anger. In doing so, she reconsiders anger, refusing to see it as only and always an impediment to rational deliberation, instead dubbing it "a political resource which is based on the public articulation of shared grievances."[14] For better or worse, she concludes, "anger"—which she defines as more communal by nature, less individualized—may indeed be "the essential political emotion . . . because it energizes groups of individuals towards a collective response to shared grievances."[15]

Wahl-Jorgensen's willingness to consider anger as a legitimate entity opens a door for us to consider dislike in general as a "political resource." To go through that door, though, we must first once more distinguish between dislike and hate. The anger of hate is one type of political resource, as it mobilizes animosity and aggression toward groups of people, and many politicians have attempted to harness this animosity, whether through a shared hatred of those groups and a shared wish to eliminate or otherwise traumatize them or through cynical promises to do so. By contrast, the anger of dislike ("based on the public articulation of grievances"), I hope to have shown, can be a powerful resource for uncovering reparative visions, yearnings for better ways, and silenced or quietened pains. We will obviously not all agree which of those visions, ways, and pains should guide us, so dislike is by no means a progressive force in and of itself. But some dislikes, some angers of dislike, can be progressive and can be the site for us to hear what is wanted from many whose marginalization has resulted in their exclusion from politics.

These dislikes are spoken emotively, hence violating Habermas's concern regarding emotions and the "irrational," but as Peter Stallybrass and Allon White note acerbically, "It is indeed one of the most powerful ruses of the dominant to pretend that critique can only exist in the language of 'reason,' 'pure knowledge' and 'seriousness.'"[16] Dislikes are spoken in a "negative" register, not in the supposedly more "constructive," "positive" language of likes. They may sound like snobbery to ears trained by Bourdieu. And since they may have built up over time, causing yet more frustration and alienation, they may at times be impolite, rude, profane, and/or caustic. But as communities of listeners—which cultural studies academics should be—we should challenge ourselves to listen beyond the possible rudeness, profanity, and actual or perceived snobbery of dislike's frames and modes to hear what is being said. By developing a richer understanding of dislike, moreover, we might better play a role in helping others to understand and appreciate how the angers of dislike work.

Dislike's "negativity," rudenesses, and incivility should not deter us. Granted, defenses of civility are at times crudely mobilized to defend the angers of hate. But drawing from Michael Schudson, Zizi Papacharissi notes that critiques of incivility also too often aim to curtail what it is possible to say and to limit who can lodge their grievances.[17] Political activists have repeatedly needed to challenge calls for "civility," and in doing so, they give us a vocabulary for valuing the adoption of a negative, emotional register that focuses on what is wrong and what is missing. In "The Uncivil Tongue," Nina M. Lozano-Reich and Dana Cloud criticize "invitational" models of deliberation by noting that the uninvited and excluded may by nature need to be rude, "uncivil," and confrontational to be heard. Women of color, they decry, "have been silenced through civilizing strategies . . . [such that] it has taken decades of critical feminist scholarship to resist politics of civility and overcome oppressive stereotypes so that women of color can be viewed as speaking subjects, and not as uncivilized subjects needing a firm hand."[18] Marginalized individuals and communities have often been shamed into silence through reprimands to an impolite, uncivil, insufficiently "respectable" mode of registering complaint, so that form negates substance.[19] Papacharissi thus encourages us to regard rudeness, negativity, or incivility as entirely acceptable *if the substance requires it*, and her litmus test is whether an utterance aims to challenge and improve civil society, not whether it is couched in friendly, chummy terms.[20] In a powerful article on "the uses of anger" to women of color, Audre Lorde proclaims, "We cannot allow our fear of anger to deflect us nor to seduce us" into silence, for "it is not the anger of other women that will destroy us, but our refusal to stand still to listen to its rhythms, to learn within it to move beyond the manner of presentation to the substance, to tap that anger as an important source of empowerment."[21]

Heeding this call to listen to the anger of dislike's rhythms, in this book, I have aimed to push through concerns about dislike's form to examine the substance beneath. Admittedly, most of my respondents were not shouting their dislikes on the streets, choosing instead to be quieter with their dislikes. But if our culture doesn't know how to listen to dislikes, we should not be surprised by many dislikers' choice to lie low. Let us return briefly to Sara Ahmed's feminist killjoy, who refuses to stay silent as her family makes sexist assertions at the dinner table. Ahmed champions the killjoy and her willfulness:

> We have to become willful, perhaps, to keep going the way we are going, if the way you are going is perceived to be "the wrong way." We all know the experience of "going the wrong way" in a crowd. Everyone seems to be going the opposite way than the way you are going. No one person has to push or shove for you to feel the collective momentum of the crowd as a pushing and shoving. For you to keep going you have to push harder than any of those individuals who are going the right way. The body "going the wrong way" is the one that is experienced as "in the way" of the will that is acquired as momentum. For some bodies mere persistence, "to continue steadfastly," requires great effort, an effort that might appear to others as stubbornness or obstinacy, as insistence on going against the flow. You have to become insistent to go against the flow; you are judged to be going against the flow because you are insistent. A life paradox: you have to become what you are judged as being.[22]

This focus on the killjoy's or disliker's impact on and interactions with others might then allow us a broader interpretation of Ahmed's proposal that "one feminist project could be to give the killjoy back her voice."[23] For if expressions of dissatisfaction, alienation, anger, annoyance, and dislike are truly to be given voice, this requires that we know how to listen and know how to allow the disliker passage rather than contributing—knowingly or not—to the momentum that resists them.

This book has aimed to contribute to this project of giving dislikers their voice by offering ways in which we can hear value, depth, and meaning in that voice. Many others are working on this project of amplifying citizens' voices, so my saber-rattling here comes not from the front lines. From my position in a rear flank, though, I've seen and heard too many voices excused when they work within dislike's register, suggesting to me that we still don't truly understand and appreciate that register. Let media and cultural studies not contribute to the momentum working against the disliker, then, cued only by the Bourdieuian suspicion of dislike and what it has to tell us. Let us instead find more ways to give the voices of dislike and disapproval passage. In making this argument, I have tried to find in dislike a world of reactions to our lived environments that may otherwise go undetected and unobserved. At one level, I hope that by doing so, I have offered some ways of thinking about and interpreting dislike that could be exported out of the realm of textual dislike to reconsider how dislike, anger, annoyance, and alienation are articulated in society more broadly. If we can hear what is being said when someone calls Caillou "a whiny little piece of crap," castigates *Basketball Wives* as "the worst mess on television" that is "horrible, horrible, horrible," or dismisses *Family Guy* as being "a combination of fart jokes and really low-grade dick jokes," perhaps this will set us on a path toward understanding better what is being said in protests and expressions of political dislike, even if they too are couched in profane, negative, emotional, and/or excessive terms.

I would hope this book's focus on textual dislike might open up doors for understanding dislike more generally. But at another level, and more humbly, "dislike more generally" was not its topic, as instead it has been about textual, media dislike. Here, I hope to have offered some ways to hear more than just snobbery. To a degree, the book has been a "defense" of dislike; but I do not wish to swing the pendulum too far the other way, and here I wish to acknowledge yet again that some expressions of dislike are purely snobbish, dismissive, aggressive, toxic, and/or outright abusive. As Papacharissi asks us to do with expressions of political dislike, though, I ask us not to stop at the form and instead to listen to whether and when something more meaningful and more important is being uttered (and if not, let us move on).

Pierre Bourdieu, and the fear of being snobs, may have scared us away from hearing what else dislike has to tell us. But Charlotte Brunsdon offers an important reminder in her own work on discourses of quality, namely, that while, in the wake of Bourdieu, "'quality,' for some good reasons, has become a bad word," the "consequence of this is that only the most conservative ideas about quality are circulating, and will therefore win the day."[24] Later, she adds, "we do not defeat the social power which presents certain critical judgments as natural and inevitable by refusing to make critical judgments," and she underlines that "it is not the exercise of judgment which is oppressive but the withholding of its grounds."[25] These words were rewritten on the second page of a notebook I kept as a graduate student, in which I wrote down smart thoughts from smart people. They have inspired a lot of my thinking on this topic, as they lay down an admittedly challenging gauntlet: to recognize that some dislikers are snobs, are giving voice to regressive beliefs, are silencing others with their voices but also to appreciate that other dislikers have much to tell us, and thus we cannot simply ignore the disliker. As an entire "outrage industry" thrives,[26] and as the internet seems ever fuller of "dark participation,"[27] we cannot throw out the baby of progressive dislikes and the complexities therein with that dark bathwater. To hear what progressive dislikes are saying—to return to Nick Couldry's terms—we need to listen beyond the roar of the traffic, to acknowledge dislike not just as the absence of like, not as an always-already "negative" and destructive mode, but at least potentially as a legitimate, "positive," and constructive reaction and expression that is common to all our textual travels.

ACKNOWLEDGMENTS

I start these acknowledgments by extending thanks to the University of Wisconsin–Madison and the Wisconsin Alumni Research Foundation for supporting my research so generously through a Romnes Faculty Fellowship and a Vilas Mid-Career Investigators Award. The funds that accompany the Hamel Family Distinguished Chair pulled everything across the finish line, too, so my humble thanks are also extended to the Hamel family for their generosity and support of my department and of me.

My other key and considerable debt of gratitude must be paid to the wonderful research assistants who worked on this project, finding people to talk to, interviewing them, and all the while learning on the job how to get better and better. In Malawi, Stanslous Ngwire had uncanny powers to get people to open up. In the United States, I benefited immensely from being able to talk everything through with Sarah Murray in the project's early days and to learn from her perceptive, expansive commentary and analysis. It is no wonder, then, that her comments on a full draft of the book were, years later, immeasurably helpful. Nicholas Benson, Jacqueline Land, Caroline Leader, Abigail M. Letak, Taylor Cole Miller, and Tony Tran were all superb too. Audience research is arduous, challenging work, yet all showed themselves beautifully adept; and if this book took a while to write, it's in part because they offered me such a wealth of material to work through and consider. And thanks to Leah Steuer for reading through a stack of lit for me and for explaining its plumbing.

Wrestling with that material when it came in and knowing what questions to ask in the first place were tasks aided by a cadre of amazing colleagues. Nick Couldry always sees the bigger frames and stakes in my work and always helps direct me to them. Melissa Click has never stopped challenging me to think more and better about dislike. Matt Hills was one of the very first people to encourage me to do more with dislike, and his work lights a path forward. Aswin Punathambekar has been a constant and sustaining source of critical questioning, helpful ideas, and big-picture thinking. And Adrienne Shaw's insights about audiences and methodology always school me in the best ways.

Every one of my coauthors and coeditors for my scholarly work has pushed me to be better and opened new doors for me; thanks therefore go to Robin Andersen, Nicholas Benson, Kristina Busse, Bertha Chin, C. Lee Harrington, Kyra Hunting, Derek Johnson, Jeffrey P. Jones, Amanda D. Lotz, Nick Marx, Taylor Cole Miller, Jason Mittell, Sarah Murray, Amanda Ochsner, Laurie Ouellette, Meagan Rothschild, Cornel Sandvoss, Adrienne Shaw, Ethan Thompson, and Dannagal Young. Thanks also go to those who questioned me at Chinese University of Hong Kong, Drexel University, Indiana University, Microsoft Research New England, Soochow University, University of California at Los Angeles, University of Michigan, University of Sunderland, Yunnan University, and numerous conferences.

Chapter 2 draws in small part from work previously published with Sarah Murray in "Hidden: Studying Media Dislike and Its Meaning," *International Journal of Cultural Studies* 19, no. 4 (2016), while one section of chapter 4 includes some material previously published in "Scales of Cultural Influence: Malawian Consumption of Foreign Media," *Media, Culture & Society* 36, no. 7 (2014). Thanks to Sage and Murray for allowing me to use that work again here. And many thanks to Eric Zinner, NYU Press's truly wonderful editor.

More generally, the spirit of pushing, prodding, polishing, and perfecting ideas that pervades the weekly Media and Cultural Studies Colloquium at UW-Madison has helped me in so many ways, and I'm thankful to every faculty member, grad student, and visitor who has helped keep that spirit alive but especially to Michele Hilmes for her instrumental role in modeling best practices for, well, absolutely everything. My Media and Cultural Studies colleagues in Madison are second to none. I would be truly lucky to have just one of Eric Hoyt, Derek Johnson, Jason Kido Lopez, Lori Kido Lopez, or Jeremy Morris as a friend and colleague, but to have had them all has been gloriously gluttonous. I have benefited from their intellects, their wisdom, and their supreme competence but also from how simply awesome they are as friends. I've shared many a Manhattan, joke, Indian buffet, rant, taco, or game of

BSG, *Betrayal*, or *Dominion* with them. They've seen "Dark Jonathan" but are instrumental in rescuing me from his grasp and in keeping me happy and hopeful. Derek in particular has been a supremely generous, wise, thoughtful, and brilliant presence whose counsel and friendship I profit from constantly: I could write a full acknowledgments section extolling just his virtues alone.

The MCS graduate students have been an amazing lot. I've learned as much from my advisees as I could hope they'd learn from me and thus wish to thank in particular Kim Bjarkman, Erin Copple Smith, Camilo Díaz Pino, Evan Elkins, Elizabeth Ellcessor, Daphne Gershon, Kyra Hunting, Wan-Jun Lu, Nick Marx, Myles McNutt, Taylor Cole Miller, Sarah Murray, Laura Schumacher, Matt Sienkiewicz, Leah Steuer, and Tony Tran for their ideas, friendship, and tolerance. Thanks, too, to Andrew Bottomley, Christopher Cwynar, Kit Hughes, Nora Patterson, and Jennifer Smith, who have all been especially sterling colleagues and friends, and to all the MCS graduate students with whom I've shared Vilas Hall.

Three other comrades in arm have kept me going, transitioning seamlessly from discussing heavy ideas to everything else that matters. Speaking with David Craig always makes me feel better about things, even if we're bemoaning all the things; he embodies intellectual curiosity and collegial enthusiasm, while making me laugh a lot. Amanda Lotz is the pacesetter to beat all pacesetters, in part because she's so adept at cutting out and/or working around the crap, even while acknowledging it when it needs to be acknowledged. When I grow up, I want to be more like Amanda. Jeffrey Jones "gets" me and opened up countless extra doors for me by inviting me into the Peabody world, but even long before that, he'd always been the superb friend, listener, and motivator that he's steadfastly remained.

Thanks also go to my family: my parents, Anne Gray and Ian Gray; my wife, Monica Grant; and the dynamo of warmth, energy, boundless love, curiosity, silliness, imagination, cool dance moves, and goodness that is my daughter, Abigail Gray. Monica and Abby had to share me with this book for too long: thanks for your patience, love, and support. *Dislike-Minded* is dedicated, though, to my brother, Matthew Gray, since it began with him. Matt can offer the most hilarious and graphic denunciations of countless media, and this book started as an exercise in trying to appreciate the complexity and legitimacy of his critiques.

NOTES

INTRODUCTION

1. Lamere 2009.
2. See Nakamura 2016.
3. For more on the fallibility and skew of social media metrics, see Baym 2013.
4. Miller 1988, 31.
5. Barker and Brooks 1998, 6.
6. Willard Gaylin, cited in Sternberg and Sternberg 2008, 16.
7. Sternberg and Sternberg 2008, 16.
8. Otto Kernberg, cited in Sternberg and Sternberg 2008, 17; see also Niewert 2009.
9. Sternberg and Sternberg 2008, 19.
10. See Ahmed 2004a, 2004b.
11. Sternberg and Sternberg 2008, 59–65, 73.
12. See, in particular, Wanzo 2015; Morimoto and Chin 2017; Pande 2018; Stanfill 2018; Woo 2018; and K. Gray 2020, though obviously some of these scholars' work was shared in conferences prior to publication.
13. See Stanfill 2020b; and Proctor and Kies 2018b.
14. See, in particular, Phillips 2015; and Buckels, Trapnell, and Paulhus 2014.
15. Mortensen 2018; see also Chess and Shaw 2015.
16. Pande 2018; Salter and Blodgett 2017; Scott 2019; Holladay and Click 2019.
17. For a fuller account, I cosign some of Carl Wilson's more involved critique. See Wilson 2007.
18. Jane 2014, 2019.
19. J. Gray 2003, 2005.
20. Jane 2014, 177.
21. J. Gray 2005, 851–52.
22. J. Gray 2003.
23. Jenkins 1992; Fiske 1989b.
24. Jenkins 1992, 18, 23.
25. Penley 1997, 3.
26. Jenkins 1992, 23.
27. See Jenkins 2006.
28. obsession_inc 2009.
29. See, for instance, Busse 2013.
30. Stein 2019, 83.

31. Jenkins 1992, 18.
32. Bourdieu 1984.
33. Bourdieu 1984, 7.
34. Fiske 1987, 1989a, 1989b; Radway 1987; D'Acci 1994; Jenkins 1992.
35. Morley 1992, 30.
36. Fiske 1989a.
37. Hoggart 1957; Hall and Morley 2018.
38. Couldry 2003, 2.
39. Couldry 2003, 11.
40. Couldry 2006, 1–2.
41. Couldry 2006, 3.
42. Couldry 2006, 7.
43. Radway 1988.
44. Hill 2019, 11.
45. Halberstam 2011; Griffin 2017, chap. 4.
46. Gray and Murray 2016.
47. Since being gay is a punishable offense in Malawi, we did not ask about sexual identification.
48. Asking about citizenship in the current political climate strikes me as invasive, so we never inquired about nationality.
49. Jane 2014, 186.
50. I also encouraged each of my US interviewers to name subjects themselves, partly so that confidentiality could be maintained to an even more stringent degree (I do not know the real names of my subjects), partly so that we could experiment with different naming strategies. One of my interviewers developed a novel way of pseudonymizing that warrants sharing. Taylor Cole Miller used pseudonyms as an ice-breaker, asking his subjects early in the interview to come up with a name based on their media consumption. He would then ask them to explain why they chose that name, thereby artfully kicking off discussion, asking a quick question about fandom, and allowing the subject to choose their own name. Other interviewers had their own systems, but in each case I encouraged interviewers to devise the system beforehand, so that names would be assigned more or less randomly (although within gender identification), rather than trying to match a name to an interviewee.
51. I did not feel culturally knowledgeable enough to rename the Malawians myself, and I could not reach Ngwire to solicit names from him.
52. Since most of the interviews were conducted by others, now that I have introduced my interviewers, I will often refer to "our" (not "my") respondents telling "us" (not "me") something, but to be clear, only one interviewer was present in any interview.
53. Nooney 2013; Anable 2018, 3, 5.
54. Practically, too, I wanted to be an ethical employer, allowing graduate students to benefit from the experience of conducting interviews not "only" by gaining

experience soliciting and conducting interviews but also by—in most cases—helping them to garner data for their own projects, in the process ensuring that my personal research funding could supplement the comparatively smaller funds they had from other sources.
55. I coded the interviews myself, by hand and without software help, a process that required me to read each transcript many times over but that therefore helped me to get a better sense of the texture of comments and of the various speakers, such that when I selected a quotation from their interviews, I understood the context in which it was spoken.
56. Ngai 2005, 7. See Ahmed 2004b especially for her own stellar exploration of hate.
57. See Gregg and Seidworth 2010, for instance.
58. Anable 2018, viii–ix.
59. Cavalcante 2018, 22.

CHAPTER 1. THE AUDIENCE FOR DISLIKE

1. Andreeva and Johnson 2019.
2. Television by the Numbers 2015.
3. McIntyre 2019.
4. Barthes 1977, 157, 162, 163.
5. Barthes 1973.
6. Barthes 1977, 164.
7. Genette 1997.
8. For more on media paratexts, see J. Gray 2010.
9. Genette 1997, 3.
10. Genette 1997, 408.
11. Bennett and Woollacott 1987; Bakhtin 1981; Volosinov 1973; Kristeva 1980.
12. Couldry 2000, 70–71.
13. J. Gray 2010.
14. Ahmed 2010b, 31.
15. Barthes 1977, 164.
16. Certeau 1984; Fiske 1987; Jenkins 1992.
17. See Pande 2018 for a more resounding challenge to the assumed progressivism of fandom.
18. Condit 1989, 110.
19. Fiske 1989b, 37.
20. Fiske 1989b, 35.
21. Livingstone 1990, 18.
22. Abercrombie and Longhurst 1998, 107.
23. see, in particular, Bausinger 1984; Morley 1986, 1992.
24. Morley 1992, 215.
25. Ahmed 2010a, 1–2.
26. Ahmed 2010a, 3.

27. See A. Gray 1992; Radway 1987.
28. Silverstone 1999, 138.
29. Hartley 1996, 7.
30. Martin 2019, 176.
31. Martin 2019, 176.
32. Martin 2019, 178.
33. Martin 2019, 178.
34. Ahmed 2010b, 32.
35. Ahmed 2010b, 37.
36. Gilbert 2019, 68.
37. Haggins 2007, 1.
38. Ahmed 2010a, 1.
39. Ahmed 2010a, 3.
40. Cavalcante 2018, 125.
41. Cavalcante 2018, 122.
42. Cavalcante 2018, 124.
43. Cavalcante 2018, 126.
44. See Hochschild 2003 on emotional labor; and Cavalcante 2018, 130, on affective resilience.
45. Cavalcante 2018, 139.
46. See Bonilla-Silva 2019; Wilkins 2012.
47. Bausinger 1984, 349; Morley 1986.
48. Wilson 2007, 3.
49. De Kosnik 2018, 262.
50. Romano 2013.
51. Frith 2004, 32.
52. Frith 2004, 33.
53. Quoted in Morley 2000, 151.
54. Bodroghkozy 1992.
55. Ngai 2005, 3.
56. Lewis 1991, 134.
57. Rorty 1992, 102–3.
58. Fish 1980b, 74.
59. Fish 1980b, 77.
60. Iser 1980, 56.
61. Mittell 2004, 105.
62. Couldry 2000, 70–71.
63. Hill 2019, 59–60.
64. See Habermas 1989.
65. Newcomb and Hirsch 1983.
66. See Dahlgren 1995; Hartley 1996; J. Jones 2004; Van Zoonen 2004.

CHAPTER 2. WHAT'S WRONG AND WHAT'S MISSING

1. Silverstone 1994, 3.
2. In this respect, enunciations of dislike are not unique, nor do I mean to suggest as much: fan objects are regularly loved for things they're perceived to be doing that other texts aren't.
3. Silverstone 1994, 40.
4. Willis 1990, 2; Hermes 2005, 3.
5. Hartley and Potts 2014, 71.
6. Silverstone 1994; Winnicott 1974.
7. Hills 2002, 108.
8. Ahmed 2010b, 29, 34.
9. Ryan and Kellner 1988, 77.
10. Sandvoss 2005, 96.
11. Sandvoss 2005, 100.
12. Barker and Brooks 1998, 60.
13. Silverstone 1999, 55.
14. Certeau 1984.
15. Fiske 1989b, 10–11, 28.
16. Radway 1987.
17. D'Acci 1994, 195–98.
18. Jenkins 1992, 27, 284.
19. Jenkins 1992, 114.
20. Bobo 1995.
21. Busse 2017.
22. Buckingham 1987; Fiske 1989a.
23. Ang 1985; Katz and Liebes 1990.
24. Gillespie 1995.
25. See obsession_inc 2009.
26. Scott 2019.
27. Pande 2018, 44, 109, 110.
28. Shaw 2014.
29. Penley 1997, 3; Stein 2019, 83.
30. McCulloch 2019, 229.
31. Cavalcante 2018, 13, 68.
32. Cavalcante 2018, 68.
33. Cavalcante 2018, 71.
34. Cavalcante 2018, 133.
35. Cavalcante 2018, 134.
36. Coleman 1998, 176, 179.
37. Coleman 1998, 183.
38. Cornwell and Orbe 2002, 35.
39. Gilbert 2019, 66.

40. Kimberlé Williams Crenshaw coined "intersectionality" to consider how race, gender, class, and sexuality interact to shape the multiple dimensions of especially Black women's lives (Crenshaw 1989), though the term now generally refers to similarly multidimensional accounts and considerations of identity. Here these women bemoaned the lack of shows considering feminism from a woman-of-color perspective.
41. Rivera 2019, 184.
42. Rivera 2019, 185.
43. Shaw 2014, 41.
44. Coleman 1998; Cornwell and Orbe 2002.
45. Warner 2015, 137.
46. Gates 2018, 176.
47. See, for instance, hooks 1992; H. Gray 1995; Smith-Shomade 2012; Martin 2019, 2021; K. Gray 2020.
48. For a fuller explanation of respectability politics, especially as regards Black women, see Higginbotham 1992. I use the term, though, to refer to requirements, imposed from within the community as much as from without at times, that Black women "uplift" themselves with their speech, dress, sexual behavior, and general comportment.
49. Gates 2018, 180–81.
50. Click and Smith-Frigerio 2019.
51. Radway 1987, 50.
52. Eliasoph 1998. See also Croteau 1995; Hay 2007.
53. Eliasoph 1998, 19.
54. Eliasoph 1998, 22, 63.
55. Theodoropoulou 2007.
56. J. Gray 2019.
57. Yin 2020.
58. Higginbotham 1992.
59. McRobbie 2009, 18.
60. Ahmed 2010a, 3.
61. See Petersen 2017.
62. See Warner 2015.
63. For a wonderful account of media activism, for contrast, see L. Lopez 2016.

CHAPTER 3. FALLEN FROM GRACE, OR, WHEN SEQUELS ATTACK

1. Reinhard 2018, 14.
2. D. Johnson 2007.
3. See, for instance, Blodgett and Salter 2018; K. Gray 2020; Harman and Jones 2013; Hills 2018; D. Johnson 2013b, 2018; P. Johnson 2020; G. Jones 2018; Pande 2018; Proctor and Kies 2018a; Salter and Blodgett 2017; Scott 2019; Stanfill 2020a.
4. Jenkins 1992.
5. Hills 2005a.

6. See especially Rebecca Williams 2015, 28–30.
7. See, for instance, Forrest and Koos 2002; Hassler-Forest and Nicklas 2015; Heinze and Krämer 2015; Hutcheon 2006; D. Johnson 2013a; Loock 2014; Loock and Verevis 2012; Rosewarne 2020; Sanders 2015; Verevis 2006.
8. Burke 2015, 130.
9. Barker and Brooks 1998, 154.
10. Barker, Arthurs, and Harindrinath 2001, 137.
11. Chin and Gray 2001.
12. See Amesley 1989; Saler 2012.
13. Shaw 2014.
14. Hills 2015, 577–78.
15. J. Gray 2010.
16. See Barker and Mathijs 2016.
17. Berardinelli 2012.
18. O'Hehir 2012.
19. Gonzalez 2012.
20. Stevens 2012.
21. Uhlich 2012.
22. Hornaday 2012.
23. Corliss 2012.
24. Foundas 2012.
25. Stanfill 2020a.
26. Sandvoss 2005, 104–5.
27. Menta 2017.
28. Moye 2017.
29. Tran 2018.
30. See Yamamoto 2017.
31. Scott 2019.
32. See D. Johnson 2018.
33. See Bradley and Jacobs 2017.
34. Morten Bay's (2018) analysis of *Last Jedi* hatred quantifies some of these comments as coming from Russian bots, presumably designed to amplify antagonisms among the US population; but some is not all, and it worked by amplifying what was already there.
35. See Blodgett and Salter 2018; B. Jones 2018.
36. D. Johnson 2018, 87.
37. Scott 2019; Pande 2018.
38. Jane 2019, 56–57.
39. Holladay and Click 2019.
40. Jane 2019, 43.
41. Bollas 1993, 269.
42. Hills 2017, 221.
43. Hills 2017, 222.

CHAPTER 4. PERFORMING IDENTITY THROUGH DISLIKE

1. Bourdieu 1984.
2. Bourdieu 1984, 7.
3. Bourdieu 1984, 92.
4. Bourdieu 1984, 66, 26.
5. Bourdieu 1984, 53, 28.
6. For examples of this, see Levine 1990.
7. Bourdieu 1984, 57.
8. Raymond Williams 1958; Hoggart 1957; Thompson 1963.
9. Willis 1990; Hall 1980; Morley and Brunsdon 1999; Brunsdon 1997; Fiske 1989a, 1989b.
10. Jenkins 1992, 16.
11. Alters 2003.
12. Gilbert 2019, 69.
13. Gilbert 2019, 71.
14. Gilbert 2019, 74.
15. Jensen 1992.
16. Pearson 2019, 216.
17. Newman and Levine 2012, 2.
18. Newman and Levine 2012, 2, 3.
19. Fiske 1989b; Glynn 2000.
20. Fiske 1992; Thornton 1996, 11.
21. Harman and Jones 2013, 952.
22. Huyssen 1986.
23. See Bryson 1996.
24. See Adorno and Simpson 1941; Arewa 2006, 2013.
25. See also Jones 2015.
26. See, respectively, Hobson 1987; Radway 1987; Fiske 1989a; Jenkins 1992.
27. See Bourdieu 1993, 2002.
28. Newman and Levine 2012, 7.
29. Newman and Levine 2012, 74.
30. ADrinkWithDave 2011.
31. Schroeder 2012.
32. Savage et al. 2013.
33. Wilson 2007, 99.
34. This section draws from research previously published in J. Gray 2014.
35. See, for example, Artz and Kamalipour 2003; Golding and Harris 1993; Hamm and Smandych 2005; Herman and McChesney 1997; Katz and Liebes 1990; Mattelart 1983; Schiller 1976; Sreberny-Mohammadi 1997; Tomlinson 1997.
36. These locations were selected for me, not with any particular rationale, since I was following my wife's project.

37. I would regularly identify myself as Canadian, and my knowledge of and interest in soccer during Euro 2008 and the World Cup in 2010 signaled in other ways that I wasn't a usual American; but I was still aware that a white man with a seemingly US accent asking about interactions with US media might elicit particular responses, whereas Ngwire could solicit different responses.
38. Here I discuss responses to film and television, though for a discussion of music consumption and of how it gave rise to performances of regional identities, see J. Gray 2014.
39. Gillespie 1995.
40. See also B. Jones 2015.
41. Hermes 2005, 4.
42. Jenkins 1992, 2006.
43. See Jenkins 1992.
44. Fiske 1989b.
45. Gillespie 1995; Lembo 2000.
46. Abercrombie and Longhurst 1998, 97.
47. Sandvoss 2005, 48, 64–65.
48. Butler 2006, xv.
49. Butler 2006, xv.
50. Warhol 2003.
51. Hills 2005b, ix.
52. Hills 2005b, xi, citing Hills 2002, 159.
53. Quoted in Morley 2000, 96.
54. Quoted in Harman and Jones 2013, 961.
55. Holladay and Click 2019, 147, 148, 149.
56. For more on the hegemonic presence of such judgments, see Petersen 2017.
57. Martin 2019, 170.
58. Martin 2019, 171.
59. Joseph 2018, 3, 15.
60. On respectability politics, see Higginbotham 1992.
61. Joseph 2018, 132.
62. Rivera 2019, 193.
63. Rivera 2019, 195.
64. Slang for "fresh off the boat," often a phrase of derision directed at newer arrivals from older, more-established immigrant communities and individuals in Vancouver.
65. T. Tran 2020.
66. Ahmed 2010a, 2.
67. R. Peterson 1992, 254.
68. See Anable's discussion of "groping in the dark to sense the embodied and structural limits of what media histories and analyses can reveal" and "to explore a potentially vast space that can be apprehended only a small section at a time" (2018, 3, 5).
69. See, for instance, Bhavnani 1991; Croteau 1995; Eliasoph 1998; Hay 2007.

CHAPTER 5. THE MULTIPLICITIES OF DISLIKE

1. Wilson 2007, 11, 76.
2. Ebert 2007, 2012, 2013.
3. Ebert 2007, 126, 21.
4. Ebert 2007, 138.
5. Ebert 2007, 73.
6. kermodeandmayo 2010.
7. Smith 2014.
8. Jenkins, Ford, and Green 2013.
9. Ebert 2007, 68.
10. Ebert 2007, 72.
11. Ebert 2007, 268.
12. See Sontag 1964; Ross 1989.
13. Juul 2013, xi.
14. Juul 2013, 2, 34.
15. Juul 2013, 2.
16. Juul 2013, 30.
17. Juul 2013, 26.
18. Juul 2013, 50.
19. Frith 2004, 19.
20. Halberstam 2011.
21. Hill 2015, 176.
22. Sconce 2007, 275.
23. Sconce 2007, 276.
24. Ngai 2005, 271.
25. Ngai 2005, 261–62.
26. Ahmed 2004b, 29.
27. Gilbert 2019, 63.
28. Joseph 2018, 120.
29. Joseph 2018, 121, 125.
30. Sontag 1964; Ross 1989.
31. Test 1991, 14.
32. Goldfarb 1991, 1, 10–11.
33. Bakhtin 1981, 23.
34. Bakhtin 1981, 23.
35. Bakhtin 1984, 21, 122–23.
36. See, for instance, Sloterdijk 1987.
37. Phillips 2015, 29.
38. Phillips 2015, 30.
39. Scott 2018, 144–45.
40. Phillips 2018.
41. See, for instance, Harman and Jones 2013.

42. For more on intersectionality, see Crenshaw 1989.
43. Geertz 1993, 9.
44. Caldwell 2008, 3.
45. Morley 1992, 156–57.
46. For more on self-deception, see J. Lopez 2016.
47. Hills 2002, 68.
48. Hills 2002, 67.
49. Crenshaw 1997.
50. See McRobie 2008.
51. Barker, Arthurs, and Harindrinath 2001, 35.
52. Mittell 2004, 176.
53. L. Lopez 2016.
54. Newcomb and Hirsch 1983.
55. See Bhavnani 1991; Croteau 1995; Eliasoph 1998; Hay 2007.
56. Sperber 1991, 30.
57. Fish 1980a.
58. Morley 1992, 54.
59. Martin 2019.

CONCLUSION

1. Vonnegut 1999, 124.
2. Abercrombie and Longhurst 1998, 68; Bird 2003, 3.
3. Sandvoss 2005, 4.
4. See also J. Gray 2007; De Kosnik 2017; Hinck 2019; Jenkins and Shresthova 2012; Jenkins, Peters-Lazaro, and Shresthova 2020; Punathambekar 2007; Sandvoss 2012; Van Zoonen 2004; Wahl-Jorgensen 2019.
5. Grossberg 1992, 57.
6. Grossberg 1992, 53.
7. J. Jones 2004, 16–17.
8. See Sandvoss 2019 for an example.
9. Habermas 1989. For brief histories of the dualism in thinking about politics between rationality and emotions, see both Papacharissi 2015, 9–12; and Wahl-Jorgensen 2019, 20–36.
10. Fraser 1992.
11. Hartley 1996, 71.
12. Marcus 2002, 75, 45.
13. Wahl-Jorgensen 2019, 25.
14. Wahl-Jorgensen 2019, 92.
15. Wahl-Jorgensen 2019, 169, 170.
16. Stallybrass and White 1986, 43.
17. Schudson 1997; Papacharissi 2004.
18. Lozano-Reich and Cloud 2009, 223–24. See also Zagacki and Boleyn-Fitzgerald 2006; Solomon 1988.

19. See Anzaldúa 1999; Bederman 1995; Ehrenreich and English 2005; Higginbotham 1992; Oravec 2003.
20. Papacharissi 2004.
21. Lorde 1997, 281, 282.
22. Ahmed 2010a, 6.
23. Ahmed 2010a, 3.
24. Brunsdon 1997, 124.
25. Brunsdon 1997, 130.
26. Berry and Sobieraj 2014.
27. Quandt 2018.

REFERENCES

Abercrombie, Nicholas, and Brian Longhurst. 1998. *Audiences: A Sociological Theory of Performance and Imagination*. London: Sage.
Adorno, Theodor, and George Simpson. 1941. "On Popular Music." *Studies in Philosophy and Social Science* 11 (1): 17–48.
ADrinkWithDave. 2011. "MON March 28: Premiere Episode/Gil Ozeri." YouTube, March 29, 2011. https://www.youtube.com/watch?v=fE9UYGskoec.
Ahmed, Sara. 2004a. "Affective Economies." *Social Text* 22 (2): 117–39.
———. 2004b. *The Cultural Politics of Emotion*. New York: Routledge.
———. 2010a. "Feminist Killjoys (and Other Willful Subjects)." *Scholar and Feminist Online* 8 (3): 1–8. http://sfonline.barnard.edu.
———. 2010b. "Happy Objects." In *The Affect Theory Reader*, ed. Melissa Gregg and Gregory J. Seidworth, 29–51. Durham, NC: Duke University Press.
Alters, Diane. 2003. "'We Hardly Watch That Rude, Crude Show': Class and Taste in *The Simpsons*." In *Prime Time Animation: Television Animation and American Culture*, ed. Carol A. Stabile and Mark Harrison, 165–84. London: Routledge.
Amesley, Cassandra. 1989. "How to Watch *Star Trek*." *Cultural Studies* 3 (3): 323–39.
Anable, Aubrey. 2018. *Playing with Feelings: Video Games and Affect*. Minneapolis: University of Minnesota Press.
Andreeva, Nellie, and Ted Johnson. 2019. "Cable Ratings 2019: Fox News Tops Total Viewers." *Deadline*, December 27, 2019. https://deadline.com.
Ang, Ien. 1985. *Watching Dallas: Soap Opera and the Melodramatic Imagination*. Translated by Della Couling. London: Methuen.
Anzaldúa, Gloria. 1999. *Borderlands / La Frontera: The New Mestiza*. San Francisco: Aunt Lute Books.
Arewa, Olufunmilayo B. 2006. "From JS Bach to Hip Hop." *North Carolina Law Review* 84:5–642.
———. 2013. "Making Music: Copyright Law and Creative Processes." In *A Companion to Media Authorship*, ed. Jonathan Gray and Derek Johnson, 69–87. Malden, MA: Wiley-Blackwell.
Artz, Lee, and Yahya R. Kamalipour, eds. 2003. *The Globalization of Corporate Media Hegemony*. Albany: SUNY Press.
Bakhtin, Mikhail Mikhailovich. 1981. *The Dialogic Imagination*. Translated by Caryl Emerson and Michael Holquist. Edited by Michael Holquist. Austin: University of Texas Press.

———. 1984. *Rabelais and His World*. Translated by Hélène Iswolsky. Cambridge, MA: MIT Press.
Barker, Martin, Jane Arthurs, and Ramaswami Harindranath. 2001. *The Crash Controversy: Censorship Campaigns and Film Reception*. London: Wallflower.
Barker, Martin, and Kate Brooks. 1998. *Knowing Audiences: Judge Dredd, Its Friends, Fans and Foes*. Luton, UK: University of Luton Press.
Barker, Martin, and Ernest Mathijs, eds. 2016. "The World Hobbit Project." Special issue, *Participations: Journal of Audience and Reception Studies* 13 (2).
Barthes, Roland. 1973. *Mythologies*. Translated by Annette Lavers. St. Albans, UK: Paladin.
———. 1977. "From Work to Text." In *Image Music Text*, translated by Stephen Heath, 155–64. Glasgow: Fontana Collins.
Bausinger, Herman. 1984. "Media, Technology and Everyday Life." *Media, Culture and Society* 6 (4): 343–51.
Bay, Morten. 2018. "Weaponizing the Haters: *The Last Jedi* and the Strategic Politicization of Pop Culture through Social Media Manipulation." ResearchGate, October 2018. www.researchgate.net.
Baym, Nancy. 2013. "Data Not Seen: The Uses and Shortcomings of Social Media Metrics." *First Monday* 18 (10). https://firstmonday.org.
Bederman, Gail. 1995. *Manliness and Civilization: A Cultural History of Gender and Race in the United States, 1880–1917*. Chicago: University of Chicago Press.
Bennett, Tony, and Janet Woollacott. 1987. *Bond and Beyond: The Political Career of a Popular Hero*. London: Macmillan.
Berardinelli, James. 2012. "The Hobbit: An Unexpected Journey." *Reel Reviews*, December 10, 2012. www.reelviews.net.
Berry, Jeffrey M., and Sarah Sobieraj. 2014. *The Outrage Industry: Political Opinion Media and the New Incivility*. New York: Oxford University Press.
Bhavnani, Kum-Kum. 1991. *Talking Politics: A Psychological Framing for Views from Youth in Britain*. Cambridge: Cambridge University Press.
Bird, S. Elizabeth. 2003. *The Audience in Everyday Life: Living in a Media World*. New York: Routledge.
Blodgett, Bridget, and Anastasia Salter. 2018. "*Ghostbusters* Is for Boys: Understanding Geek Masculinity's Role in the Alt-Right." *Communication, Culture and Critique* 11 (1): 133–46.
Bobo, Jacqueline. 1995. *Black Women as Cultural Readers*. New York: Columbia University Press.
Bodroghkozy, Aniko. 1992. "'Is This What You Mean by Color TV?' Race, Gender, and Contested Meanings in NBC's Julia." In *Private Screenings: Television and the Female Consumer*, ed. Lynn Spigel and Denise Mann, 143–68. Minneapolis: University of Minnesota Press.
Bollas, Christopher. 1993. *Being a Character: Psychoanalysis and Self Experience*. New York: Routledge.
Bonilla-Silva, Eduardo. 2019. "Feeling Race: Theorizing the Racial Economy of Emotions." *American Sociological Review* 84 (1): 1–25.

Bourdieu, Pierre. 1984. *Distinction: A Social Critique of the Judgement of Taste*. Translated by Richard Nice. London: Routledge and Kegan Paul.

———. 1993. *The Field of Cultural Production*. New York: Columbia University Press.

———. 2002. *Masculine Domination*. Translated by Richard Nice. Stanford, CA: Stanford University Press.

Bradley, Bill, and Matthew Jacobs. 2017. "Surprise, Surprise: The 'Alt-Right' Claims Credit for 'Last Jedi' Backlash." *Huffington Post*, December 20, 2017. www.huffpost.com.

Brunsdon, Charlotte. 1997. *Screen Tastes: Soap Operas and Satellite Dishes*. London: Routledge.

Bryson, Bethany. 1996. "'Anything but Heavy Metal': Symbolic Exclusion and Musical Dislikes." *American Sociological Review* 61 (5): 884–99.

Buckels, Erin E., Paul D. Trapnell, and Delroy L. Paulhus. 2014. "Trolls Just Want to Have Fun." *Personality and Individual Differences* 67:97–102.

Buckingham, David. 1987. *Public Secrets: East Enders and its Audience*. London: BFI.

Burke, Liam. 2015. *The Comic Book Film Adaptation*. Jackson: University Press of Mississippi.

Busse, Kristina. 2013. "Geek Hierarchies, Boundary Policing, and the Gendering of the Good Fan." *Participations: Journal of Audience and Reception Studies* 10 (1). www.participations.org.

———. 2017. *Framing Fan Fiction: Literary and Social Practices in Fan Fiction Communities*. Iowa City: University of Iowa Press.

Butler, Judith. 2006. *Gender Trouble*. New York: Routledge.

Caldwell, John Thornton. 2008. *Production Culture: Industrial Reflexivity and Critical Practice in Film and Television*. Durham, NC: Duke University Press.

Cavalcante, Andre. 2018. *Struggling for the Ordinary: Media and Transgender Belonging in Everyday Life*. New York: NYU Press.

Certeau, Michel de. 1984. *The Practice of Everyday Life*. Translated by Steven F. Rendall. Berkeley: University of California Press.

Chess, Shira, and Adrienne Shaw. 2015. "A Conspiracy of Fishes, or, How We Learned to Stop Worrying about #GamerGate and Embrace Hegemonic Masculinity." *Journal of Broadcasting and Electronic Media* 59:208–20.

Chin, Bertha, and Jonathan Gray. 2001. "'One Ring to Rule Them All': Pre-viewers and Pre-texts of the *Lord of the Rings* Films." *Intensities* 2. www.cult-media.com.

Click, Melissa, and Sarah Smith-Frigerio. 2019. "One Tough Cookie: Exploring Black Women's Responses to *Empire*'s Cookie Lyon." *Communication, Culture & Critique* 12:287–304.

Coleman, Robin R. Means. 1998. *African American Viewers and the Black Situation Comedy: Situating Racial Humor*. New York: Garland.

Condit, Celeste Michelle. 1989. "The Rhetorical Limits of Polysemy." *Critical Studies in Mass Communication* 6 (2): 103–22.

Corliss, Richard. 2012. "*The Hobbit*: Why Go There and Back Again?" *Time*, December 5, 2012. https://entertainment.time.com.

Cornwell, Nancy C., and Mark P. Orbe. 2002. "'Keepin' It Real' and/or 'Sellin' Out to the Man: African-American Responses to Aaron McGruder's *The Boondocks*." In *Say It Loud! African-American Audiences, Media, and Identity*, ed. Robin R. Means Coleman, 27–43. New York: Routledge.

Couldry, Nick. 2000. *Inside Culture: Re-imagining the Method of Cultural Studies*. London: Sage.

———. 2003. *Media Rituals: A Critical Approach*. London: Routledge.

———. 2006. *Listening beyond the Echoes: Media, Ethics, and Agency in an Uncertain World*. Herndon, VA: Paradigm.

Crenshaw, Kimberlé Williams. 1989. "Demarginalizing the Intersection of Race and Sex: A Black Feminist Critique of Antidiscrimination Doctrine, Feminist Theory, and Antiracist Politics." University of Chicago Legal Forum. https://philpapers.org.

———. 1997. "Beyond Racism and Misogyny: Black Feminism and 2 Live Crew." In *Feminist Social Thought: A Reader*, ed. Diana T. Meyers, 246–63. New York: Routledge.

Croteau, David. 1995. *Politics and the Class Divide: Working People and the Middle Class Left*. Philadelphia: Temple University Press.

D'Acci, Julie. 1994. *Defining Women: Television and the Case of Cagney and Lacey*. Chapel Hill: University of North Carolina Press.

Dahlgren, Peter. 1995. *Television and the Public Sphere: Citizenship, Democracy and the Media*. London: Sage.

De Kosnik, Abigail. 2017. "Memory, Archive, and History in Political Fan Fiction." In *Fandom: Identities and Communities in a Mediated Era*, ed. Jonathan Gray, Cornel Sandvoss, and C. Lee Harrington, 2nd ed., 270–84. New York: NYU Press.

———. 2018. "Filipinos' Forced Fandom of US Media: Protests against *The Daily Show* and *Desperate Housewives* as Bids for Cultural Citizenship." In *The Routledge Companion to Media Fandom*, ed. Melissa Click and Suzanne Scott, 262–70. New York: Routledge.

Ebert, Roger. 2007. *Your Movie Sucks*. Kansas City, MO: Andrews McMeel.

———. 2012. *A Horrible Experience of Unbearable Length: More Movies That Suck*. Kansas City, MO: Andrews McMeel.

———. 2013. *I Hated, Hated, Hated This Movie*. Kansas City, MO: Andrews McMeel.

Ehrenreich, Barbara, and Deirdre English. 2005. *For Her Own Good: Two Centuries of the Experts' Advice to Women*. 2nd ed. New York: Anchor Books.

Eliasoph, Nina. 1998. *Avoiding Politics: How Americans Produce Apathy in Everyday Life*. Cambridge: Cambridge University Press.

Fish, Stanley. 1980a. *Is There a Text in This Class? The Authority of Interpretive Communities*. Cambridge, MA: Harvard University Press.

———. 1980b. "Literature in the Reader: Affective Stylistics." In *Reader-Response Criticism: From Formalism to Post-Structuralism*, ed. Jane Tompkins, 70–100. Baltimore: Johns Hopkins University Press.

Fiske, John. 1987. *Television Culture*. London: Methuen.

———. 1989a. *Reading the Popular*. London: Unwin Hyman.

———. 1989b. *Understanding Popular Culture*. London: Unwin Hyman.

———. 1992. "The Cultural Economy of Fandom." In *The Adoring Audience: Fan Culture and Popular Media*, ed. Lisa A. Lewis, 30–49. New York: Routledge.
Forrest, Jennifer, and Leonard R. Koos, eds. 2002. *Dead Ringers: The Remake in Theory and Practice*. Albany: SUNY Press.
Foundas, Scott. 2012. "*The Hobbit*: Slouching toward Erebor." *Village Voice*, December 5, 2012. www.villagevoice.com.
Fraser, Nancy. 1992. "Rethinking the Public Sphere: A Contribution to the Critique of Actually Existing Democracy." In *Habermas and the Public Sphere*, ed. Craig Calhoun, 109–42. Cambridge, MA: MIT Press.
Frith, Simon. 2004. "What Is Bad Music?" In *Bad Music: The Music We Love to Hate*, ed. Christopher J. Washburne and Maiken Derno, 15–36. New York: Routledge.
Gates, Racquel. 2018. *Double Negative: The Black Image and Popular Culture*. Durham, NC: Duke University Press.
Geertz, Clifford. 1993. *The Interpretation of Cultures*. London: Fontana.
Genette, Gérard. 1997. *Paratexts: Thresholds of Interpretation*. Translated by Jane E. Lewin. Cambridge: Cambridge University Press.
Gilbert, Anne. 2019. "Hatewatch with Me: Anti-fandom as Social Performance." In *Anti-fandom: Dislike and Hate in the Digital Age*, ed. Melissa A. Click, 62–80. New York: NYU Press.
Gillespie, Marie. 1995. *Television, Ethnicity and Cultural Change*. London: Routledge.
Glynn, Kevin. 2000. *Tabloid Culture: Trash Taste, Popular Power, and the Transformation of American Television*. Durham, NC: Duke University Press.
Goldfarb, Jeffrey C. 1991. *The Cynical Society: The Culture of Politics and the Politics of Culture in American Life*. Chicago: University of Chicago Press.
Golding, Peter, and Phil Harris, eds. 1993. *Beyond Cultural Imperialism: Globalization, Communication and the New International Order*. London: Sage.
Gonzalez, Ed. 2012. "The Hobbit: An Unexpected Journey." *Slant*, December 8, 2012. www.slantmagazine.com.
Gray, Ann. 1992. *Video Playtime: The Gendering of a Leisure Technology*. New York: Routledge.
Gray, Herman. 1995. *Watching Race: Television and the Struggle for Blackness*. Minneapolis: University of Minnesota Press.
Gray, Jonathan. 2003. "New Audiences, New Textualities: Anti-fans and Non-fans." *International Journal of Cultural Studies* 6 (1): 64–81.
———. 2005. "Anti-fandom and the Moral Text: *Television without Pity* and Textual Dislike." *American Behavioral Scientist* 48 (7): 840–58.
———. 2007. "The News: You Gotta Love It." In *Fandom: Identities and Communities in a Mediated Era*, ed. Jonathan Gray, Cornel Sandvoss, and C. Lee Harrington, 75–87. New York: NYU Press.
———. 2010. *Show Sold Separately: Promos, Spoilers, and Other Media Paratexts*. New York: NYU Press.
———. 2014. "Scales of Cultural Influence: Malawian Media Consumption of Foreign Media." *Media, Culture & Society* 36 (7): 982–97.

———. 2019. "How Do I Dislike Thee? Let Me Count the Ways." In *Anti-fandom: Dislike and Hate in the Digital Age*, ed. Melissa A. Click, 25–41. New York: NYU Press.
Gray, Jonathan, and Sarah Murray. 2016. "Hidden: Studying Media Dislike and Its Meaning." *International Journal of Cultural Studies* 19 (4): 357–72.
Gray, Kishonna L. 2020. *Intersectional Tech: Black Users in Digital Gaming*. Baton Rouge: LSU Press.
Gregg, Melissa, and Gregory J. Seidworth, eds. 2010. *The Affect Theory Reader*. Durham, NC: Duke University Press.
Griffin, F. Hollis. 2017. *Feeling Normal: Sexuality and Media Criticism in the Digital Age*. Bloomington: Indiana University Press.
Grossberg, Lawrence. 1992. "Is There a Fan in the House? The Affective Sensibility of Fandom." In *The Adoring Audience: Fan Culture and Popular Media*, ed. Lisa A. Lewis, 50–65. New York: Routledge.
Habermas, Jürgen. 1989. *The Structural Transformation of the Public Sphere: An Inquiry into a Category of Bourgeois Society*. Translated by Thomas Burger. Cambridge, UK: Polity.
Haggins, Bambi. 2007. *Laughing Mad: The Black Comic Persona in Post-soul America*. New Brunswick, NJ: Rutgers University Press.
Halberstam, J. 2011. *The Queer Art of Failure*. Durham, NC: Duke University Press.
Hall, Stuart. 1980. "Encoding, Decoding." In *Culture, Media, Language: Working Papers in Cultural Studies, 1972–1979*, ed. Stuart Hall et al., 128–38. London: Hutchinson.
Hall, Stuart, and David Morley. 2018. *Essential Essays: Foundations of Cultural Studies and Identity and Diaspora*. Durham, NC: Duke University Press.
Hamm, Bernd, and Russell Smandych, eds. 2005. *Cultural Imperialism: Essays on the Political Economy of Cultural Domination*. Peterborough, ON: Broadview.
Harman, Sarah, and Bethan Jones. 2013. "Fifty Shades of Ghey: Snark Fandom and the Figure of the Anti-fan." *Sexualities* 16 (8): 951–68.
Hartley, John. 1996. *Popular Reality: Journalism, Modernity, Popular Culture*. London: Arnold.
Hartley, John, and Jason Potts. 2014. *Cultural Science: A Natural History of Stories, Demes, Knowledge and Innovation*, New York: Bloomsbury.
Hassler-Forest, Dan, and Pascal Nicklas, eds. 2015. *The Politics of Adaptation: Media Convergence and Ideology*. New York: Palgrave Macmillan.
Hay, Colin. 2007. *Why We Hate Politics*. London: Polity.
Heinze, Rüdiger, and Lucia Krämer, eds. 2015. *Remakes and Remaking: Concepts—Media—Practices*. New York: Transcript-Verlag.
Herman, Edward, and Robert McChesney. 1997. *The Global Media: The Missionaries of Global Capitalism*. Washington, DC: Cassell.
Hermes, Joke. 2005. *Re-reading Popular Culture*. Malden, MA: Blackwell.
Higginbotham, Evelyn Brooks. 1992. "African-American Women's History and the Metalanguage of Race." *Signs* 17 (2): 251–74.
Hill, Annette. 2015. "Spectacle of Excess: The Passion Work of Professional Wrestlers, Fans and Anti-fans." *European Journal of Cultural Studies* 18 (2): 174–89.

———. 2019. *Media Experiences: Engaging with Drama and Reality Television*. New York: Routledge.

Hills, Matt. 2002. *Fan Cultures*. New York: Routledge.

———. 2005a. "Patterns of Surprise: The 'Aleatory Object' in Psychoanalytic Ethnography and Cyclical Fandom." *American Behavioral Scientist* 48 (7): 801–21.

———. 2005b. *The Pleasures of Horror*. New York: Routledge.

———. 2015. "Afterword: The Hope of the Doctor." *Implicit Religion* 18 (4): 575–78.

———. 2017. "'The One You Watched When You Were Twelve': Regenerations of *Doctor Who* and Enduring Fandom's 'Life-Transitional Objects.'" *Journal of British Cinema and Television* 14 (2): 213–30.

———. 2018. "An Extended Foreword: From Fan Doxa to Toxic Fan Practices?" *Participations: Journal of Audience and Reception Studies* 15 (1). www.participations.org.

Hinck, Ashley. 2019. *Politics for the Love of Fandom: Fan-Based Citizenship in a Digital World*. Baton Rouge: Louisiana State University Press.

Hobson, Dorothy. 1987. "Housewives and the Mass Media." In *Culture, Media, Language: Working Papers in Cultural Studies, 1972–1979*, ed. Stuart Hall et al., 105–14. London: Hutchinson.

Hochschild, Arlie. 2003. *The Managed Heart: Commercialization of Human Feeling*. Berkeley: University of California Press.

Hoggart, Richard. 1957. *The Uses of Literacy*. London: Chatto and Windus.

Holladay, Holly Willson, and Melissa Click. 2019. "Hating Skyler White: Gender and Anti-fandom in AMC's *Breaking Bad*." In *Anti-fandom: Dislike and Hate in the Digital Age*, ed. Melissa A. Click, 147–65. New York: NYU Press.

hooks, bell. 1992. *Black Looks: Race and Representation*. Boston: South End.

Hornaday, Ann. 2012. "A Long, Strange Cinematic Trip." *Washington Post*, December 14, 2012. Archived at www.rottentomatoes.com.

Hutcheon, Linda. 2006. *A Theory of Adaptation*. New York: Routledge.

Huyssen, Andreas. 1986. *After the Great Divide: Modernism, Mass Culture, Postmodernism*. Bloomington: Indiana University Press.

Iser, Wolfgang. 1980. "The Reading Process: A Phenomenological Approach." In *Reader-Response Criticism: From Formalism to Post-Structuralism*, ed. Jane Tompkins, 50–69. Baltimore: Johns Hopkins University Press.

Jane, Emma A. 2014. "Beyond Antifandom: Cheerleading, Textual Hate and New Media Ethics." *International Journal of Cultural Studies* 17 (2): 175–90.

———. 2019. "Hating 3.0: Should Anti-fan Studies Be Renewed for Another Season?" In *Anti-fandom: Dislike and Hate in the Digital Age*, ed. Melissa A. Click, 42–61. New York: NYU Press.

Jenkins, Henry. 1992. *Textual Poachers: Television Fans and Participating Culture*. New York: Routledge.

———. 2006. *Convergence Culture: When Old and New Media Collide*. New York: NYU Press.

Jenkins, Henry, Sam Ford, and Joshua Green. 2013. *Spreadable Media: Creating Value and Meaning in a Networked Culture*. New York: NYU Press.

Jenkins, Henry, Gabriel Peters-Lazaro, and Sangita Shresthova, eds. 2020. *Popular Culture and the Civic Imagination: Case Studies of Creative Social Change*. New York: NYU Press.

Jenkins, Henry, and Sangita Shresthova, eds. 2012. "Transformative Works and Fan Activism." Special issue, *Transformative Works and Cultures* 10. http://journal.transformativeworks.org.

Jensen, Joli. 1992. "Fandom as Pathology: The Consequences of Characterization." In *The Adoring Audience: Fan Culture and Popular Media*, ed. Lisa A. Lewis, 9–29. New York: Routledge.

Johnson, Derek. 2007. "Fan-tagonism: Factions, Institutions, and Constitutive Hegemonies of Fandom." In *Fandom: Identities and Communities in a Mediated Era*, ed. Jonathan Gray, Cornel Sandvoss, and C. Lee Harrington, 285–300. New York: NYU Press.

———. 2013a. *Media Franchising: Creative License and Collaboration in the Culture Industries*. New York: NYU Press.

———. 2013b. "Participation is Magic: Collaboration, Authorial Legitimacy, and the Audience Function." In *A Companion to Media Authorship*, ed. Jonathan Gray and Derek Johnson, 135–57. Malden, MA: Wiley-Blackwell.

———. 2018. "From the Ruins: Neomasculinity, Media Franchising, and Struggles over Industrial Reproduction of Culture." *Communication, Culture, and Critique* 11 (1): 85–99.

Johnson, Poe. 2020. "Playing with Lynching: Fandom Violence and the Black Athletic Body." *Television and New Media* 21 (2): 169–83.

Jones, Bethan. 2015. "Antifan Activism as a Response to MTV's *The Valleys*." *Transformative Works and Culture* 19. https://journal.transformativeworks.org.

———. 2018. "#AskELJames, *Ghostbusters*, and #Gamergate: Digital Dislike and Damage Control." In *A Companion to Media Fandom and Fan Studies*, ed. Paul Booth, 415–29. Malden, MA: Wiley-Blackwell.

Jones, Jeffrey P. 2004. *Entertaining Politics: New Political Television and Civic Culture*. Lanham, MD: Rowman and Littlefield.

Joseph, Ralina. 2018. *Postracial Resistance: Black Women, Media, and the Uses of Strategic Ambiguity*. New York: NYU Press.

Juul, Jesper. 2013. *The Art of Failure: An Essay on the Pain of Playing Video Games*. Cambridge, MA: MIT Press.

Katz, Elihu, and Tamar Liebes. 1990. *The Export of Meaning: Cross-Cultural Readings of Dallas*. Oxford: Oxford University Press.

kermodeandmayo. 2010. "Sex and the City 2 Reviewed by Mark Kermode." YouTube, June 1, 2010. https://www.youtube.com/watch?v=uHeQeHstrsc.

Kristeva, Julia. 1980. *Desire in Language: A Semiotic Approach to Literature and Art*. Translated by Thomas Gora et al. Edited by Leon Roudiez. Oxford, UK: Basil Blackwell.

Lamere, Paul. 2009. "Paul's Music Wreckommender." *Music Machinery* (blog), November 22, 2009. https://musicmachinery.com.

Lembo, Ron. 2000. *Thinking through Television*. Cambridge: Cambridge University Press.
Levine, Lawrence W. 1990. *Highbrow/Lowbrow: The Emergence of Cultural Hierarchy in America*. Cambridge, MA: Harvard University Press.
Lewis, Justin. 1991. *The Ideological Octopus: An Exploration of Television and Its Audience*. London: Routledge.
Livingstone, Sonia. 1990. *Making Sense of Television: The Psychology of Audience Interpretation*. Oxford, UK: Pergamon.
Loock, Kathleen, ed. 2014. "Serial Narratives." Special issue, *Literatur in Wissenschaft und Unterricht* 47 (1–2).
Loock, Kathleen, and Constantin Verevis, eds. 2012. *Film Remakes, Adaptations and Fan Productions*. New York: Palgrave Macmillan.
Lopez, Jason Kido. 2016. *Self-Deception's Puzzles and Processes: A Return to a Sartrean View*. Lanham, MD: Lexington Books.
Lopez, Lori Kido. 2016. *Asian American Media Activism: Fighting for Cultural Citizenship*. New York: NYU Press.
Lorde, Audre. 1997. "The Uses of Anger." *Women's Studies Quarterly* 25 (1–2): 278–85.
Lozano-Reich, Nina M., and Dana L. Cloud. 2009. "The Uncivil Tongue: Invitational Rhetoric and the Problem of Inequality." *Western Journal of Communication* 73 (2): 220–26.
Marcus, George E. 2002. *The Sentimental Citizen: Emotion in Democratic Politics*. University Park: Pennsylvania State University Press.
Martin, Alfred L., Jr. 2019. "Why All the Hate? Four Black Women's Anti-fandom and Tyler Perry." In *Anti-fandom: Dislike and Hate in the Digital Age*, ed. Melissa A. Click, 166–83. New York: NYU Press.
———. 2021. *The Generic Closet: Black Gayness and the Black Cast Sitcom*. Bloomington: Indiana University Press.
Mattelart, Armand. 1983. *Transnationals and the Third World: The Struggle for Culture*. South Hadley, MA: Bergin and Garvey.
McCulloch, Richard. 2019. "A Game of Moans: Fantipathy and Criticism in Football Fandom." In *Anti-fandom: Dislike and Hate in the Digital Age*, ed. Melissa A. Click, 227–48. New York: NYU Press.
McIntyre, Hugh. 2019. "These Were the 10 Bestselling Albums in the World in 2018." *Forbes*, March 14, 2019. www.forbes.com.
McRobbie, Angela. 2009. *The Aftermath of Feminism: Gender, Culture and Social Change*. New York: Routledge.
McRobie, Heather. 2008. "Conservatives for Hillary Clinton?" *The Guardian*, August 5, 2008. www.theguardian.com.
Menta, Anna. 2017. "Racist Attacks against Kelly Marie Tran Posted to Rose Tico's 'Wookieepedia' Page." *Newsweek*, December 19, 2017. www.newsweek.com.
Miller, Mark Crispin. 1988. *Boxed In: The Culture of TV*. Evanston, IL: Northwestern University Press.
Mittell, Jason. 2004. *Genre and Television: From Cop Shows to Cartoons in American Culture*. New York: Routledge.

Morimoto, Lori Hitchcock, and Bertha Chin. 2017. "Reimagining the Imagined Community: Online Media Fandoms in the Age of Global Convergence." In *Fandom: Identities and Communities in a Mediated Era*, ed. Jonathan Gray, Cornel Sandvoss, and C. Lee Harrington, 2nd ed., 174–89. New York: NYU Press.

Morley, David. 1986. *Family Television*. London: Comedia.

———. 1992. *Television, Audiences and Cultural Studies*. London: Routledge.

———. 2000. *Home Territories: Media, Mobility and Identity*. London: Routledge.

Morley, David, and Charlotte Brunsdon. 1999. *The Nationwide Television Studies*. London: Routledge.

Mortensen, Torill Elvira. 2018. "Anger, Fear, and Games: The Long Event of #GamerGate." *Games and Culture* 13 (8): 787–806.

Moye, David. 2017. "Kelly Marie Tran of 'Last Jedi' Facing Racist, Sexist Comments Online." *Huffington Post*, December 27, 2017. www.huffpost.com.

Nakamura, Reid. 2016. "Hate Drives TV Viewers to Return to Shows, New Study Finds." *The Wrap*, June 29, 2016. www.thewrap.com.

Newcomb, Horace M., and Paul M. Hirsch. 1983. "Television as a Cultural Forum: Implications for Research." *Quarterly Review of Film Studies* 8 (3): 45–55.

Newman, Michael Z., and Elana Levine. 2012. *Legitimating Television: Media Convergence and Cultural Status*. New York: Routledge.

Ngai, Sianne. 2005. *Ugly Feelings*. Cambridge, MA: Harvard University Press.

Niewert, David. 2009. *The Eliminationists: How Hate Talk Radicalized the American Right*. New York: Routledge.

Nooney, Laine. 2013. "A Pedestal, a Table, a Love Letter: Archaeologies of Gender in Videogame History." *Game Studies* 13 (2). http://gamestudies.org.

obsession_inc. 2009. "Affirmational Fandom vs. Transformational Fandom." June 1, 2009. https://obsession-inc.dreamwidth.org.

O'Hehir, Andrew. 2012. "'The Hobbit': Middle-Earth Faces a Phantom Menace." *Salon*, December 13, 2012. www.salon.com.

Oravec, Christine L. 2003. "Fanny Wright and the Enforcing of Prudence: Women, Propriety, and Transgression in Nineteenth-Century Public Oratory of the United States." In *Prudence: Classical Virtue, Postmodern Practice*, ed. Robert Hariman, 189–228. University Park: Pennsylvania State University Press.

Pande, Rukmini. 2018. *Squee From the Margins: Fandom and Race*. Iowa City: University of Iowa Press.

Papacharissi, Zizi. 2004. "Democracy Online: Civility, Politeness, and the Democratic Potential of Online Political Discussion Groups." *New Media and Society* 6 (2): 259–83.

———. 2015. *Affective Publics: Sentiment, Technology, and Politics*. New York: Oxford University Press.

Pearson, Roberta. 2019. "'I Just Hate It Now': The Supracultural Anti-fans of BBC Radio 3." In *Anti-fandom: Dislike and Hate in the Digital Age*, ed. Melissa A. Click, 205–26. New York: NYU Press.

Penley, Constance. 1997. *NASA/TREK: Popular Science and Sex in America*. London: Verso.

Petersen, Anne Helen. 2017. *Too Fat, Too Slutty, Too Loud: The Rise and Reign of the Unruly Woman*. New York: Plume.
Peterson, Richard A. 1992. "Understanding Audience Segmentation: From Elite and Mass to Omnivore and Univore." *Poetics* 21:243–58.
Phillips, Whitney. 2015. *This Is Why We Can't Have Nice Things: Mapping the Relationship Between Online Trolling an d Mainstream Culture*. Cambridge, MA: MIT Press.
———. 2018. "Am I Why I Can't Have Nice Things? A Reflection on Personal Trauma, Networked Play, and Ethical Sight." In *A Networked Self and Love*, ed. Zizi Papacharissi, 202–12. New York: Routledge.
Proctor, William, and Bridget Kies. 2018a. "Editors' Introduction: On Toxic Fan Practices and the New Culture Wars." *Participations: Journal of Audience and Reception Studies* 15 (1). www.participations.org.
———, eds. 2018b. "Toxic Fan Practices." *Participations: Journal of Audience and Reception Studies* 15 (1). www.participations.org.
Punathambekar, Aswin. 2007. "Between Rowdies and *Rasikas*: Rethinking Fan Activity in Indian Film Culture." In *Fandom: Identities and Communities in a Mediated Era*, ed. Jonathan Gray, Cornel Sandvoss, and C. Lee Harrington, 198–209. New York: NYU Press.
Quandt, Thorsten. 2018. "Dark Participation." *Media and Communication* 6 (4): 36–48.
Radway, Janice. 1987. *Reading the Romance: Women, Patriarchy, and Popular Literature*. London: Verso.
———. 1988. "Reception Study: Ethnography and the Problems of Dispersed Audiences and Nomadic Subjects." *Cultural Studies* 2 (3): 359–76.
Reinhard, CarrieLynn D. 2018. *Fractured Fandoms: Contentious Communication on Fan Communities*. Lanham, MD: Lexington Books.
Rivera, Michelle M. 2019. "Just Sexual Games and Twenty-Four-Hour Parties? Anti-fans Contest the Global Crossover of Reggaetón Music Online." In *Anti-fandom: Dislike and Hate in the Digital Age*, ed. Melissa A. Click, 184–204. New York: NYU Press.
Romano, Aja. 2013. "The Rise of the Anti-fandom Fandom." *Daily Dot*, May 22, 2013. www.dailydot.com.
Rorty, Richard. 1992. "The Pragmatist's Progress." In *Interpretation and Overinterpretation*, by Umberto Eco, 89–108. Cambridge: Cambridge University Press.
Rosewarne, Lauren. 2020. *Why We Remake: The Politics, Economics and Emotions of Film and TV Remakes*. New York: Routledge.
Ross, Andrew. 1989. *No Respect: Intellectuals and Popular Culture*. New York: Routledge.
Ryan, Michael, and Douglas Kellner. 1988. *Camera Politica: The Politics and Ideology of Contemporary Hollywood Film*. Bloomington: Indiana University Press.
Saler, Michael. 2012. *As If: Modern Enchantment and the Literary Prehistory of Virtual Reality*. Oxford: Oxford University Press.
Salter, Anastasia, and Bridget Blodgett. 2017. *Toxic Geek Masculinity in Media: Sexism, Trolling, and Identity Politics*. New York: Palgrave Macmillan.
Sanders, Julie. 2015. *Adaptation and Appropriation*. New York: Routledge.

Sandvoss, Cornel. 2005. *Fans: The Mirror of Consumption*. London: Polity.
———. 2012. "Enthusiasm, Trust and Its Erosion in Mediated Politics: On Fans of Obama and the Liberal Democrats." *European Journal of Communication* 27 (1): 68–81.
———. 2019. "The Politics of Against: Political Participation, Anti-fandom, and Populism." In *Anti-fandom: Dislike and Hate in the Digital Age*, ed. Melissa A. Click, 125–46. New York: NYU Press.
Savage, Mike, Fiona Devine, Niall Cunningham, Mark Taylor, Yaojun Li, Johs. Hjellbrekke, Brigitte Le Roux, Sam Friedman, and Andrew Miles. 2013. "A New Model of Social Class? Findings from the BBC's Great British Class Survey Experiment." *Sociology* 47 (2): 219–50.
Schiller, Herbert. 1976. *Communication and Cultural Domination*. Armonk, NY: M. E. Sharpe.
Schroeder, Joanna. 2012. "Two and a Half Shades of Masculinity." Good Men Project, January 11, 2012. https://goodmenproject.com.
Schudson, Michael. 1997. "Why Conversation Is Not the Soul of Democracy." *Critical Studies in Mass Communication* 14 (4): 1–13.
Sconce, Jeffrey. 2007. "Movies: A Century of Failure." In *Sleaze Artists: Cinema at the Margins of Taste, Style, and Politics*, ed. Jeffrey Sconce, 273–309. Durham, NC: Duke University Press.
Scott, Suzanne. 2018. "Towards a Theory of Producer/Fan Trolling." *Participations: Journal of Audience and Reception Studies* 15 (1): 143–59. www.participations.org.
———. 2019. *Fake Geek Girls: Fandom, Gender, and the Convergence Culture Industry*. New York: NYU Press.
Shaw, Adrienne. 2014. *Gaming at the Edge: Sexuality and Gender at the Margins of Gamer Culture*. Minneapolis: University of Minnesota Press.
Silverstone, Roger. 1994. *Television and Everyday Life*. London: Routledge.
———. 1999. *Why Study the Media?* London: Sage.
Sloterdijk, Peter. 1987. *Critique of Cynical Reason*. Translated by Michael Eldred. Minneapolis: University of Minnesota Press.
Smith, Patrick. 2014. "11 Film Posters Improved by Mark Kermode's Scathing Reviews." *BuzzFeed*, November 28, 2014. www.buzzfeed.com.
Smith-Shomade, Beretta E., ed. 2012. *Watching While Black: Centering the Television of Black Audiences*. New Brunswick, NJ: Rutgers University Press.
Solomon, Robert C. 1988. "On Emotions and Judgments." *American Philosophical Quarterly* 25 (2): 183–91.
Sontag, Susan. 1964. "Notes on Camp." *Partisan Review* 31 (4): 515–30.
Sperber, Dan. 1991. *On Anthropological Knowledge*. Cambridge: Cambridge University Press.
Sreberny-Mohammadi, Annabelle. 1997. "The Many Faces of Imperialism." In *Beyond Cultural Imperialism: Globalization, Communication and the New International Order*, ed. Peter Golding and Phil Harris, 48–68. London: Sage.
Stallybrass, Peter, and Allon White. 1986. *The Politics and Poetics of Transgression*. London: Methuen.

Stanfill, Mel. 2018. "The Unbearable Whiteness of Fandom and Fan Studies." In *A Companion to Fandom and Fan Studies*, ed. Paul Booth, 305–17. Oxford, UK: Wiley-Blackwell.

———. 2020a. "Introduction: The Reactionary in the Fan and the Fan in the Reactionary." *Television and New Media* 21 (2): 123–34.

———, ed. 2020b. "Reactionary Fandom." Special issue, *Television and New Media* 21 (2).

Stein, Louisa. 2019. "Dissatisfaction and *Glee*: On Emotional Range in Fandom and Feels Culture." In *Anti-fandom: Dislike and Hate in the Digital Age*, ed. Melissa A. Click, 81–101. New York: NYU Press.

Sternberg, Robert J., and Karin Sternberg. 2008. *The Nature of Hate*. Cambridge: Cambridge University Press.

Stevens, Dana. 2012. "Bored of the Rings: *The Hobbit* Looks like Teletubbies and Is Way Too Long." *Slate*, December 7, 2012. https://slate.com.

Television by the Numbers. 2015. "Sunday Final Ratings." https://tvbythenumbers.zap2it.com.

Test, George A. 1991. *Satire: Spirit and Art*. Tampa: University of South Florida Press.

Theodoropoulou, Vivi. 2007. "The Anti-fan within the Fan: Awe and Envy in Sport Fandom." In *Fandom: Identities and Communities in a Mediated Era*, ed. Jonathan Gray, Cornel Sandvoss, and C. Lee Harrington, 316–27. New York: NYU Press.

Thompson, E. P. 1963. *The Making of the English Working Class*. New York: Vintage.

Thornton, Sarah. 1996. *Club Cultures: Music, Media and Subcultural Capital*. Middletown, CT: Wesleyan University Press.

Tomlinson, John. 1997. "Cultural Globalization and Cultural Imperialism." In *International Communication and Globalization*, ed. Annabelle Mohammadi, 170–90. London: Sage.

Tran, Kelly Marie. 2018. "I Won't Be Marginalized by Online Harassment." *New York Times*, August 21, 2018. www.nytimes.com.

Tran, Tony. 2020. "Imagining the Perfect Asian Woman through Hate: Michelle Phan, Anti-Phandom, and Asian Diasporic Beauty Cultures." *Communication, Culture, and Critique*, May 15, 2020. https://doi.org/10.1093/ccc/tcz057.

Uhlich, Keith. 2012. "The Hobbit: An Expected Journey." *Time Out New York*, December 10, 2012. www.timeout.com.

Van Zoonen, Liesbet. 2004. *Entertaining the Citizen: When Politics and Popular Culture Converge*. Lanham, MD: Rowman and Littlefield.

Verevis, Constantin. 2006. *Film Remakes*. Edinburgh: Edinburgh University Press.

Volosinov, Valentin Nikolaevic. 1973. *Marxism and the Philosophy of Language*. Translated by Ladislav Metejka and I. R. Titunik. London: Seminar.

Vonnegut, Kurt. 1999. *Palm Sunday: An Autobiographical Collage*. New York: Dial.

Wahl-Jorgensen, Karin. 2019. *Emotions, Media, and Politics*. London: Polity.

Wanzo, Rebecca. 2015. "African American Acafandom and Other Strangers: New Genealogies of Fan Studies." *Transformative Works and Cultures* 20. https://journal.transformativeworks.org.

Warhol, Robyn R. 2003. *Having a Good Cry: Effeminate Feelings and Pop-Culture Forms*. Columbus: Ohio State University Press.

Warner, Kristen J. 2015. "They Gon' Think You Loud Regardless: Ratchetness, Reality Television, and Black Womanhood." *Camera Obscura* 30:129–53.

Wilkins, Amy. 2012. "Not Out to Start a Revolution: Race, Gender, and Emotional Restraint among Black University Men." *Journal of Contemporary Ethnography* 4 (1): 34–65.

Williams, Raymond. 1958. *Culture and Society: 1780–1950*. London: Chatto and Windus.

Williams, Rebecca. 2015. *Post-object Fandom: Television, Identity and Self-Narrative*. New York: Bloomsbury.

Willis, Paul. 1990. *Common Culture: Symbolic Work at Play in the Everyday Cultures of the Young*. Milton Keynes, UK: Open University Press.

Wilson, Carl. 2007. *Let's Talk about Love: A Journey to the End of Taste*. New York: Bloomsbury.

Winnicott, D. W. 1974. *Playing and Reality*. Harmondsworth, UK: Penguin.

Woo, Benjamin. 2018. "The Invisible Bag of Holding: Whiteness and Media Fandom." In *The Routledge Companion to Media Fandom*, ed. Melissa Click and Suzanne Scott, 245–52. New York: Routledge.

Yamamoto, Jen. 2017. "Racists Urge Boycott of 'Star Wars: Episode VII' over Black Lead." *Daily Beast*, April 13, 2017. www.thedailybeast.com.

Yin, Yiyi. 2020. "An Emergent Algorithmic Culture: The Data-ization of Online Fandom in China." *International Journal of Cultural Studies* 23 (4): 475–92.

Zagacki, Kenneth S., and Patrick A. Boleyn-Fitzgerald. 2006. "Rhetoric and Anger." *Philosophy and Rhetoric* 39 (4): 290–309.

INDEX

2 Live Crew, 202
13 Reasons Why, 95–96, 111

Abercrombie, Nicholas, and Longhurst, Brian, 39, 158, 213
activism, 71, 106, 205–6, 215, 218, 232n63
adaptation, 107–8, 115–18, 122, 128, 135; and fidelity, 115–18
Adorno, Theodor, 144
affect, 24–25, 37, 48–49, 50, 58, 78, 110, 173, 182
agency, 15, 30, 40–41, 158–59, 166; obstructed, 58
Ahmed, Sara, 37, 41, 45–46, 49, 78, 104, 173, 188, 219
algorithms, 2, 4, 40
alienation, 3, 11, 14, 46, 78, 83–85, 173, 195, 218–20
Alters, Diane, 140
America's Next Top Model, 167, 189
American Idol, 28
Anable, Aubrey, 23, 24–25, 235n68
anger, 5–7, 129–33, 217–19
antifans, 8–11, 43, 56, 90, 98, 133–34; competitive, 98, 186
Arewa, Olufunmilayo, 144
Aristotle, 5, 7
audience, definition, 36
audiences: active, 13, 37–38, 40, 81–82, 155–56; African American, 43, 48–49, 55, 85–86, 89, 91–95, 104, 105, 166–67, 170–71, 189, 195, 208–9; and class, 12, 48, 73–74, 136–43, 145–49, 155, 194–95; and fatigue, 43; and femininity, 50; 69–70, 77, 87–90, 93, 103–4, 134, 144, 152, 157, 160–61, 164–66, 167, 169–71, 189, 195–97; feminists, 41, 44–45, 49, 87–89, 95, 100–105, 110–14, 148, 160–64, 166, 171–73, 196, 200–202, 206, 210–11, 219; and generation, 46, 119–21, 134–35, 145, 152–53, 155, 195–97; Latinx, 90, 167–68; Malawian, 20, 21, 149–56, 195–97; and masculinity, 77, 125, 128–33, 157, 162–65, 195–96; national, 55, 72, 144, 149–56, 168–69, 195–97; parents, 50, 52, 58, 74–76, 93, 140, 155, 182, 189–90, 206; queer, 13, 22–23, 46–47, 49–50, 82, 84–87, 90, 100, 144, 185–86, 190; and race, 22–23, 45, 48–49, 85, 87–88, 90, 91–94, 101–2, 144, 166–72, 189, 194–95, 209, 219; reluctant, 39–58, 65–66; straight, 22–23, 103; transgender, 49–50, 84–85; white, 22–23, 57, 87–89, 101–3, 128–33, 141, 161, 166, 171, 193; workplace, 42–43, 46, 48, 53
audience studies, 9, 12, 15, 16, 60, 66, 80–81, 108, 135, 207–8
author, 34
Avengers: Endgame, 29

Bachelor, The, 77, 142–43, 171, 179
bad media, 53, 144, 183, 185, 187–88
bad readings, 59–60
Bakhtin, Mikhail, 35, 191–92
Barker, Martin, and Brooks, Kate, 4, 81, 116–17
Barker, Martin, and Mathijs, Ernest, 124
Barker, Martin, Arthurs, Jane, and Harindrinath, Ramaswami, 117, 205

Barthes, Roland, 32–33, 37–38
Basketball Wives, 55–56, 91–94, 105, 166, 176, 195
Bausinger, Herman, 50
Bay, Michael, 179–80
Baym, Nancy, 227n3
Beauty and the Beast, 109
Beckett, Samuel, 188
Beguiled, The, 211
Being Mary Jane, 170
belabored consumption, 46–51
Bennett, Tony, and Woollacott, Janet, 35
Berardinelli, James, 124–25
Bird, S. Elizabeth, 213
Bledel, Alexis, 134
Bodroghkozy, Aniko, 57
Bollas, Christopher, 134–35
Bond and Beyond: The Political Career of a Popular Hero (Bennett and Woollacott), 35
book covers, 34
Bourdieu, Pierre, 12–14, 136–149, 173–75, 177, 180, 194, 221
Boyega, John, 129–30
Bratz dolls, 75, 182
Breaking Bad, 96, 133, 165, 195
Brooks, Kate, 4, 81, 116–17
Brunsdon, Charlotte, 139, 221
BTS, 29
Burke, Liam, 116
Butler, Judith, 158–59

Caillou, 179, 182, 189–90, 206
Caldwell, John Thornton, 198
camp, 183, 190
Caplan, Lizzy, 147–48
Cavalcante, Andre, 25, 49–50, 84–85
celebrity, 7–8, 22, 71, 152, 166, 186
citizenship, 66, 213–20
Click, Melissa, and Smith-Frigerio, Sarah, 94
Coleman, Robin R. Means, 85–86, 91
Condit, Celeste, 38
convergence culture, 10
Corliss, Richard, 126–27
Cornwell, Nancy, and Orbe, Mark, 85–86, 91
Couldry, Nick, 19–20, 36, 221
Crash, 117, 205
The Cash Controversy: Censorship Campaigns and Film Reception (Martin, Arthurs, and Harindranath), 117, 205
Crenshaw, Kimberlé, 202, 232n40
cultural capital, 136–38, 140, 143–44, 145
cultural forum, 66, 207–8
cultural imperialism, 150–56, 168–69
cultural omnivore, 173
cynicism, 191

D'Acci, Julie, 13, 82
de Certeau, Michel, 37–38, 81–82
De Kosnik, Abigail, 53
deal-breakers, 88, 100, 109–15, 121, 133, 166, 200
deception, 198–202
Dion, Céline, 8, 51, 178
disappointment, 10, 80–99, 105–6, 107–35
discursive mantras, 200, 202, 208
disinterest, 5, 25, 39, 54
dislike: aestheticization of, 177–83; as cancerous, 201; engaged, 5, 7–8, 10, 45; joys of, 177–94; multiplicities of, 176–212, 215; sociality of, 202–12; mundane, 5, 203; as political resource, 227; ubiquity and inescapability, 39–59, 65, 69, 79, 98–99, 182, 187, 192–93; unmet expectations, 80–99, 107, 215; worst violator, 69–77, 79–80, 86, 105
Disney, 52, 131, 160, 169
Distinction: A Social Distinction of the Judgement of Taste (Bourdieu), 12–13, 137–39, 145–46
Dunham, Lena, 87–88, 105, 201

Ebert, Roger, 178, 180, 181–82
Eco, Umberto, 60

Eliasoph, Nina, 95
Entourage, 178–79

Facebook, 102
failure, 3–4, 19–20, 69, 99, 183–87
Family Guy, 51, 100, 113, 163
fandom, 3, 6–7, 9–11, 13, 37, 43, 56, 78–9, 82–84, 91, 94, 95, 98, 107–10, 112–15, 117, 121, 128–33, 140, 144, 155–56, 158, 163, 199, 213–14, 229n17; affirmative, 10, 83; checkups, 114; cyclical, 100; end of, 107–15; forced, 53; moral economy of, 12–13; reactionary, 7, 129; toxic, 7, 83, 109, 129–33, 157, 166; transformative, 10, 82–83, 95, 99; wounds within, 112–13
fan studies, 3–4, 6–7, 9–12, 83, 95, 102, 109–110, 116, 164
fantagonism, 109
fauxtrage, 201–2
feminist killjoy, 41, 44, 49, 104, 173, 219
Fish, Stanley, 62–63, 207–8
Fiske, John, 13, 37–39, 81–82, 84, 139, 143, 158
Foundas, Scott, 127
Fox News, 27–28, 201–2
Fractured Fandoms: Contentions: Contentious Communication on Fan Communities (Reinhard), 109
Fraser, Nancy, 216
Frith, Simon, 57, 185
Frozen, 52, 75, 160

Game of Thrones, 10–11, 46, 59, 111–13, 146, 199–200, 206
GamerGate, 7
Gates, Racquel, 93–94
Geertz, Clifford, 198
generational consciousness, 134–35
Genette, Gérard, 33–35
genre, 4, 58–59, 63–65, 69, 78–79, 90, 144, 146, 205–6
Gilbert, Anne, 46, 87, 140, 188–89

Gillespie, Marie, 155
Gilmore, Rory, 115–22, 134
Gilmore Girls, 54, 58, 88, 115–22, 134, 157, 161
Girls, 46, 54, 87–88, 101, 142–43, 161, 201
Glynn, Kevin, 143
Goldfarb, Jeffrey, 191
Gonzalez, Ed, 125–26
Gray, Jonathan, 8–11, 33, 123
Gray, Jonathan, and Chin, Bertha, 117
Green, Leila, 165
Griffin, F. Hollis, 20
Grossberg, Lawrence, 214

Habermas, Jürgen, 216, 218
Haggins, Bambi, 58–59
Halberstam, J., 20, 185–86
Hall, Stuart, 14, 139
Harman, Sarah, and Jones, Bethan, 144
Hartley, John, 42, 216
Hartley, John, and Potts, Jason, 68
hate, 5–9, 22, 128–33, 193–94, 217, 229n56
hatewatching, 46, 99, 140, 167, 177, 188–89
hegemony, 13, 105, 131, 164, 166, 167, 185, 208
Hermes, Joke, 68, 158
Higginbotham, 104, 232n48
Hill, Annette, 19–20, 66, 186
Hills, Matt, 77–78, 79, 110, 122, 135, 159, 199–200
Hobbit, The, 122–28, 134
Holladay, Holly Willson, and Click, Melissa, 7, 133, 165
Hollywood, 11, 125, 127–28, 156, 169, 188
Hornaday, Ann, 126
Huyssen, Andreas, 144
hype, 27–29, 89, 181

identification, 83, 115, 121
identity, performance of, 22–23, 115, 136–75, 188, 194–98, 199, 215
interpretive communities, 207–8

intersectionality, 88–89, 91, 95, 99, 101–4, 145, 161, 171, 194–98, 200, 232n40
intertextuality, 35
interviewee demographics, 21–22
Iser, Wolfgang, 62–63

Jackson, Peter, 123–28
Jane, Emma, 8–9, 22, 133, 134
Jenkins, Henry, 10, 11–12, 13, 37–38, 82–83, 109, 139, 158
Jenkins, Henry, Ford, Sam, and Green, Joshua, 181
Jensen, Joli, 140
Jerry Springer Show, The, 84–85
Johnson, Derek, 132
Jones, Jeffrey, 214
Joseph, Ralina, 167–68, 189
Judge Dredd, 81, 116–17
Juul, Jesper, 183–85

Kardashians, 52, 71–72, 142, 164, 190, 196–97
Kermode, Mark, 178–80, 182
Knowing Audiences: Judge Dredd, Its Friends, Fans and Foes (Barker and Brooks), 4, 81, 116–17
Kristeva, Julia, 35

laughter, 191–92
Law and Order, 61–62
Legitimating Television: Media Convergence and Cultural Status (Newman and Levine), 140–41, 147–49, 195
Letak, Abigail M., 110
Lewis, Justin, 60
Little Mermaid, The, 132
Livingstone, Sonia, 39
Lopez, Lori Kido, 206, 232n63
Lord of the Rings, 117, 123–28
Lorde, Audre, 219
loveshock, 110
Lozano-Reich, Nina M., and Cloud, Dana, 218

Mad Men, 89, 161
Madden, 164
making do, 14, 81–82
Malawi, 20, 21, 149–56, 195–96, 197
Manigault Stallworth, Omarosa, 8–9
Marcus, George E., 216–17
Martin, Alfred, 43, 166–67, 208
Mary Tyler Moore Show, The, 161
McCulloch, Richard, 84
McRobbie, Angela, 104
Menta, Anna, 129
Mercury Theatre on the Air, 60
methods, 19–25, 228n50, 228n52, 228–9n54, 235n37
#metoo movement, 115
Mickey Mouse Clubhouse, 179, 189
Miller, Mark Crispin, 3
Mindy Project, The, 114, 169
misogyny, 70, 87–88, 105, 133, 148, 165, 176, 189, 202, 211
Mittell, Jason, 64, 205–6
Modern Family, 86–87
Morley, David, 13, 40–41, 50, 57, 139, 198, 207–8
myth of mediated center, 19

negativity, 18, 72, 73, 218, 221
Newcomb, Horace and Hirsch, Paul, 207
Newman, Michael, and Levine, Elana, 140–41, 147–49, 195
Newsroom, The, 69–70, 157
Ngai, Sianne, 24, 58, 188
Nielsen ratings, 2, 20, 27–28
Nigerian film and television, 151–56, 195, 197
noise, 57
Nooney, Laine, 23

O'Hehir, Andrew, 125
objects: bad, 64, 105, 166, 183, 189–90; fan, 10, 13, 77–79, 83, 97, 98, 110, 113–15, 135, 231n2; happy, 45, 78, 110; object relations theory, 77–79; tran-

sitional, 77–79, 135; unhappy, 77–80, 91, 166
Other, the, 5, 55, 79, 149, 158
Ozeri, Gil, 148

Pande, Rukmini, 7, 83, 132, 229n17
Papacharissi, Zizi, 218, 220, 237n9
paratexts, 33–36, 52, 61, 63–64, 123, 124, 181, 189, 229n8
participatory culture, 10, 138, 158, 214
Pearson, Roberta, 140
Penley, Constance, 10, 83
performance: of class, 12–13, 137–43, 146–49, 195–97; deceptive, 198–202; of gender, 144–45, 147–48, 156–67, 169–71, 195–97, 200–201; of generation, 145, 195–97; intersectional, 194–98; of nation, 149–56, 195–97; of race, 144–45, 166–72, 195, 202; silent, 172–74
Peterson, Richard, 173
Phillips, Whitney, 192–93
poaching, 10, 13, 37, 81–84, 91, 95, 96
poetry of putrescence, 177–83, 188, 192
politics, 66, 95, 199–202, 207, 214–221
privilege, 12, 83, 88, 100–105, 139, 143
public sphere, 66, 216

quality television, 146–47, 162, 200, 221

racism, 7, 45, 48, 93, 94, 100, 105, 113, 128–33, 167, 202, 210–11, 218–19
Radway, Janice, 13, 82, 94–95
reality television, 74, 93, 105, 136, 139, 141–42, 146, 180, 183, 190
refractive audience analysis, 108, 118, 128–29
reggaetón, 90, 167–68
Reinhard, CarrieLynn, 109
representation, failure of, 7, 19, 49–50, 68–96, 99, 105–6
resilient reception, 49–50, 230n44
respectability politics, 18, 94, 104–5, 167, 218–19, 232n48

reviews, 122–28, 131, 177–81, 213
ridicule, 191–93
Ridley, Daisy, 129, 131
Rivera, Michelle, 90, 167–68
Romano, Aja, 56
Rorty, Richard, 60
rudeness, 218
Ryan, Michael, and Kellner, Douglas, 78

Salter, Anastasia, and Blodgett, Bridget, 7
Sandvoss, Cornel, 79, 129, 158, 213
satire, 191–92
Savage, Mike, 149
Schroeder, Joanna, 148–49
Schumer, Amy, 88–89, 105, 171
Sconce, Jeffrey, 187–88
Scott, Suzanne, 7, 83, 131, 132, 193
self-deception, 8, 198–202, 237n46
Sepinwall, Alan, 87
Shaw, Adrienne, 83, 90, 121
Sherlock, 143
shit: and alchemy, 82; cheap, 52; just, 81–84; and *The Phantom Menace*, 210; piece of, 54; pointless, 51; racist, 48, 87; singing in, 187–90, 192; toxic masculine, 163
Signs, 179
Silverstone, Roger, 41–42, 67, 68, 77, 81
Smash, 140, 188
snobbery, 4, 12, 14, 141–42, 144–48, 173, 180, 195, 218, 220–21
soap opera, 139, 144, 155, 165, 206
spectacles of failure, 183–87
Sperber, Dan, 207
sperosemic reading, 122
sports, 46, 53, 98, 143, 162–63, 164–65, 184, 186
Stallybrass, Peter, and White, Allon, 218, 237
Stanfill, Mel, 129
Star Wars Episode VII: The Force Awakens, 129–32, 209–10

Star Wars Episode VIII: The Last Jedi, 29, 129–32, 193, 233n34
Stein, Louisa, 10, 83–84
Sternberg, Robert, and Sternberg, Karin, 6
Stevens, Dana, 126
Strong, Catherine, 165
stuplimity, 188
Super Bowl, 28–30, 32, 36–37
Supernatural, 100
Swift, Taylor, 88–89, 157, 200, 209, 210–11

taste, 12, 137–49, 180, 190
Test, George, 191
textuality, 7–9, 10–11, 30–39, 52, 56–66, 67–69, 77–80, 82, 84, 99, 104, 108, 110, 114, 122, 129, 133, 140, 181
Theodoropoulou, Vivi, 98
Thornton, Sarah, 143–44
tone policing, 18, 104
Tonight Show with Jimmy Fallon, The, 97
toxic white masculinity, 7, 71, 83, 128–33, 162–63, 166
Tran, Kelly Marie, 7, 129–30
Tran, Tony, 169
Transparent, 64
trolling, 7, 129–33, 192–94, 210
True Blood, 42
Tumblr, 56, 100, 206
Twitter, 2, 130

Two and a Half Men, 42–43, 45, 51, 70, 105, 147–49, 157, 190, 195

Uhlich, Keith, 126
Unbreakable Kimmy Schmidt, 101, 113; 171–72
Undercover Boss, 73–74, 76

Volosinov, Valentin, 35
Vonnegut, Kurt, 213

Wahl-Jorgensen, Karin, 217
War of the Worlds, 60
Warhol, Robyn, 159
Warner, Kristen, 93–94
Way We Were, The, 89–90
White, Skyler, 133, 165
whiteness, 22–23, 57, 87–89, 101–3, 128–33, 161, 166, 171, 193, 209
Williams, Raymond, 139
Williams, Rebecca, 110
Willis, Paul, 68, 139
Wilson, Carl, 51, 149, 178, 227n17
Winnicott, D. W., 77–78
Wookieepedia, 129
World Hobbit Project, The (Barker and Mathijs), 124
work, the, 31–36, 38, 60–65

Yin, Yiyi, 98

ABOUT THE AUTHOR

Jonathan Gray is Hamel Family Distinguished Chair of Communication Arts at University of Wisconsin–Madison and the author or coeditor of numerous books, including *Television Entertainment, Show Sold Separately: Promos, Spoilers, and Other Media Paratexts, Fandom: Identities and Communities in a Mediated World, Satire TV: Politics and Comedy in the Post-Network Era,* and *Keywords for Media Studies.*

www.ingramcontent.com/pod-product-compliance
Lightning Source LLC
Chambersburg PA
CBHW020401080526
44584CB00014B/1128